W9-DHU-292

Happy Birthday
1988

Mom

And then the purple walked sadly away.

A Monster is Bigger than 9

Edited by
Claire Ericksen

Illustrated by
Mary Ericksen

The Green Tiger Press, Inc.
San Diego
1988

*These are the people at the Northfield Day Care
who listened to the children, and recorded the quotations
which make up this book:*

Claire Ericksen
Mary Williams
Cindy Veach
Jan Roberts
Jan Schoger
Gwen Lee
Laura Smith
Caterine Lewis
Denise Cherrington
Sarah Voegele
Mary Ericksen

Text copyright © 1988 by Claire Ericksen
Illustrations copyright © 1988 by Mary Ericksen
The Green Tiger Press, Inc.
Library of Congress Catalog Card No. 88-80350
Manufactured in Hong Kong
2 4 6 8 10 9 7 5 3 1

ISBN 0-88138-099-7

INTRODUCTION

All parents hear their children saying strange and wonderful things. Often they plan to record these sayings, but usually, in the hustle and bustle of raising a family, they forget.

Claire Ericksen and other teachers at the Northfield Day Care have been listening attentively to their extended family of preschoolers since 1970, and they have been faithfully recording their bits of humor, wisdom, naivete and insight since that time. This collection results from those rich years of experience, and is a tribute to those particular children who attended the Northfield Day Care. It is also a celebration of childhood, the short but crucial years where each of us begins to build a foundation of originality and independence which will enable us to survive in an extremely complicated world. As this book reveals so clearly, the world of childhood involves much more than playing and motor development. Many of the quotes included in this book have to do with feelings, ideas, cultural traditions, community, nature and language, topics frequently associated with the exclusively "adult" world.

A Monster is Bigger Than 9 is a rare glimpse into growth and learning, not the growth that psychologists refer to in their books on child development, but the ongoing moment-by-moment growth that unself-consciously occurs as preschool children speak their intentions and conclusions to each other.

Comments like "Don't talk with your mouth open!" or "Look how well that doesn't work!" are beautiful small satires on the adult obsessions of appraising and advising. What adults do, children mimic, but—fortunately—not always getting the words or meaning exactly right. Children mirror adult manners and styles as in a funhouse looking glass; the image returned is often distorted or offbeat, clever and personalized. Perceptions have not yet been channeled by routine procedures.

Ericksen and her staff have devoted much love, time and energy to children through the years. Now they give them, and us, something more— a collection of spontaneous sayings by children who probably have no recollection of the marvelous things they said. It is a gift returned to the givers. It is a gift for the childhood in all of us.

Joan Wolf
Northfield, Minnesota

"Can you think of something bigger than nine?"
"Yes. A monster. A monster is bigger than nine."

That's my picture. It was an accident.

I'm picking up trash so spring can come.

I caught a jelly fish. I caught a peanut butter and jelly fish.

The sky is pitch blue today.

Winter, spring, summer, fall ... and then you're dead. But it's okay.

I cut my finger so deep it went past the blood.

There are no back doors in fairyland.

I have long legs. They reach my body all the way.

... looking at a mess of toys:
We did it by itself.

I'm getting dizzy from coloring this circle.

You have to whisper to talk to yourself.

I hate Return of the Jedi now. Now I like Barbie with boots.

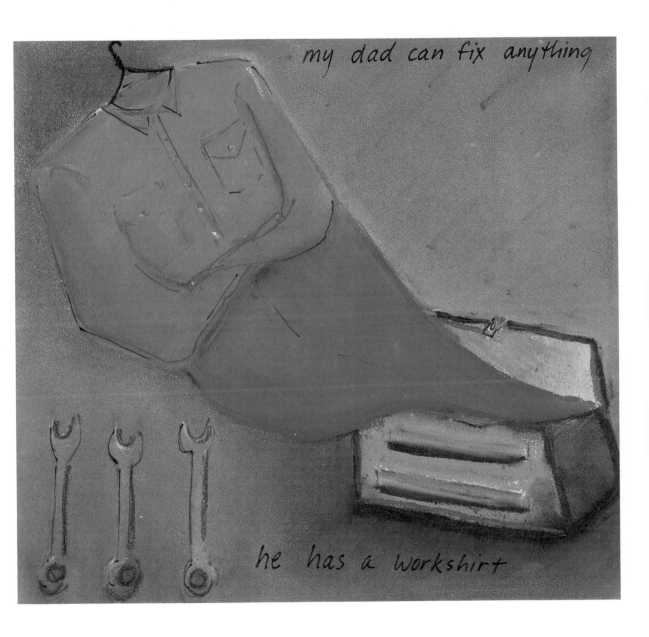

My dad can fix anything because he has a work shirt.

Take off my hat. My bones are roasting.

Is that you? I can't see you because you don't have your glasses on.

... *four-year-old girl:*
I've been smoking for fifteen years and I'm not a bit dead.

I know what's inside bubbles ... rainbows.

Listen to the sun!

I know what "maybe" means. Maybe means "no."

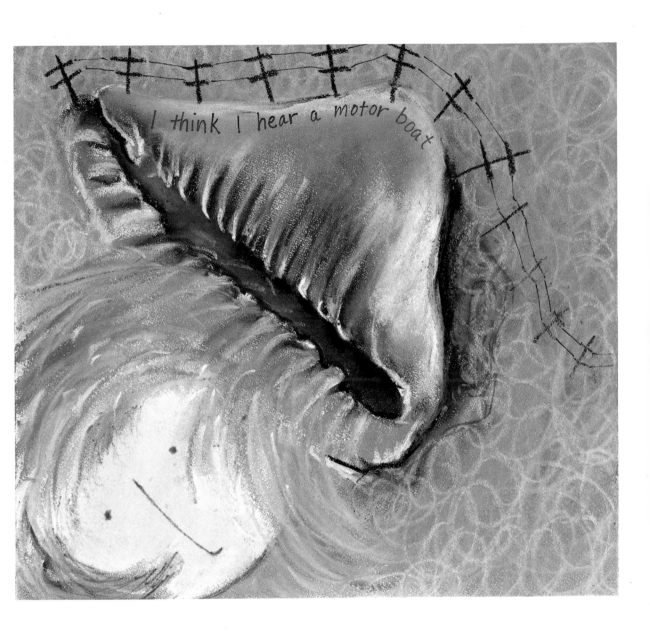

Listening to a conch shell:
Shhh. I think I hear a motor boat.

The earth is up in the sky.

My dream made me believe it.

The polka dots on my arm mean they are shivering.

This soup is full of things my mother likes.

... *girl to stuffed kitten:*
If you like my picture, smile.

I'm glad you're letting your hair grow because you need long hair
to get married.

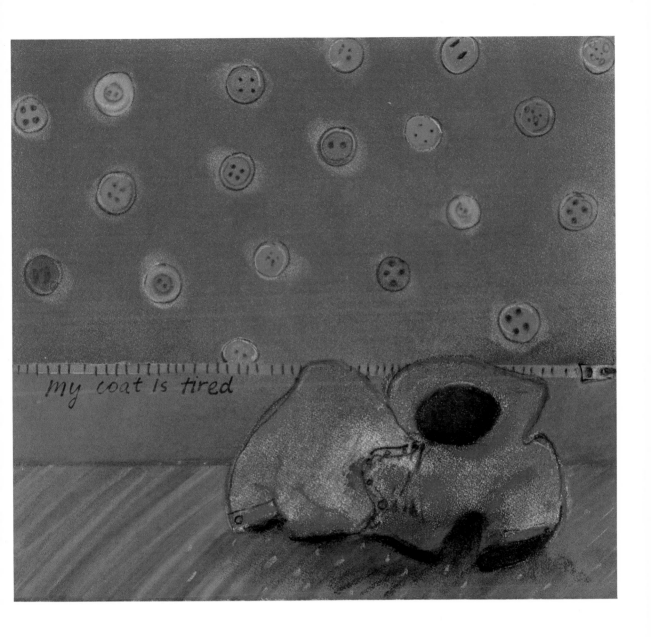

My coat is tired. It didn't sleep at all last night.

Ladies and girls are the juiciest people.

Be careful! Don't touch those blocks together—they're made of wood and they might start on fire.

What if orange were colored green?

... *drawing a bird:*
I feel like my body is changing into a bird.

My mouth got sick because the story was too long.

Don't blow up his balloon. You might catch his sad germs.

The sun's not open today.

When it's winter, I might be a baby again.

... reluctantly admitting a newcomer to a game:
Well, if he's going to be a mouse, he's going to have to be toasted.

Let's play the good guys are bad and the bad guys are good.

I think I hear a robin crowing.

... walking through a puddle:
Pretend this is the desert and this is all sand.

What happens at the end of the year—does time stop?

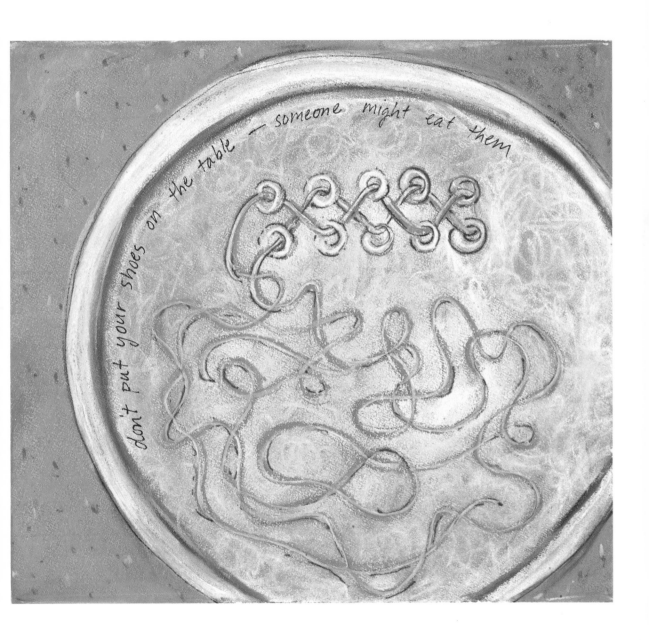

You shouldn't put your shoes on the table. Someone might eat them.

. . . watching the river:
Does the water ever all run out?

Poor people are too poor to have points on their houses.

. . . watching a teacher chip ice from the sidewalk:
Why are you killing the ice?

The wind is so strong it's blowing me back to heaven!

The air is bumping into me.

Should we make a sand castle? First we need a lot of sand and
then we need a lot of castle.

Now I'm four because I went to Mike's birthday. When you go to birthdays you get older.

Sometimes witches are doctors. Grandma said so. They say "wooka wooka wooka" and you're all better.

New shoes don't stay new long, but old shoes stay old long.

Girls can't dance with boys because girls do pretty dances and boys do dumb dances.

Come on, let's go tap dance in the sandbox.

I thought my feet hurt, but I was only thirsty.

I'm going to start thinking when I'm three and a half.

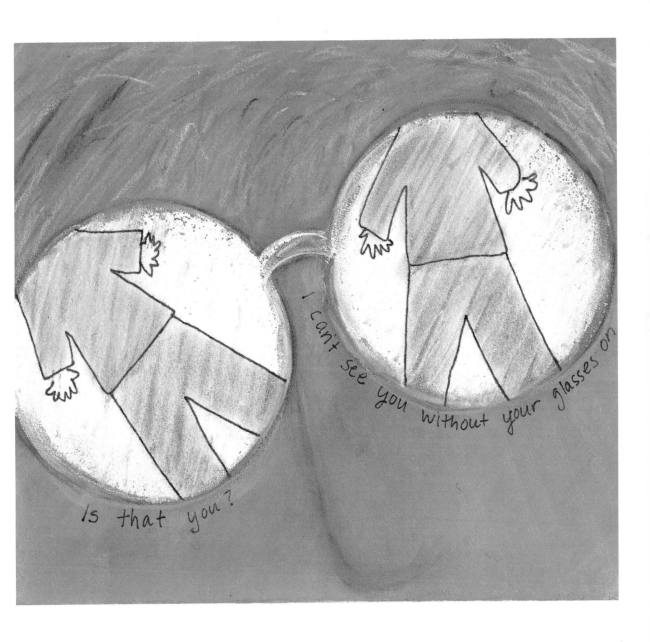

Is that you? I can't see you because you don't have your glasses on.

Black comes before brown like five before six.

I need to go in and get some fresh air.

Get a thousand candles ... this birthday cake is for teacher.

Look! I found a thumb attack!

"Are those gerbils girls or boys?"
"You can't really tell because they don't have any clothes on."

You have to study to become a genius if you want to live forever.

"There aren't any dinosaurs left in Minnesota."
"Yes, there are—but they're all plastic."

My mom has a white coat that's red.

Did you know that all cats are girls and all dogs are boys?

... *crying:*
He called me "person."

The dwarfs live in a little cottage-cheese.

... *pointing to cobwebs:*
Are those Halloween decorations?

My dad took out the sliver with the pleasers.

My mother went to a cardboard meeting last night.

Let's play Thanksgiving. I'll be the cook and you can be the turkey. Get in the oven.

Exactly when am I going to know all about life?

The witch was so scary it made my throat hurt.

If Mommy and Daddy fell into the river, my big brother would have to pour milk on my cereal.

We played this two other agos.

If I have a baby I hope it's just a doll.

Let's make rootbeer. You mix whiskey and ice cream.

"I love pizza so much I think I'll marry it."
"No, you can't. You can kiss it or hug it, but you can't marry it."

Can I please have some dry water?

She screamed me over.

You draw something and I'll say it's good even if it isn't.

I can't think. I left my brains at home.

I bit my tongue. I thought it was a carrot.

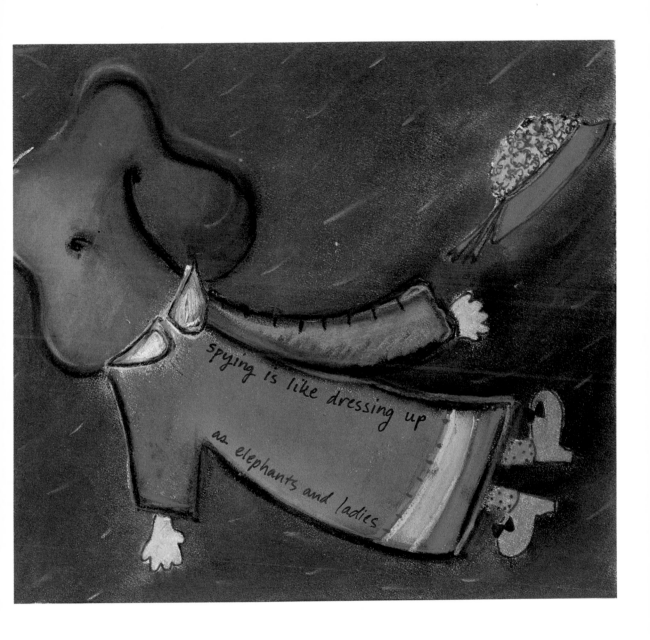

Spying is dressing up like ladies or elephants so you don't know who you are.

Outer space is farther away than China because you can dig to China.

Everytime I see a graveyard my throat starts to hurt.

When you grow up, you start to like beer.

We have a runny nose together.

I know these are your mittens. I heard you wearing them yesterday.

Here ... hold my snowball. Don't eat it.

We have bad furniture at our house. Sometimes it hits you in the stomach.

"There is no sun today."
"That's because it's Thursday. There's no sun on Thursday."

"These lilacs smell like tacos."
"No. Only the leaves smell like tacos."

Take him to the dentist. He's dead.

Sarah with the nice soft hair I can see your underwear.

Pretend you like me, okay?

How can everyone be sure that all pigs like corn?

If you don't wear your socks, your feet will get sick and the fireman will give you a ticket.

Say, do you know why we have butts? So we can ride trikes!

What color is the pink panther?

Something stinks like raccoons in here. I hope it's lunch.

I'm never scared of anything. But my tummy is.

"All we have to do is water the dirt and a new swingset will grow."
"No. We're digging for a new swingset—it's underground. Under
   all this dirt, there's more grass."

Don't say "stomach." There are no stomachs allowed at day care.

I don't smell anything. You smelled it all away.

Did you hear the bad news? The dinosaurs all died.

She's been talking to strangers so she has to sleep in the kitchen.

Do you know what color I wish it was? Summer!

Can I please have some dry water?

You can't make a picture of teacher because you don't have a gray marker.

Your eyes are so clean I can see myself in them.

For Christmas, I want a stuffed snowflake.

. . . pointing to a paper clip:
Please pass the trombone.

. . . visiting a retirement center:
When those people were little they used to go to day care.

"Pretend I'm eighty years old."
"No way."
"Well then, pretend I'm one."

Teacher: If you plant 3 trees today, and 3 tomorrow, how many
will you have?
Children: A woods!

"There aren't any single clouds today."
"That's because they are all hiding behind the blue."

After a compliment on a painting:
I didn't do it. My arm did.

Let's pretend we're having fun.

... looking at a dead bird in the spring:
It's dead. I think the Romans did it.

Skeletons don't have bones ... only Indians do. They have
bone-arrows.

My brother gave me his shoes because he ran out of them.

When you're done purpling, can I purple?

Do you know how dinosaurs cook people? They roast them over
volcanoes.

Children are sometimes heroes. Worms are never heroes. Worms are always losers.

. . . looking for a fur collar:
Help me find the pet part.

Now are you happy at me?

Please inside this out.

You have blue teeth because you're old.

Me and she are married. She's the grandma and I'm the baby grandma.

Pizza is my favorite dessert.

I always sleep with my eyes open so I can see my dreams.

I wish I was a little baby so that I wouldn't know that someday I was going to die.

Who wants to play with me? It has to be a boy or a girl.

I didn't get enough sleep tomorrow.

One time I was born in France.

I'm allergic to milk. Can I have some chocolate milk?

. . . outside in the fall:
I just love it when it leaves outside.

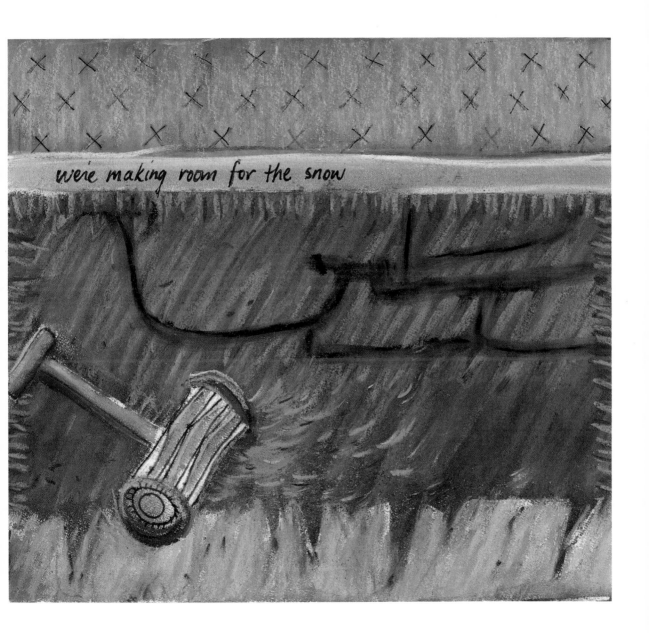

We're cutting the grass to make room for the snow.

The clock is fast, but time is slow.

Watching the river:
Does the water ever all run out?

Teacher, when you get little and I get big, I'll let you use my blanket.

I can spell 'Nell' ... N – e – eleven.

... in the wind:
Mr. Nobody is bumping into me.

Anyone who knows what "irritate" means can come to my birthday ... except teachers.

When I grow up, I'm going to be an artist. Then I'll draw so many pictures I won't be afraid of the dark anymore.

KU-731-144

INSTITUTE OF ECONOMICS
AND STATISTICS
WITHDRAWN

TJ 163.2
TRA

Transitions to Alternative
Energy Systems

WITHDRAWN

WITHDRAWN

Westview Replica Editions

The concept of Westview Replica Editions is a response to the continuing crisis in academic and informational publishing. Library budgets for books have been severely curtailed. Ever larger portions of general library budgets are being diverted from the purchase of books and used for data banks, computers, micromedia, and other methods of information retrieval. Interlibrary loan structures further reduce the edition sizes required to satisfy the needs of the scholarly community. Economic pressures on the university presses and the few private scholarly publishing companies have severely limited the capacity of the industry to properly serve the academic and research communities. As a result, many manuscripts dealing with important subjects, often representing the highest level of scholarship, are no longer economically viable publishing projects--or, if accepted for publication, are typically subject to lead times ranging from one to three years.

Westview Replica Editions are our practical solution to the problem. We accept a manuscript in camera-ready form, typed according to our specifications, and move it immediately into the production process. As always, the selection criteria include the importance of the subject, the work's contribution to scholarship, and its insight, originality of thought, and excellence of exposition. The responsibility for editing and proofreading lies with the author or sponsoring institution. We prepare chapter headings and display pages, file for copyright, and obtain Library of Congress Cataloging in Publication Data. A detailed manual contains simple instructions for preparing the final typescript, and our editorial staff is always available to answer questions.

The end result is a book printed on acid-free paper and bound in sturdy library-quality soft covers. We manufacture these books ourselves using equipment that does not require a lengthy make-ready process and that allows us to publish first editions of 300 to 600 copies and to reprint even smaller quantities as needed. Thus, we can produce Replica Editions quickly and can keep even very specialized books in print as long as there is a demand for them.

WITHDRAWN

About the Book and Editors

Transitions to Alternative Energy Systems:
Entrepreneurs, New Technologies, and Social Change
edited by Thomas Baumgartner and Tom R. Burns

This book offers a comparative analysis of seven case studies that provide insight into the factors that have facilitated or blocked the emergence of alternative energy production and use systems. The authors suggest that the actors (public or private, individual or collective) who provide information and know-how are extremely important in determining the speed with which a new energy technology is adopted. They stress the importance of incorporating legal, organizational, institutional, and social factors with economic and technical considerations in planning and managing the energy transition process.

Thomas Baumgartner is presently working as a research consultant based in Zurich. Tom R. Burns is professor of sociology at the University of Uppsala, Sweden, and head of policy research at SIFO, the Swedish Institute for Opinion Research.

WITHDRAWN

Transitions to Alternative Energy Systems
Entrepreneurs, New Technologies, and Social Change

edited by Thomas Baumgartner
and Tom R. Burns

Westview Press / Boulder and London

A Westview Replica Edition

All rights reserved. No part of this publication may be reproduced or
transmitted in any form or by any means, electronic or mechanical, including
photocopy, recording, or any information storage and retrieval system,
without permission in writing from the publisher.

Copyright © 1984 by Westview Press, Inc.

Published in 1984 in the United States of America by
   Westview Press, Inc.
   5500 Central Avenue
   Boulder, Colorado 80301
   Frederick A. Praeger, President and Publisher

Library of Congress Cataloging in Publication Data
Main entry under title:
Transitions to alternative energy systems.
   (A Westview replica edition)
   1. Renewable energy sources. 2. Energy policy. I. Baumgartner, Thomas
(Thomas Martin) II. Burns, Tom R.
TJ163.2.T7   1984   333.79'15   82-11089
ISBN 0-86531-907-3 (pbk.)

Printed and bound in the United States of America

10 9 8 7 6 5 4 3 2 1

Contents

PART I
THE SHAPING OF ALTERNATIVE
ENERGY SYSTEMS

PART II
CONSUMER-ORIENTED TECHNOLOGIES

PART III
PRODUCER-ORIENTED TECHNOLOGIES

PART IV
ANALYSIS, THEORY, AND NORMATIVE CONCLUSIONS

Tables

Figures

Foreword:
Toward a Sustainable Future

Denis Hayes

The industrial world was built to run on cheap oil, and now the cheap oil has run out. For a while longer, the West will depend for its energy upon expensive oil --much of it obtained from sources that are geographically remote or politically unstable. But in the near future, the world must shift from oil to other sources of energy. TRANSITIONS TO ALTERNATIVE ENERGY SYSTEMS explores how such change can best be encouraged.

Three proven energy sources are available to replace oil and gas: nuclear power, solid fossil fuels, and renewable energy resources. None is without problems. But the problems associated with renewable energy development appear to be solvable, while those afflicting the nuclear and fossil options appear to be intractable.

In assessing something as sweeping as an energy transition, it is often helpful to view issues in a broad context. In looking at the consequences of choosing nuclear power of coal as the centerpiece of a global energy strategy, let's hypothesize that each of these sources provides half the commercial energy needed by the entire world fifty years hence.

To produce this amount of energy from nuclear power would require the annual use of between seven million and twenty million kilograms of some fissile isotope --probably plutonium-239. In the hands of a sophisticated bomb maker, four kilograms can make a nuclear explosive. Even if the lower end conventional projections of energy demand prove to be too high by a factor of almost two, there would still be enough plutonium in circulation each

---

Denis Hayes, the author of SMART ENERGY, served as Director of the U.S. Solar Energy Research Institute under the Carter Administration.

year to manufacture one million bombs. If 1 percent of it
were diverted, 10,000 Hiroshima-sized bombs could be
built each year! If, through unprecedented controls,
losses could somehow be held to one hundreth of one percent, 100 new atom bombs could be produced annually. The
inevitability of 'normal' losses during production would
allow a thief --or a nation-- that operated within the
credible margin of error to divert huge amounts of bomb-
grade material without detection. It would not lead to
the kind of world that most of us find very attractive.

Coal, oil shale, and bituminous sands face a similarly unsolvable problem. The energy they contain cannot be
released without producing carbon dioxide. A 1,000 MW
coal-fired power plant emits about 270 kilograms of
carbon dioxide a second, or 16 metric tons a minute. No
economically plausible way to capture any significant
fraction of this gas has yet been suggested. If, fifty
years from now, half the world's energy were obtained
from solid fossil fuels, atmospheric carbon dioxide would
be increasing at almost 4 percent per year. If all the
world's coal were burned, atmospheric carbon dioxide
could increase eightfold. The climatic consequences of a
doubling of carbon dioxide are uncertain, but a near-con-
sensus in the atmospheric research community holds that
they would be dire. These include the parching of the
North American breadbasket and the flooding of the
Netherlands and of the rice-producing river deltas of
East Asia. Because of industrial development, the atmos-
phere already contains much more carbon dioxide than at
any time since the evolution of Homo sapiens. We would be
wise not to pursue an energy strategy calculated to accelerate the rate of increase.

Through elimination, then, we can conclude that renewable energy sources will quickly have to play an important --indeed, a dominant-- role. Fortunately, renewable sources are huge; many technologies exist to harness
them; and promising research is underway in fields
ranging from photo-electrochemistry to biotechnology that
will doubtless yield even more elegant technologies to-
morrow.

Yet, a decade after the first Arab oil embargo, the
world has made far less progress in pursuit of a solar
future than might have legitimately been expected. In
part this has been due to the power of vested economic
interests, In part it has been due to ignorance at high
levels of government. In part it has been due to simple
bureaucratic inertia.

However, perhaps the most important single reason
that so little has been accomplished is that, because
'energy' is connected to everything else, change is ne-

cessarily very complex. Change in western cultures tends
to be linear. A problem is found and 'solved'. Then another problem is found and solved. But solving the energy
crisis in this fashion is like attacking a large field of
bamboo with a machete. Each time a problem is cut down,
two more spring up to take its place. And at the root,
they are all connected.

It is in analyzing this broader context of the energy
crisis that TRANSITIONS TO ALTERNATIVE ENERGY SYSTEMS
makes its most vital contribution. Neither a guide to
technology nor an ideological tract, the book carefully
examines a diverse array of specific case studies involving the introduction of renewable energy technologies
in particular settings.

Some of the examples appear to have been spectacular-
ly successful. Others were failures. Both types have much
to teach us, if only we are willing to open our eyes and
learn from them.

There is, of course, already a fairly well developed
literature in the field of technology diffusion. The rapid
market penetration of automobiles, jet airplanes, television, and computers have been examined with care by other
books. But energy sources in general, and decentralized
energy resources in particular, possess characteristics
that deserve the kind of detailed attention this volume
provides. By probing beneath the surface in several different countries, the authors add breadth to a field too
long dominated by U.S. experiences.

Is there a simple lesson to be distilled from this
volume? I thinks so, though the authors never explixitly
draw a 'political' conclusion.

What the book makes clear to me is the fact that the
'free market' approach to energy being taken by the Reagan
and the Thatcher governments stands no chance of success.
Although the price of fuel is the most important single
determinant of energy usage, ultimate decisions are often
shaped by a combination of other elements. An energy policy that ignores institutional issues, environmental effects, social impacts, and political consequences can produce bad results, but will more likely produce no results
at all.

To be sure, free market rethoric has its attractions;
moreover, the track records of most public sector energy
efforts have been deplorable bad. There is perhaps no
stronger argument for the free market than the complete
botch being made by the Reagan Department of Energy.

Yet it is impossible to reconcile a free market approach with a field in which oil production is governed by
a global cartel and in which oil transportation and oil
refining are dominated by an oligopoly. When Adam Smith

formulated his concept of the marketplace, he was not
thinking of such 'natural monopolies' as electric utilities. If there is something to be learned from experiences in the environmental field over the last decade, it
is that market signals will not by themselves internalize
the costs of pollution, nor assign appropriate future
rents to depletable resources. These necessary chores
must be performed by governments.

The governments of the world, then, do not have the
option of piously washing their hands of the energy crisis. They must be involved; they must pursue wise policies; and they must prove far more effective in the future than they have in the past. Through its careful analysis of past programs to promote renewable resource development, Tom Baumgartner's new book provides the public
sector with precisely the kind of guidance it needs.

NOTES

1. Today, official U.S. inventories of plutonium and
highly enriched uranium show losses of enough material to
make more than 800 atom bombs. Such statistical uncertainties would quickly reach even more terrifying propor-
tions with the creation of a huge, world-wide nuclear
program.

Preface

The studies and analyses reported here were supported by research grants from the Swedish Building Research
Council and the Norwegian Oil and Energy Department. The
empirical research was carried out in 1979-80. The preliminary reports from the end of that period were all
updated, revised, translated and edited in late 1981 and
early 1982. The developments reported in Chapters 3 to 9
reflect, therefore, the state of affairs circa 1981.

In our view, the studies are important both as
contributions to debates and policy formulation relating
to energy issues and, more generally, as contributions
to knowledge about technological innovation and development.

The studies offer important insights into, and empirical descriptions of, the development of new technologies and their diffusion. The studies provided, in
part, a basis for the theory and the policy proposals
formulated in Chapters 11 and 12, respectively. The
theory treats technological development as a complex social process. Multiple actors, including diverse types
of entrepreneurs and change agents are involved in it.
The process entails social learning, the exercise of
economic and social power, and even struggle and conflict, as actors advocate different technological solutions and socio-technical systems. The unpredictable
and unplannable character of many technological developments is stressed. This implies strictly limited possibilities for effective government regulation of technological development. Several possible government roles
in such developments are specified and analyzed within
the framework presented in the book.

In addition to its value in increasing our knowledge of technological development, the empirical and
theoretical research reported here has direct implications for current energy issues and future energy developments. The research results are of continuing rele-

vance in today's context in spite of some changes in legislation, subsidy rules and market development that
have taken place since the studies and analyses were
carried out. In part this assessment rests on our firm
conviction that high levels of uncertainty and confusion
negatively affect the decisions and actions of potential
entrepreneurs, change agents and technology users, which
are essential to the successful introduction and development of new technologies. In our view the context for
new energy developments in early 1984 is no better, in
some ways even worse, than that prevalent during the
1970s, the period covered by our empirical studies.

The production and use of alternative energy technologies remain largely marginal, with partial achievements only in a few narrow, specialized market niches.
The developments in the 1970s, particularly those associated with the second oil price shock of 1979 and 1980
were to some extent encouraging. Entrepreneurs, change
agents, and users interested in developing alternative
energy technologies found conventional energy price and
supply developments favoring risk taking and investment
efforts, both essential to new energy developments.

But the early 1980s have again been characterized
by increased uncertainty and other unfavorable developments. The oil price declined in 1982 and 1983. Many
hope, some believe, that this will continue in the future. Energy surpluses have appeared in most OECD countries in connection with the deep economic recession.
Public and private utilities struggle to sell their surplus electricity, gas, coal and oil, even when this
means selling at cost or even at a loss, thereby under-
mining policies favoring conservation and substitution.
At the same time, energy policies oriented toward alternative and new energy developments remain in most instances fragmented, in some cases outright contradictory. Obvious barriers are unidentified or ignored. Governments hesitate to formulate strong policies and effective programs directed at consumers and energy consumption patterns. There is still an underlying hope
that market developments (including shifts in oil markets) will produce a breakthrough in supply, that the
cheap and easy supply of the "oil age" will be substantially restored.

Not surprisingly, the status of new or alternative
energy developments appear discouraging at this point in
time. In some cases, for example heat pumps in Germany,
sales have actually been falling. In others, such as
solar collectors in California and windmills in Denmark,
sales have stagnated or grown much less than forecasted
at the beginning of the decade.

The lessons that are to be learned from the past

have yet to be recognized or understood. Policy remains at best confused, at worst dream-like in the face of (i) long-term forecasts of oil supply imbalances and (ii) substantial opposition to nuclear and coal as alternative energy sources, an opposition which appears even more determined and organized than during the 1970s. Alarming reports are appearing daily in Europe about pollution threats to remaining forest areas and to people's health. These and other signals raise the spectre of future energy crises, particularly once OECD countries start again to achieve a sustainable economic recovery. This will set the stage for policy and institutional crises, crises which may, as during the 1970s and early 1980s, inhibit effective economic recovery and the pursuit of balanced, rational strategies to deal with long-term energy problems.

The arguments found in this book do not advocate or imply radical changes in current energy supply and consumption patterns. However, they do speak for the systematic encouragement of entrepreneurs and change agents to initiate new developments in saving energy and in introducing and developing new and alternative energy supply systems. The aim in the short to medium term should be to increase flexibility (and variety) in energy production and consumption and to progressively accumulate knowledge of and experience with alternative energy systems, particularly non-polluting and low-risk systems. Such a development would provide a favorable context (or point of departure) in the late 1980s and early 1990s for attacking effectively and systematically world energy problems. The long-term future developments cannot be planned or foressen, only prepared for intelligently.

Thomas Baumgartner and Tom R. Burns

Acknowledgments

We are grateful to our families and friends who organized their lives to make our travelling possible and who supported our often extravagant demands and behavior when working on this book.

This study has been supported by the Swedish Building Research Council (Project Nr. 790452-0) and the Norwegian Oil and Energy Department.

The seven case studies presented here are condensed versions of reports originally written in Swedish, Norwegian, German and English. They have been translated and edited by T. Baumgartner. The individual authors should not be blamed for style and formulation

Thomas Baumgartner and Tom R. Burns

Part I

The Shaping of Alternative Energy Systems

1
Introduction

Tom R. Burns and Thomas Baumgartner

The energy crisis is in large part a problem of mal-
adjustment: Established energy-producing and energy-using
systems are based on relative energy costs and energy
availability in forms (above all petroleum) which belong
to the past. At the same time, the energy forms which
will replace them are not yet apparent. This creates uncertainty and confusion as well as social conflicts which
tend to block or slow down the emergence of alternative
energy systems. The same applies also to those industries
geared to producing goods and services useful for complementing alternative energy forms.

This is not the first time in human history that
societies have faced the challenge of such an energy transition. For instance, Europe made the revolutionary transition from wood to coal use in the 18th and 19th centu-
ries. Such a transition usually entails difficult economic and socio-political adaptations, with substantial
changes in production systems, the distribution of social
power, and life styles. The energy crisis of the 1970s
has been particularly abrupt and difficult, since the
prices of the major energy resource multipled several
times in short, dramatic spurts and did so on a world-
wide basis. The ensuing confusion and uncertainty has
hindered the emergence of a consensus about likely and
desirable futures.

Tom R. Burns is Professor of Sociology at the University
of Uppsala and Head of Policy Research at SIFO, the Swedish Institute for Opinion Research. Thomas Baumgartner
has degrees in economics from the Universities of Zurich
and of New Hampshire. He is presently working as a research consultant based in Zurich. Both work on the development of a framework for modeling and analyzing actor-
system dynamics, applying it to contemporary societal problems such as energy, inflation, industrial democratiza-
tion, and socio-economic development.

4

New industries, their production processes, the
goods and services they produce, and their distribution
and utilization make up complex socio-technical systems.
The problem is that the "new" has to grow within the
framework of the "old" socio-technical systems and institutional framework. The "new" cannot be clearly perceived
and is created based on our experience with the "old."
Social actors --private and public, individual and col-
lective-- play the roles of entrepreneurs and change
agents pushing new products and establishing and developing new systems. They bring about --or try to bring a-
bout-- organizational and institutional changes which
will facilitate or validate the new products and systems.
In many instances, particular interest groups and social
agents are threatened by the developments associated with
the innovations. They may resist the developments and
succeed in reorienting or blocking them.

Also, existing values and beliefs, and institutional
and physical infrastructures make some of the possible
energy developments appear economically gainful. Others
appear unprofitable, wasteful, even though some of them
may be the first steps toward the solutions of the future. In this way, institutional arrangements --and the
social power constellations which support them-- select
out and shape with considerable bias innovations designed
to solve problems of the energy crisis. As a result, the
innovations and industries emerging are likely to be less
effective or optimal than would have been the case if the
necessary re-thinking and re-assessment of policies and
institutional changes had been carried out in a systematic way and at an early stage.

This book is addressed to those persons and groups
interested in bringing about transitions to new energy
systems, especially:

o   enterpreneurs and companies interested in deve-
    loping new products and markets connected with
    alternative energy systems;

o   government agencies responsible for developing
    alternative energy supplies;

o   politicians determined to deal with the energy
    crisis and to promote alternative energy deve-
    lopments; and

o   social groups and movements committed to develo-
    ping alternative energy systems, energy conser-
    vation and environmental protection.[1]

The book should also be of interest to social scientists curious about how innovations are introduced and
markets developed within industrialized societies. As
Freeman et al (1978) point out, none of the main schools
of economic thought --and the same holds largely for

sociology and political science-- has devoted much attention to the detailed investigation and analysis of the
sources and consequences of technical change. The research reported here redresses this neglect to some extent, at the same time that it offers a number of insights into the development of new energy systems.
 The research reported here investigated alternative
energy innovations and the development of new energy systems through a series of case studies. These describe and
analyze several of the key technical, socio-economic and
political processes whereby new energy technologies have
been introduced and systems producing and utilizing them
have been established and have grown.[2]
 Two types of technological innovation were investigated: The introduction, development and use of technologies (1) to provide energy to households and small buildings, and (2) to exploit new energy forms on a relatively large scale for the production of heat and electricity
by utilities and industry.[3]
 The case studies reported on are the following:

(1) the introduction and wide-spread use of solar water
    heating in Israel;
(2) the emergence and development of solar water heating
    in California;
(3) the introduction and diffusion of small windmills for
    the production of electricity in Denmark;
(4) the growing production and use of heat pumps in West
    Germany;
(5) the history and recent development of geothermal
    electricity production in California;
(6) the increasing use of wood for the cogeneration of
    steam and electricity by utilities and factories
    in Northern New England in the USA; and
(7) the development of peat for cogeneration in Finland.

 Extensive interviews in the field and by telephone
were conducted for the studies at the beginning of the
1980s. Also, when available, use was made of documents,
reports and available statistics. In general, we found
documentary material and statistics to be scarce, reflecting the recency of the developments described in the
studies.
 The studies provide insight into the factors facilitating and blocking the introduction of new energy technologies and the emergence of new markets and entirely
new industries. A general overview of the studies suggests
that not only physical infrastructures but institutional
and cultural contexts --and the power of different interest groups-- are critical factors determining the fate
of such innovations and developments. Moreover, social
agents who control and provide know-how and information
play a strategic role in determining the speed of adoption

and diffusion of new energy technologies. In general,
failure to develop adequate information and knowledge systems --technical as well as commercial-- and to provide
complementary service systems can retard if not block new
and useful energy developments.

The introduction of a new energy technology --or any
technology for that matter-- is not simply a matter of
taking an invention and producing it for someone to use
somewhere. It involves ultimately the shaping and development of social and technical systems for producing, distributing, and utilizing the technology. In many instances, existing socio-technical systems can be adapted and
exploited in establishing and developing the new. Invariably, system development entails a historical process,
the making of many different decisions and the solving of
a variety of technical, economic, and socio-political problems. Multiple actors and groups are directly and indirectly engaged in such historical developments.

Our case studies examine some of the ways new systems have emerged and developed in diverse socio-political, economic, and technical contexts. Of major interest
has been the role of entrepreneurs, change agents, and
policy-makers --private and public-- in initiating and
establishing new energy systems. Attention has also been
given to those social agents and interests as well as
structural conditions which retard or reorient new developments. The outcome of such struggles and contradictions
determines to a great extent the direction and speed of
social adaptation and restructuring in response to the
oil crisis.

The general motivation for our investigation has
been to determine the social processes, social organizations, and the strategies of entrepreneurs and change
agents which have brought about important alternative
energy developments. More specific research questions
were:[4]

(1) How has an energy-related innovation been in-
    troduced? A historical perspective on the inno-
    vation and the social agents pushing or oppo-
    sing it is a central feature of our methodology.

(2) Who were the key actors involved in the intro-
    duction and development of the innovation? What
    were their interests and motives, their strate-
    gies for organizing and bringing about necessa-
    ry social changes? For example, entrepreneurs
    establish new markets; they educate potential
    users; social movements bring about attitude
    changes as well as political and legal changes
    on different political levels.

(3) What were the major facilitating and constrai-
    ning factors in the course of the development

and introduction of new energy equipment? Who
were major opponents, if any, and what means
did they use to oppose or reorient the new developments?

(4) How were major constraints or problems overcome,
and which actors or coalitions of actors were
involved and to what key problems and constraints were they linked?

(5) What strategies, means of organization, and
other social technologies did these actors
use to solve key problems and overcome constraints?

(6) What role did state and municipal agencies play
in initiating, facilitating, or obstructing
--intentionally or unintentionally-- the new
developments?

(7) What appear to be current constraints and opportunities for further development? Which actors
seem to be most active in pushing for further
developments or in opposing them? What are the
prospects for the future?

Our studies do not provide answers to all of these
questions, in part because of the limited resources available to carry out the investigations. In part, they do
not because the persons interviewed and the documents
examined were not always providing answers. Despite these
limitations, we believe the studies provide considerable
insight into technological developments, in particular
developments related to the introduction and use of alternative energy technologies. They also point up the various roles played by different actors, their strategies
and the inter-linkages among them.

The research reported here does not suggest a blue-
print for the future. No one is in a position to provide
one since the transition will entail further innovations
and creative activity not yet known or fully worked out.
However, useful guidelines and lessons for managing the
future of the transition can be gained from the cumulati-
ve experience of developing alternative energy systems,
for example:

o   There are various development patterns of new
     energy systems, products, markets, know-how and
     expertise.

o   Entrepreneurs and companies interested in new
     products and markets are important in overco-
     ming strategic problems, but they may use quite
     different means to deal with them.

o   The challenges and risks involved in product and
     market developments generate different growth

patterns. Growth may be slow but steady, or it
may be rapid, in some instances, followed by
stagnation and unfulfilled expectations

o   The complex of laws and rules affecting the
     production, distribution, and use of energy
     equipment and facilities can provide many, of-
     ten contradictory signals.

o   Taxation and subsidies can have a significant
     impact on the introduction and development of
     alternative energy systems but they can have
     counterproductive effects if they are insigni-
     ficant, too complex, and contradictory in their
     signals.

o   Social movements, such as the ecological and
     conservationist movements, are potentially power-
     ful forces both for bringing about changes in
     laws and policies and in educating potential
     consumers in appropriate attitudes and practi-
     ces.

It is our hope that entrepreneurs, policy-makers
and others interested in the introduction of alternative
energy technologies and the transition to alternative
energy systems can use the insights and conclusions provided in this book to develop more effective strategies
and policies to bring about such developments. In part,
this means being able to cope effectively with the uncertainties and conflicts which such developments entail,
and which our studies point up. In part, it means mobilizing resources --not only technical and financial, but
social and political-- and forming coalitions and exercising social power to change conditions which retard, distort or block the transition. In many instances, this
means identifying and overcoming the opposition and inertia of vested interests connected with fossil fuels and
nuclear power.
     The next chapter provides a short theoretical in-
troduction to the shaping and reshaping of socio-technical systems. Part II of the book includes the four case
studies of consumer-oriented technologies, solar, wind
and heat pumps. Part III covers producer-oriented technologies, geothermal power, wood and peat. Chapter 10 in
Part IV discusses some of the comparative observations
and draws general conclusions from our empirical studies.
In Chapter 11, we suggest some elements of a theory of
new technology development. The concluding Chapter 12 indicates a number of policy and normative implications of
our studies and related analysis.

NOTES

1. Woodward (1984) uses the same approach to study municipal activities in favor of energy conservation and the use of alternative energy technologies in the housing sector in a number of European and American cities.
2. We distinguish three main elements in discussing alternative energy technologies:
(a) The energy flows and materials (solar, wind,forests, petroleum, uranium, etc.) which are potentially available for exploitation as energy sources.
(b) The technologies designed to tap energy flows and materials and to transform them into usable energy (in boilers, generators, collectors, heat pumps, windmills, etc.).
(c) The socio-technical systems --with a certain social organization, organized knowledge and expertise, and occupations and professions involved-- which produce technologies, distribute them and use them in the exploitation of energy flows and materials.
Spencer (1983) suggests a somewhat similar set of distinctions.
3. Wood and peat are not "new" energy sources but the technologies which our case studies look at are.
4.The theoretical and methodological framework on which the research has been largely based is found in Burns et al (1984) and Baumgartner et al (1984).

BIBLIOGRAPHY

Baumgartner, T., T.R. Burns and P. DeVillé 1984 The Shaping of Socio-economic Systems. London: Gordon and Breach.
Burns, T.R., T. Baumgartner and P. DeVillé 1984 Man, Decisions, Society. London: Gordon and Breach.
Freeman, C., C. Cooper and K. Pavitt 1978 "Policies for Technical Change." In C. Freeman and M. Jahoda (eds.), World Futures: The Great Debate. London: Robertson.
Spencer, R.D. 1983 "Renewable Energy in Sweden and Denmark: Wood, Straw, Wind, and Biogas." Report to the Thomas J. Watson Foundation.
Woodward, A. 1984 International Innovations in Energy. Communities' Conservation and Planning. Uppsala: Institute of Sociology.

2
Technology, Society, and Social Change

Tom R. Burns and Thomas Baumgartner

INTRODUCING NEW TECHNOLOGIES INTO SOCIAL SYSTEMS:
COMPATIBILITY ANALYSIS

Technologies are tools used in social action to
solve certain problems, to produce certain products, or
to earn income and consume. Certain concepts, standards,
and norms guide the organization of production and consumption processes and the concrete relationships among
the actors engaged in them. Thus one can speak of a socio-
technical system (Baumgartner et al, 1984).
Technology is only one component linked to a number
of other components in a social system designed to solve
problems and to accomplish tasks. Technology involves,
besides the obvious physical tools and equipment, the use
of skills and know-how. It involves a cognitive framework
made up, among other things, of underlying assumptions,
concepts, and principles about social and physical realities. And it involves social organization of the actors
using the technology.
This perspective on technology leads one to ask how
well any particular technique or equipment fits into, or
is compatible with, the various components available in a
social system (either in the existing socio-technical
systems or those capable of being developed at acceptable
costs). In other words, how appropriate are the material
social and cultural structures of any ongoing system for
a new technology? This is a particularly pertinent question if the system's infrastructures have been shaped and
developed to match quite specific, for example very large-
scale and capital-intensive technologies, and the new technological development in question involves small-scale
and labor-intensive technologies.
Technologies may fail to be developed or they
may be misutilized because various components in socio-
technical systems are inappropriate or are missing. Social
learning and restructuring of some kind will inevitably
take place in such cases. It may have negative or coun-

11

ter-productive effects. That is, learning not only relates to operating a given technology more efficiently, or making suitable innovations and adaptations in introducing it into existing socio-technical systems. Learning may also entail growing mistrust of the technology or its advocates. Ultimately this can lead to passive or active resistance to the new technology and its supporting agents. Industrialization in its historical development suffered from a number of such critical developments. Nuclear power is a recent, well-publicized example.

Compatibility analysis consists of examining the extent to which and in what ways a given new technology will fit into an ongoing social system, the degree to which it can be effectively used, and the positive as well as negative consequences of introducing it as such (Baumgartner et al, 1984). This entails investigating how the technology would relate to key social agents and groups involved, their social organization and power relations; how it would fit into and affect their ways of acting and interacting; how it would fit into and alter existing material and social conditions; the extent to which it would tend to generate opposition and conflicts, ultimately blocking its introduction or causing its non-optimal use.

Compatibility analysis of a technology and the social system into which it is introduced requires at least a rough model of the social system. This provides, as well, the basis for assessing social and economic impacts of new technologies.

The introduction and use of a new technology involves establishing socio-technical systems, or reshaping already existing ones. Such systems are the frames within which social agents will produce, distribute, and use the technology. The method of compatibility analysis considers in what concrete ways the introduction and use of a new technology will interact with the infrastructures and conditions in production, distribution and use settings. Key conceptual elements of such compatibility analysis are:

(1) Technology and material infrastructures. The effective use of a new technology requires the presence of complementary technologies. These may not be available or may be inappropriate, thus blocking the effective introduction and development of the new technology. Physical conditions, including climatic and geographic factors, are obviously important for the introduction and utilization of a new technology. Underdeveloped transport and communication systems hamper and constrain the use of many technologies; lack of maintenance and repair facilities, or their use for other purposes may similarly lead to misuse of the technology.

(2) Cultural infrastructures. The cognitive frames and values in a given culture may prevent the correct

perception of a technology, preventing its introduction
or distorting its development. Essential activities, such
as maintaining and repairing equipment, may be given a
low value in society, thus generating rapid deterioration
of equipment. Lack of experience with small-scale technologies may make it difficult in the short run to acquire
suitable cognitive frames to recognize the potential of
the technology and to push development in the most appropriate direction. Engineering and measurement norms may
fail to consider parameters essential for the correct design of the technology.

(3) Organizational and social infrastructures. Established or customary ways for actors to be organized
may prevent the effective production and utilization of
the technology. Persons with established authority, but
lacking real knowledge or expertise relating to the new
technology, may dominate social initiatives and the formulation of policies and rules governing the introduction
and use of the technology. Similarly, social agents with
vested interests in established socio-technical systems
may be in a position to block or hold back new developments (for example by refusing to allocate to them research
funds). Those actors with the technological know-how and
the entrepreneurial drive may lack sustained influence or
opportunities to bring about the restructuring and adaptations necessary to produce and make use of the technology.

(4) External support structures and institutions.
A socio-technical system for production and use does not
operate in isolation. External conditions and networks of
agents may be essential to the success or failure of the
technology development. We have in mind educational and
research services, advisory organizations, information
networks and training institutions. Political and legal
support and government infrastructures may be only weakly
developed in areas relevant for or useful to the production and utilization of the new technology. Key political
or professional groups may be unable or unwilling to help
in bringing about or organizing the necessary organizational and legal changes for the rapid transition to systems based on the new technology.

The problem, in many instances is not one of ill
will or lack of motivation, but of false perceptions,
and of scarce educational, managerial and administrative
resources. These may have been allocated to other problems, including those bound up with competing technologies (e.g., nuclear power). But outdated policies and
vested interests have their share of   responsibility in
blocking the reallocation of scarce support structures.
This implies that strategic factors in the development of
new energy systems are those affecting the availability
of social agents and institutions supporting the produc-

tion and utilization of new energy technologies such as
solar heating or windmills.

The above is only a rough sketch of the main elements and of the method of compatibility analysis based
on social systems theory. The utilization of such an approach can, in our view, contribute to realistic perspectives on technology introduction and development in relation to historically given social systems with established
socio-technical systems.

THE SHAPING OF NEW SOCIO-TECHNICAL SYSTEMS:
ACTORS, CONSTRAINTS AND INNOVATION PROCESSES

Below we suggest implications of the framework reflected in compatibility analysis as well as in the research questions raised in Chapter 1. A number of our
points anticipate the descriptions and observations from
our case studies, and in that sense provide a set of organizing concepts and principles for the investigation
and analysis of technology introduction and development
in social systems.

(1) No technological innovation will be introduced
or incorporated into production, distribution, and use
systems (PDU systems) if there are no actors -- entrepreneurs and change agents -- who push for its introduction
and development. These actors must possess or develop the
social powers to bring about the necessary social restructuring. These include capabilities such as expert knowledge, the ability to bring about new legislation, rules
and regulations, policies, education of workers, users,
and maintenance personnel, and so forth. Inventors who
create new things -- and entrepreneurs who produce them
and shape new markets for them -- may be unprepared to
act in areas where their resources and powers are limited,
their competence and legitimation low, and opposition
great. They may also be unwilling to pay the costs of strug-
gling to overcome major institutional barriers to the widespread acceptance and use of the new technology.

In sum, the establishment and development of alternative energy systems will require actors with social power, knowledge and motivation to bring about the necessary changes in material, cultural, and social organizational conditions. Otherwise, there will be no alternative
energy systems!

(2) The introduction of new technologies entails
either building up from scratch, or making use of existing systems of production, distribution, and utilization.
The new or adapted systems vary in their degree of compatibility with conventional PDU systems. The less this fit,
the more restructuring of material, cultural and social

organizational conditions is required in order to effectively introduce the technology, other things being equal.

(3) The institutional framework favorable for one
technology may be unfavorable for another. For instance,
a large scale nuclear program does not favor a large scale
solar collector program and vice versa. Established practices and the social power of electricity utilities may
reinforce conditions that make,for example solar technology and heat pump development, less attractive than large
scale nuclear or coal fired power plants. The institutional structure of the energy supply industry therefore has
important implications for the ease with which new technologies will fit in. Along the lines of such an argument,
Lönnroth (1978:27) points out:

> The introduction and expansion of oil in Wes-
> tern Europe did obviously benefit from the very
> stable structure built by the oil companies a-
> round the production in the Middle East. This
> structure included both intra-corporate, inter-
> corporate, as well as government-corporate compo-
> nents (in particular U.S. tax policies).
> .... the early expansion of nuclear power
> in the U.S. clearly benefitted from the division
> of responsibility for the fuel cycle, when uti-
> lity involvement was limited to the operation
> of reactors. The introduction of the LWR in
> Western Europe depended to a large extent on
> a regime under which U.S. companies supplied
> reactor technology and the U.S. government
> fuel cycle services.
> ..... Conditions on the local level are im-
> portant in other cases. The expansion of dis-
> trict heating is very much dependent on the
> strength of cities and local authorities vis-
> a-vis individual property owners, and here
> countries differ with Northern and Eastern
> European countries giving the cities a stron-
> ger role than other countries. Cogeneration
> within industry and district heating networks
> depend very much on the utility structure, and
> the less centralized utility structure of e.g.
> Denmark, and to some extent Sweden and West
> Germany, seems to be more favorable than the
> more centralized French and UK utilities.

One may try to adapt new technologies or other energy innovations to existing PDU systems, but it is not always obvious how this can be done. Also, there are often
technical, physical and economic limits to such technological restructuring, at least, in the short- and medium-
run.

(4) The more the new technology to be introduced 'misfits' with major components of established socio-technical systems, and of the society as a whole, into which it is to be introduced, the greater the restructuring required -- and, in general, the higher the economic, political and social costs of introduction. This explains why so often the technology will not be introduced unless a deep crisis or catastrophe compels it. Historically, the tendency has been for societies to put off radical changes such as shifting to entirely new technologies, even if 'prophets' warn about the risks of waiting. The transitions are made when necessity and the obvious failure of conventional technologies compel them. In some instances, a new technology may be introduced relatively early, but under marginal conditions and in such ways that it fails to be used effectively or optimally.

(5) The more radical the restructuring required to introduce a new energy technology, the more likely that conflicts will be generated, above all with those who have vested interests in existing structures, that is:

- o in established material conditions, conventional technologies, physical plant and physical infrastructure.

- o in existing knowledge, expertise, educational and research systems and in the status and privileges of particular professional and occupational groupings.

- o in given social organizational conditions: authority and control, rules and procedures, and institutional arrangements generally.

Producing radical restructuring in social organizational and cultural conditions in favor of PDU systems based on new technologies typically requires a coalition of actors or even a 'social movement' cutting across institutional spheres of society. Building up such a coalition usually requires certain strategies and means to resolve conflicts between different groups and agents who have diverse interests or are located in different spheres. Political leaderships and the state are often involved in putting together or coordinating such a coalition and resolving conflicts within it as well as between it and those sceptical or opposed to the introduction and development of the new technologies.

Investigations into technological innovation and development focus typically on inventors and manufacturers, particularly well-established, large enterprises. Although these agents are obviously important, we put

equal, or in some instances greater, stress on entrepreneurs who build up new enterprises and shape new markets,
those skilled in marketing, 'cultural entrepreneurs', and
users of new technologies. The latter, in particular, are
not simply passive recipients but actors open to new opportunities, who may be involved in influencing the design of
and adaptations associated with introducing and developing new technologies. In general, a spectrum of different
actors are involved -- and provide important resources --
in the introduction and development of new energy technologies.

(6) The various social agents involved in the development process, particularly those most actively engaged,
will succeed or fail depending on such factors as:

o their collective knowledge and learning capabilities, the ability of key actors to develop designs or models of new energy PDU systems and to get them to function effectively,
or at least to identify what concrete problems have to be solved to achieve effective
functioning.

o their awareness of the need, and their readiness to try , to restructure existing laws,
institutions, policies and other relevant
regulation.

o their ability to mobilize social power in
order to bring about economic and socio-
political changes, in part to deal with any
agents or groups opposed to the introduction
and development of the new technologies.

(7) The more radical the innovation in technology
or in the socio-technical systems based on it, the more
social restructuring which must be carried out. This not
only increases the likelihood of social conflicts and
political uncertainty (see point 5),but confronts enterpreneurs and manufacturers potentially interested in the
technology with increased economic uncertainty and risks.
Extensive restructuring, particularly in areas where the
entrepreneurs and change agents lack property rights or
a political mandate, will be difficult to carry out and
the eventual outcomes are uncertain. Uncertainty will be
high about such matters as ultimate cost structures,
quality levels achievable, possibilities for further improvements, likely market demand, levels of political
support or opposition, and so forth.
Given the spectrum of new and in many instances unknown problems which must be tackled and solved, lead times for the development of new socio-technical systems are

often highly uncertain. In any case, they tend to be long,
much longer than their advocates believe, or are prepared to recognize. Under such circumstances, it is extremely difficult to make reliable and valid prognoses and assessments of cost and sales potentials and other critical
matters, for example:

- o investment costs per energy production unit;

- o price level for primary energy and raw material inputs;

- o quality of energy outputs; and

- o potential demand (and demand among different potential user groups) when price and
quality questions are difficult to answer
with any degree of certainty.

In the absence of reliable data and knowledge about such
matters, secure judgments about the ultimate cost-effectiveness, or competitiveness of a new technology, particularly one requiring substantial restructuring, cannot
be made. Often, entrepreneurs and change agents act on
faith. The all too human tendency for most others is to
stay with what is known, what 'works', what is understandable and predictable, including predictable costs,
performance characteristics, quality levels and other
important features, until the development of the alternative technology is completed, and it has been shown to
work or not, as the case may be.

(8) The above arguments suggest that relative cost
calculations for different energy systems should not be
over-emphasized. The cost calculations for the emerging,
alternative energy sources are particularly uncertain and
subject to radical shifts, until the major problems have
been identified and various proposals for solutions tried
and effective ones identified.
Relative cost calculations signal risks. They help
make entrepreneurs and policy-makers aware of problems in
introducing and developing a new technology. But such
calculations are far from safe. Relative costs and prices
for new energy technologies may change substantially as
a function of technical as well as socio-political problem-
solving. These very often go hand in hand with the introduction of new technologies into production and use. Typically, changes in laws, rules and policies, changes in
the forms and scale of production, and in distribution
and use patterns can bring about radical changes in cost
and price structures, the more so, the more innovative
and atypical the technology .

(9) As pointed out earlier, a new technology is not simply equipment with certain technical properties. Its use and development is tied up with the shaping and re-shaping of complex socio-technical systems with physical, social organizational and cultural features. For instance, the use of peat as an energy source entails more than simply replacing an oil burner. It entails replacing one energy production system by another.

Establishing and developing a relatively new system involves a variety of problems, social and political, technical and economic. These problems must be solved in order to bring about a successful development and a transition to a new framework. Economic and political resources have to be mobilized. A large number and variety of technical, economic, and socio-political decisions are distributed over the entire process of developing the technology, and determine to a large extent its ultimate development.

(10) Consideration of alternative socio-technical systems may be a rational strategy even though they initially appear to be less "efficient" than the dominant choice. Only engagement in the actual process of learning about and developing a new technology and of structuring its socio-technical systems will demonstrate its real potentialities and limitations.

It has often been argued that nuclear energy is cheaper and more efficient than for example solar energy. This may have been true in the past and may still hold but only in terms of a limited time and context perspective. For instance, we recognize now that nuclear energy is competitive today because its early R&D costs have been socialized. Tax payers have paid for it and for substantial parts of infrastructure development as well. The economics of nuclear energy would look different if every utility using it would have to pay royalties and fees to governments to compensate them for their past investments. The present profitability of nuclear power is also significantly affected by the recognition of all the follow-up costs which will have to be covered in the future. Essential tasks and costs which have been left out of all conventional cost calculations in the past are:

o   charges for maintenance downtime and work which have proved to be more significant than expected;

o   additional safety measures which become advisable or compulsory in the wake of operating experience;

o   the decommissioning of worn out power plants, possibly their dismanteling and the guarding of old sites;

o   the storage and final disposal of nuclear waste;

o   the coverage for liabilities in case of accidents.

Arguments in favor of nuclear power still stress that "technological innovations" will certainly find safe solutions at acceptable costs. But those making such arguments in favor of nuclear are often unwilling to accept a similar argument in favor of solar and other renewable energy technologies. At the same time, they refuse to recognize the possibility that acceptable and cheap solutions to the problems of nuclear energy may not be found. In our view, the cost arguments against renewable against renewable energy sources -- and in favor of nuclear -- are premature and are based on very incomplete models and analyses of the relevant socio-technical systems.

In this context the obvious must be stressed. Nuclear technology is certainly much further developed than alternative energy technologies. The uneven allocation of R&D funds in favor of nuclear has now gone on already for many years. Those funds allocated to alternative technologies have probably never reached the critical mass required for achieving real break-throughs.[2] A change in research policy would substantially increase the possibility for rapid improvements in the cost-effectiveness of alternative energy technologies.

SUMMING UP

The introduction and development of a new technology is a historical process. The process of shaping sociotechnical systems entails the solution both to technical and economic problems as well as to socio-political and cultural ones. The key point here is that there are multiple, qualitatively different problems which have to be dealt with and solved in order to shape and develop alternative energy systems. There are many different actors involved in the process of shaping systems of production, distribution, and use of the technology. Important types of actors are inventors, production engineers, financial and marketing experts, innovative consumers and opinion leaders, policy- and law-makers, as well as those involved in social and political movements, which are able to influence the normative climate and the policy processes in the society.

These actors obviously play different roles and command different competencies and power resources. The inventor has the knowledge and the capability to formulate a new idea or to bring forth a novel method. But he may lack the capital or the skill to bring the idea into effective production. Those building up production may be bad at marketing the products, at influencing the perspectives and practices of potential users, or at educating them. Educational processes are often carried out through

networks of users and potential users. These different
actors play out their roles in shaping new systems of production, distribution and use at different but overlapping times.

A variety of conditions and factors influence the
development of PDU systems, facilitating, retarding or even
blocking the introduction of new energy technologies:

o the price, quality and service advantages of
   conventional energy sources compared to alternative sources making use of new or improved
   technologies. Vested interests support conventional products and their markets.

o the availability of entrepreneurs and change
   agents who push for the introduction of new
   technologies, developing new products and new
   markets.

o sufficiently broad and powerful coalitions of
   actors to bring about required restructuring of
   material, social organizational, and cultural
   conditions to facilitate the development of new
   markets and industries based on new technologies.

In general, the entrepreneurs and change agents pushing
for alternative energy sources are relatively weak at the
present time. But there are clearly important, and still
growing, social movements supporting alternative energy
developments although their support tends to be in spirit
rather than the "nuts and bolts" of technology development. Typically, the ultimate success of new energy technologies will depend on the position taken by large corporations, utility companies, the construction industry,
powerful labor unions, and key government agencies. Historically, governments have played strategic roles in reducing the technical and market uncertainties and in
spreading the risks involved in alternative technology
developments.

Established energy industries have their lobbies
as do labor unions and communities dependent on these industries. A potentially promising alternative development
may have at best a few entrepreneurs looking for new markets. Workers who will ultimately get jobs in the new
branch and the communities who will benefit from the im-
plantation of new factories are not yet known. They make
up no lobbying force while the former groups will fight
new developments which threaten their livelihood. This
suggests the strategic importance of policies which link
new branch developments to those who may be hurt by the
decline of conventional energy systems. Apart from this,
the state, or a socio-political movement, may have an interest in the development of alternative energy technologies and may provide the lobbying force essential to push

through initial policy and institutional changes that
will then open up opportunities for entrepreneurial market development.
     Government authorities play a very decisive role
together with entrepreneurs and utilities in introducing
new energy technologies and in getting started market developments. Of course they sometimes play quite negative
roles. The government's role is important because energy
is a "product" which is rarely left to "market forces".
People depend too much on energy for the satisfaction of
their daily needs. Like food, they demand from their governments as much as possible as cheaply as possible
(Spencer, 1983). Moreover, energy-intensive industries
--and the communities and regions where these industries
are based-- usually depend on the continued availability
of cheap and reliable energy supplies. Typically, these
actors are sufficiently organized to lobby and apply effective pressure on regulators and policy-makers.
     The result is that economics and politics are inse-
parable in the energy area (Spencer, 1983). Politics centers around the issues of pricing, market entry for new
producers and distributors as well as new energy sources,
R&D funding and subsidies, the extent of monopoly control
over energy production and distribution, and the conditions under which new equipment may be used. The more social restructuring required because new energy technologies represent radical departures from conventional ones
or because powerful vested interests oppose their introduction, the more politics is required for the development of alternative energy systems (Arnestad and Burns,
1984).
     Under such conditions, any energy transition will
require the mobilization of a powerful socio-political
movement or coalition to bring about the necessary restructuring. This transformation does not only involve
the restructuring of a variety of components linked to
the effective production and use of the new energy technologies. Nor is it simply a question of structuring
sanctions and incentives to allow such technologies to
grow and develop through self-transforming processes. (We
have in mind here the possibility to generate a sufficient cashflow, to be able to attract new investors and
to get bank loans, but also to be able to benefit from
tax benefits, subsidies and other government determined
benefits.) Obtaining a mandate and the legitimation to
carry out restructuring is equally as important, if not in
some instances more so, than receiving economic and technical support.
     A mandate and the legitimacy to restructure facili-
tates and makes possible the restructuring of components
in spheres which are not subject to market rules, such as
in politics and in education, but which nevertheless affect market behavior, consumer practices, and price deve-

lopments. The different institutional areas and spheres
of social action have their own procedures and rules of
operation, their own beliefs and values. The coalition or
movement must bridge these spheres and areas so as to
link and coordinate the multiple changes making up social
transformation and the transition to new, alternative
nergy systems. Legitimacy to do so is facilitating this
task.

Our case studies demonstrate that major innovations
in alternative energy technologies have been accomplished
and that new products and markets have been shaped. But
we are still a long way from realizing the social transformation that would carry industrialized societies
through the transition to alternative energy systems. The
barriers are not only technical or economic. They are,
above all, socio-political and cultural. Vested interests
in conventional energy systems are all too powerful. The
power and authority of those pushing for alternative
energy systems are very circumscribed, not only in terms
of lobbying strength and the ability to influence policy-
making, but also in terms of technical know-how and access
to investment and R&D resources, of influence on education and research policies, as well as the various policies which influence consumer practices around housing
and the use of cars.

Undoubtedly, a much more severe crisis than the oil
crisis of the 1970s will be necessary to provide a political mandate or to establish the legitimacy to bring
about the necessary restructuring for the large-scale introduction and development of alternative energy systems.

The following seven chapters present our case studies of the introduction of alternative energy technologies and the formation of viable PDU systems based on
them.

NOTES

1. Lönnroth (1977:132-133) has argued:

Today we chiefly use electricity and different
fuels (heating oil, gasoline, town gas, etc.)
as energy carriers around which distribution
systems are built up. Solar collectors or thermal
heat pumps for home heating purposes will require a distribution system, e.g., circulating
water. Direct electric resistance heating thus
impedes the introduction of solar collectors,
while water as an energy carrier admits of much
greater flexibility.

So the freedom of action toward the renewable
alternative will very much depend on whether
we can adapt today's energy carriers (and the

distribution system) to make them fit both the
coal and/or breeder solution and the renewable
solution. ... a continued rapid electrification
probably reduces the flexibility.

2. The only exception is research on photovoltaic
cells. But they are a crucial element for space exploration with all its military implications.

BIBLIOGRAPHY

Arnestad, M. and T.R. Burns 1984 Public Policy, Power and
     Social Change: The Case of Energy. Oslo: Universi-
     tetsförlaget.
Baumgartner, T., T.R. Burns and P. DeVillé 1984 The Sha-
     ping of Socio-Economic Systems. London: Gordon and
     Breach.
Lönnroth, M., P. Steen and T.B. Johansson 1977 Energy in
     Transition. Stockholm: Secretariat for Future
     Studies (published in 1980 by University of Cali-
     fornia Press).
Lönnroth, M. 1978 The Oil Peak and Beyond. Stockholm:
     Beijer Institute and Secretariat for Future Stu-
     dies.
Spencer, R.D. 1983 "Renewable Energy in Sweden and Den-
     mark: Wood, Straw, Wind and Biogas." Report to
     the J. Watson Foundation.

Part II

Consumer-Oriented Technologies

3
Solar Branch Development in Israel

Halfdan Farstad

Israel is one of the most favored countries in the world in terms of solar radiation. It is also the country which in 1980 made the greatest active use of solar energy which contributed around 1,4 percent to a total domestic energy consumption of 7.4 million tons of oil equivalent (mtoe).

Solar energy is primarily used to produce hot sanitary water in households, industry, office buildings, and public institutions. 33 percent of all households were using solar energy for the production of hot water in the late 1970s, i.e., 300,000 to 350,000 families out of a population of 3.9m. It is expected that between 60 and 70 percent of all households will do so by the mid 1980s.

Solar energy use reduces Israeli dependence on oil by about 2 percent. Oil covers more than 99 percent of primary energy, and almost all of it is imported. This still small contribution of solar to energy supply is the consequence of the limitation of solar energy to the production of hot water. New technologies developed since the mid 1970s are now beginning to open up the markets for air conditioning and for electricity generation. These technical developments partly explain the optimism in Israel about rapid future increases in the use of solar energy. Officials in the Ministry of Energy and Infrastructure expect solar energy to contribute between 8 percent and 15 percent to domestic energy supply by the year 2000. Professor Grossmann, a successful solar energy researcher at the Technion in Haifa, claims that

Halfdan Farstad has an MA in sociology and worked for the Energy & Society Project at the University of Oslo on renewable energy problems and the history of Norwegian oil developments.

solar energy could contribute up to 25 percent of domestic energy consumption by 1990 if only the government
decided on such a development.

The solar technologies and installations used in
Israel are all of domestic design and production. The
solar energy branch has expanded parallel to the growth
of the market. In the late 1970s about 200 to 300 producers were competing in the production of solar energy
equipment. In addition, a number of companies are exclusively engaged in the distribution of this equipment.
Below we give a description of the processes behind this
development.

THE DEVELOPMENT OF SOLAR ENERGY PRODUCTION[1]

The active use of solar energy in Israel began in
the late 1940s, probably even before the proclamation of
the state of Israel in 1948. Solar use has grown at a
relatively low but more or less steady rate ever since.
Few and small fluctuations in this rate of growth are
linked to political events, national and international.
Wars and oil boycotts have sometimes pointed up the advantages of having available domestic energy resources.

The Development of the Market for Solar Hot Water Heaters

The idea of using solar energy for the heating of
water was probably imported from Florida by American
immigrants at the end of the 1940s.[2] Some people connected home made solar collectors to the ubiquitous water
tanks on the rooftops. The idea spread. Craftsmen in
different parts of the country began production of solar
collectors on a small scale. Markets were very compart-
mentalized because communication and distribution networks in Israel were underdeveloped at the time. This
partly explains the emergence of a relatively high
number of small producers.

Market segmentation contributed to the producers'
passive attitude to the marketing of solar energy
systems during the early years. Market potential was
generally thought to be limited. Hot water use, the only
solar energy application at the time, was still a luxury
only a few families could afford.

The perception of a limited market potential induced
the producers of solar collectors to concentrate on their
other lines of business and to treat solar collectors as
only one among many products. Consequently, none of the
manufacturers managed to create a market dynamic in his
favor. Other firms failed to experience competitive
pressures. Everybody remained small, and nobody managed
to widen the market. The small enterprise structure
reproduced itself and basically survived until today.

Knowledge and information about solar water heaters spread mostly by word of mouth to potential solar collector buyers. New owners of such equipment talked about it and passed information and knowledge along through local social networks. Some information and knowledge was carried outside the local milieus by passers-by whose attention was caught by the distinct appearance of solar collectors on the flat rooftops. It was such entrepreneural consumers talking about and adopting the new systems, and not the equipment producers, who played both an active and passive marketing role.

Solar water heaters made up only part of the activity of the many small multi-product enterprises. As a consequence, solar collector panels were of poor quality due to lacking technical skills. Panel frames were made of wood which soon warped, letting rainwater run over the absorption plates, ruining them quickly. Equipment lifetime was often not more than two to three years. Most collector panels also lacked insulation, giving them a low efficiency compared to the equipment of today. This was not a serious drawback in itself. Israel's sunny climate made it possible to produce hot water even with the most primitive equipment. But it limited the exportability of the equipment thus also blocking this route to market expansion and technological innovation.

Yet, this equipment, despite all its weaknesses, allowed many families to gain access to sufficient hot water for the first time in their lives. Israelis use much more water than the inhabitants of the comparable countries along the European coast of the Mediterranean. Yet, high electricity prices, and regular and long blackouts due to supply shortages severely limited the available quantity of electrically heated hot water.[3] Especially during the hot summer months, hot water use required careful planning. Solar hot water heaters provided many Israelis with a sufficient supply of hot water, at more convenient times, and generally at lower costs than electric water heaters. The increased use of solar water heaters was therefore contributing to an increased standard of living at reduced expenses. This is the main explanation for the continuous growth in the number of installed solar water heaters throughout the early period.

An important technical break-through was realized in 1954. Miromit, a producer of tubular steel furniture, designed and produced the first solar collector with a steel frame and a relatively high degree of insulation. This design resulted from research carried out by Miromit's director since the beginning of the 1950s. Miromit's collector had a considerably higher efficiency and better durability than earlier collector types. Many collectors delivered by Miromit in the mid 1950s have been functioning without serious troubles ever since.

This technological advance induced a vigorous commercial development of solar hot water systems. Potential buyers, instead of having to contact a manufacturer, were now continuously exposed to promotion, advertising and visits by salesmen. But other uses of solar energy failed to experience a similar development as we will discuss later.

About 100 enterprises were producing solar hot water equipment by the end of the 1950s. The number of installed systems grew steadily throughout that period. Sales stagnated somewhat for a short time during 1963. The decision by the Israel Electricity Company (I.E.C.) to reduce night time electricity rates for electric water heaters was the main cause. I.E.C. attempted to slow down further penetration of the market for water heaters by solar energy equipment, the main alternative to electric water heaters. The accompanying publicity campaign however failed to achieve the desired result. The campaign stressed the convenience of and added comfort from having a ready hot water supply in the house. It did not emphasize the advantage of having an electric compared to a solar water heater. The message of greater convenience and comfort reached many households. Many buyers simply decided to install a solar heater, attracted by the idea of having hot water in the house. The solar market share did not change significantly after the initial sales stagnation.

The first 100'000 units since the beginning were sold by 1965. Sales stagnated again at the end of the 1960s. They remained flat until immediately after the first oil price shock of 1973/74 because of:

1. Changes in the housing structure: The housing needs of large numbers of immigrants throughout the 1960s required the large-scale construction of apartment buildings. Solar energy water heating systems for such buildings were not in widespread use at the time. The installation of individual household units was often difficult. New pipes had to be installed. Low water pressure often limited the distance to the roof which could be overcome. Roof space was limited constraining the collector surface per household which was negatively affecting water availability and water temperature.[4]

2. Relative energy price changes: Prices of solar energy systems increased in step with inflation. Other energy prices, above all electricity rates, remained more or less constant in nominal terms, reflecting the fall in the real oil price which began in the early 1960s.

3. Legal restrictions on solar systems: A new law had been introduced authorizing municipalities to restrict the erection of solar collectors in towns. This

law was the response to the ugly looking rooftops plastered with collectors and water tanks.

The first oil price shock of 1973 and 1974 changed all this. The economics now were again favoring the use of solar energy for water heating purposes. The government frequently exhorted the population to reduce the direct and indirect consumption of fossil fuel in order to improve the difficult energy supply situation in which Israel had found itself. Local regulations to protect the look of urban architecture were now overlooked in favor of national energy policy interests.

Sales promptly increased again and are stabilizing today around 100,000 units per year. The energy minister thinks that Israeli solar collectors are the cheapest in the world, yet made of highest quality. The Energy 2000 exhibition organized in Tel Aviv in May 1981 was to be the beginning of the big export push by the solar industry.

It should be stressed that the development of the commercial solar energy sector until the first oil crises was primarily the result of private initiatives. The government has financed some research projects, but they were mostly for other than hot water applications.

Solar Research and Development

Information about solar energy research, especially in its early stages, is limited. Such research started around 1954 in Israel at about the time Miromit's director first showed an interest in solar water heating systems. The first researchers were the physicists Block, Aschbell and Robinson, the latter from the Technion in Haifa. Block worked with the idea of using tall tanks for collecting solar radiation. Robinson tried to improve the efficiency of solar collectors and worked on other improvements as well.

The best known solar energy researcher in Israel is Harry S. Tabor. He entered the field in 1953 or 1954 when he was director of the Israeli National Physics Laboratory. He had the responsibility to evaluate research proposals. One day he received the visit of an inventor who presented some ideas on the construction of solar collectors. Tabor was forced to go in some detail into the technical side of solar energy problems in order to eventually argue against the proposal. In doing so, he became fascinated with the potential of solar energy. He started out to determine the reasons for the low collector efficiency. Tabor's laboratory was at the time subordinate to the prime minister's office. Ben Gurion, the prime minister, arranged initial financial support for Tabor's group and provided continuous encouragement for the group's work on solar energy problems. This high-level political support is probably responsible that Tabor's group has been one of the main beneficiaries from government funding of solar R & D.

Energy research in the late 1950s was to a large part solar energy research. This and Ben Gurion's interest in solar energy were rather remarkable because Israel did not face oil supply problems at that time.[5] Energy prices were low and Israel had just discovered some oil on its territory.

Tabor's early work led to several internationally acclaimed papers, for example on selective solar collector surfaces. These deal with different coatings of the solar collector absorption plates. This work greatly influenced subsequent collector development. Tabor's group built a collector prototype, applying the new theoretical insights. Tabor then took the initiative to find an enterprise willing to produce the new collectors under license. Miromit was finally selected by the Ministry of Industry for this task because it was still the only producer of collectors with metal frames. Miromit then built the first modern plant in the world suitable for the mass production of solar collectors, supported in this effort by Tabor's group. The plant was ready for production in 1958.

Solar energy research had also become broader by the end of the 1950s. Besides solar collector research, Tabor's group had started projects on researching solar ponds and low temperature turbines suitable for solar energy use. The turbine, based on the Rankine cycle, was to be used both for generating electricity and for doing mechanical work, for example pumping.

The turbine was first presented at a conference in Rome in 1961. The design was operating with water and was supposed to have a higher efficiency than steam-driven turbines. Special attention had gone into minimizing maintenance requirements in order to make it suitable for use in sunny, but less developed countries where qualified technical personnel is scarce.

The turbine, like many other renewable energy systems, compensates for the low operating costs with high initial investment costs. The high turbine costs discouraged Israeli companies from starting to produce the turbine although the existing units are among the most reliable electricity generating units in the world. One member of Tabor's research group managed finally to raise enough money to found the Ormat Turbines Ltd. Ormat built a production facility but sales were disappointingly low despite realization of all the technical specifications.

The plant fortunately remained in operation. The few units produced were mostly sold to industrialized countries which in turn donated the turbines to Third World countries. Operating experience with these turbines seems to be excellent. The second oil price shock in 1979

has now generated renewed interest in this technical concept. Expectations in Israel are high that the turbine
can be successfully matched with solar ponds. A 150 kW
unit was ready for commercial production in the fall of
1979. A 5MW demonstration facility being built by Ormat
now is to be finished in 1983.

Solar ponds are one method for collecting and storing large amounts of solar energy. Shallow, often artificial, dark-bottomed ponds are filled with high-density
saltwater which ultimately separates out a top-layer of
salt-free water with a relatively low temperature. This
layer insulates the salty bottom layer of water which
accumulates and stores solar heat. The heat can be removed with a heat exchanger and can be used to drive a
Rankine cycle turbine. Or the fluid from the exchanger
can be used directly in district heating networks or for
low-temperature processes in industry. The top layer of
clean, salt-free water in the solar ponds could contribute to lessen water shortages for household consumption, irrigation and industrial processes in Israel
and other countries. Calculations suggest that a pond
with a surface of one square kilometer could annually
produce 40 GWh of electricity and up to half a million
cubic meters of clean water.[6]

Experimental solar ponds built in the early 1960s
reached stable temperatures of up to 90°C (200°F) although 80°C (180°F) were more usual. The government
stopped support for the pond project in the mid 1960s
because it estimated that electricity prices from a
solar pond and Rankine turbine system would be about
double those from a normal power plant burning oil.
Tabor's groupe restarted the research and development
work after the first oil price shock in 1974. The energy
supply and economic situation of Israel had become so
serious by that time that the government covered 80 percent of project costs instead of the usual 50 percent.
Project objective was to quickly solve the problems left
hanging when the project was stopped eight years earlier.

Three large solar ponds, one of them with a surface
of 6,500 m[2] had been built by 1979. A commercial solar
pond plant was opened in the fall of 1979. The interruption of Iranian oil supplies in 1979, the main source
of oil for Israel, led to the consideration of a plan
to convert part of the Dead Sea into a solar pond as
Dead Sea water has the required quality.[7]

The fluctuating financial support for the Tabor research group reflects a more general vacillation on the
part of the government towards solar energy. Initial
support in the 1950s was basically personal support for
Tabor and his group by the then Prime Minister Ben
Gurion. Plentiful and cheap oil in the 1960s led to a
government disinterest in further solar energy development.[8] Only the difficult supply situation in 1973 and

1974 and its economic and political consequences led to a
more positive government attitude towards energy research.
Not only was Tabor and his group able to restart the low
temperature turbine and the solar pond projects. The
Ministry of Industry began to show a much more positive
and active attitude towards all research and development
groups in the solar energy field as soon as the development and exploitation of domestic natural resources
became paramount.

The government began financing 50 percent of the
costs of proposed energy research projects if they were
deemed to positively affect the national energy supply
situation. Support could go as high as 80 percent as in
the case of Tabor's work on turbines and ponds. Support
always took the form of straight financial allocations.
Loans, subsidized or otherwise, were never given.

The administration of this government program was
transferred from the Ministry of Industry to the Ministry
of Energy when the latter was established in 1977. The
hope was to facilitate with this reorganization the realization of goals assigned to energy research. But the
Ministry of Energy chose to simply continue the existing
funding policy for solar energy research.

It should be stressed that no organized pressure
group has apparently been influencing the development
of the Israeli solar energy sector neither in positive
nor negative directions. The nearly total lack of organized interest groups in the Israeli energy field con-
trasts quite sharply with the situation in other industrialized countries. For instance, as we shall see
in Chapter 5, the introduction of wind energy in Denmark
was heavily influenced by such groups.

This short overview over the development of the
solar energy branch and of solar energy research indicates how existing structures and institutional arrangements, that is the socio-technical system, tended to
select out and shape solar energy innovations. But the
innovative developments were also transforming the existing socio-technical system, although the mutual influence process may well have led to a suboptimal outcome, especially when looked at in retrospect. Innovations emerge and socio-technical systems are transformed through the activity of entrepreneurs and change-
agents. The following section looks at a number of
central actors and the roles they played in the emergence
of the Israeli solar energy branch.

DOMINANT ACTORS AND THEIR ACTIVITIES

We have already pointed out in the section on the
development of the market for solar hot water heaters how
important a role the final buyers of these systems have

played in diffusing them throughout Israel. We will not come back to this group because we were unable to interview early adopters of solar collectors in order to elucidate their motivations, problems and experiences. The historical overview has also pointed to the importance of producers and researchers for starting, and especially for maintaining, the solar energy growth process. We will look in the following in more detail at the reasons which made them behave the way they did, which problems they confronted, and how they tried to overcome them.

We will also look at the group of national politicians and central government administrators, local authorities and the electric utility. They all seem to have played a role in shaping the emerging solar energy branch.

Equipment Producers

As already mentioned, little is known about those who introduced into Israel the idea of solar water heating systems, and how the idea took hold and led to an emergent production structure.

It is known that the development started with individual craftsmen and small entrepreneurs. They produced and sold rather simple solar water heating systems. They were not really aware of an existing market potential which they could activate with appropriate marketing and product development policies. Yet, as precursors they played an important, albeit passive, information role preparing the terrain for others to occupy. They introduced solar to consumers and made them familiar with the idea of using solar energy for the household production of hot water. They thereby drew the attention of more sophisticated and technically better skilled producers to this market potential. These original producers had in general little influence on the later developments, both in the technical and the marketing sense.

However, one important decision taken early on in the development of the solar water heater market was to offer three and then five-year guarantees in order to assure customers of the reliability of the new product even though no or little practical experience over longer time periods was available. By the mid 1960s, buyers could even acquire an eight-year guarantee against a fee of about 10 percent of the price. This marketing strategy was sufficient to establish by the mid 1960s a level of customer confidence in uninterrupted, trouble-free operation equally as high as for customary household appliances such as refrigerators, ovens, radios and television sets.[9]

Technical developments of solar water heating systems have been dominated by larger companies. They had the advantage of having access to important economic

and technical resources. Their motivation was the prospect of profits and for this purpose they were willing to
invest in research and development in two ways:
 1. They financed 20 to 50 percent of research costs
for projects located at the universities. It was this
action which made possible the existence of professional
academic research in the field of solar energy.
 2. They built up enterprise internal R&D departments.
This action especially enabled them after the oil crisis
of 1973 and 1974 to considerably and quickly broaden
product range and improve processes using solar energy.
Such product development together with quality improv-
ments is likely to produce the increase in sales and
cashflow which will make further investment in R&D
profitable.
 Sales expansion is not just a domestic phenomena.
The tough domestic competition from the smaller companies
and an awareness of having products with an unrivalled
export potential are inducing the larger companies to
prospect, develop and penetrate export markets. Active
export marketing in the late 1970s had been concentrated
on the United States and Southern Europe. Sales of solar
collectors to these areas are increasing at a significant rate. The larger enterprises are now preparing a
similar export offensive for newer solar energy equipment, among others for central heating and air-conditioning purposes.
 The larger producers have also intervened and co-
operated with the government in order to positively
influence supply and demand conditions in the solar
energy market. The organisational set-up of research and
its cofinancing not only helped enterprises to orient
solar research development. It also provided them with
informal channels through which enterprises, loosely
cooperating among themselves, could influence governmental policy. In this way they got the government to
remove special tariffs on imported raw materials such
as copper and steel which are basic inputs into the
production of solar energy equipment.
 This successful reduction of input costs led to
price falls of 10 to 15 percent for solar energy equipment. This had a significant effect on demand; the cost
effectiveness of solar energy equipment with its low
operating costs is basically determined by equipment
prices. This price reduction put solar equipment for the
first time within reach of the weaker socio-economic
groups, thereby opening up a new large market potential.

Researchers

 Solar energy researchers played a very important
role in the development of the solar energy branch. Their
technical and technological improvements were indispensa-

ble for the manufacturing of qualitatively acceptable
products. The branch certainly could not have grown as
much and as fast as it did without such products. Improved technical quality was essential for strengthening
consumer confidence in locally produced solar equipment.
Designing aesthetically more pleasing collectors allowed
outflanking regulatory resistance to solar collectors
which had at one time threatened the further expansion
of demand.

These developments were important. As already mentioned, early buyers were central in spreading knowldege
and information about solar collectors, both locally and
nation-wide. This informal consumer activity accelerated
the formation of a national market for solar water
heaters. And the creation of such a national market was
the precondition for the entrance inte the developing
industry of larger enterprises who had the resources to
support a sustained research effort for further product
and process development.

The initial involvement in the branch of researchers oriented towards product development was therefore
essential to start a positive growth circle involving
improvements in product quality, expansion of the market,
entrance of new enterprises with their resources, and
so on.

Another factor was also important for sustaining
this positive growth circle. Consumers need to acquire
sufficient information to separate low quality from high
quality brands and products within an emergent product
application. This can create a substantial psychological
and time-cost barrier dissuading many potential buyers
from even trying. Early quality together with the already mentioned guarantees were therefore an important
factor in lowering resistance by individual consumers
to consider the adoption of solar hot water systems.

This process of technical development has greatly
benefited from the close cooperation between, and mutual
dependence, of researchers and producers. It led to a
rapid realization of new ideas and inventions, and therefore helped to sustain the market growth dynamic.[10]
Another result of this rapid diffusion of technical improvements was the achievement of an international
leadership position. This has had limited commercial
consequences up to today because other countries were
disinterested in solar energy utilization. The second
oil price shock has now transformed this situation and
the potential for a rapid expansion of exports of solar
technology and equipment is now existing.

Academic solar energy researchers have won international acclaim for some of their theoretical work. But
the development of new types of solar energy uses and
equipments not related to household and industrial hot
water production has not yet led to a breakthrough in

38

terms of commercial mass production. This might now also
change since the second oil price shock and the uncertain
oil supply situation of Israel make worthwhile every
effort to lessen oil consumption.

Scientific research and development have mainly been
motivated by a desire to make Israel's energy supply
less dependent on international developments. However,
some projects have been initiated in the past for ideal-
istic and for ideological reasons, the Rankine cycle
turbine being one such case. Important scientific find-
ings have been the result of work done by researchers
who became engaged more or less incidentally in the
solar energy field. Natural scientists having finished
their degrees, looking for jobs, got by coincidence involved in solar energy research and did some pioneer work.

Finally it should be mentioned that groups of
nuclear physicists apparently have resisted the allocation of relatively large sums of money to solar energy
research. They seem to have preferred transferring part
of these funds to research on fusion energy, obviously
for professional reasons. However, their arguments have
not met much favor in other milieus.

National Politicians and Central Government Administrators

Politicians have by and large faced solar energy
developments in a passive manner. Ben Gurion, the
prime minister for most of the time between 1948, the
declaration of the state of Israel, and 1963, was one of
the most important exceptions. His support for Tabor's
research in the 1950s has been decisive as pointed out
above. The ending of government support coincides with
Ben Gurion's retirement.

Oil market developments in 1973 and 1974, and especially the oil boycott by OPEC, changed many a politician's mind towards a more positive attitude to the
development of solar energy. However, it is more correct
to say that individual politicians, political parties,
and the administration together take a neutral stand
towards the different energy forms. Israel's politicians
have become very pragmatic about energy questions. There
are indications that they feel unsure about the importance of and potential for developing national renewable energy resources, including solar energy. Yet,
this neutrality and uncertainty luckily adds up today
to a nearly complete consensus to promote the development and use of solar energy technologies. Financial
support has again become fairly generous and other
political support measures are also taken. Below we
discuss the economic incentives available and the legal
support measures which have been passed in favor of
solar energy.

Economic incentives in support of solar energy:
Financial support and incentives have been introduced
both on the producer and the consumer side. On the
producer side, an important source of funds for supporting research is now administered by the Research and
Development Department of the Ministry of Energy. Funds
are available both for academic research and for enterprise product development. However, the practical organization of research in Israel makes such a neat
distinction impossible.

Research projects at the universities, apart from
special basic research projects, are never fully financed
by government funds. Solar energy research as a rule is
cofinanced by the ministry and the enterprises involved.
And this is independent of who initiates the project, a
university researcher or an enterprise. University
projects are commonly benefiting from a 50 percent
government grant.[11] Universities are therefore forced to
look for enterprises willing to cooperate with them. Cooperating enterprises are likely to be able to make
eventual use of research results for their commercial and
industrial activities.

On the consumer side, it is subsidies for energy
economizing which can be used for the financing of
solar energy equipment. The introduction of these subsidies in April 1978 was above all intended to get
industry to economize energy. Loans were therefore the
only instrument. A first extension of the law in July
1978 also made hotels and other service enterprises
eligible for support. In April 1979, it became possible
to get grants, and not only loans, for introducing
energy saving measures. Big energy consumers can apply
to the Ministry of Energy to get a 15 percent contribution to install solar energy equipment. There is no
upper limit on the value of these grants. On top of this
they usually get a loan for 40 percent of total investment costs. Repayment is over 10 years, and the loans
carry a real interest rate of 6 percent.

Industrial energy consumers usually accept an offer
of getting a 50 percent grant to use one of a number of
special consulting firms approved by the ministry to
identify energy saving possibilities. The grants are
given on the condition that the client eventually accepts
and realizes the recommended plans proposed by the consultant. There is no upper limit on the value of these
grants either.

The Ministry of Energy planned in 1980 to extend the
subsidy to organized groups of consumers in the residential sector. This would enable private housing co-
operatives and apartment houseowners to get grants to
install collective solar hot water systems. However,
solar energy equipment designed for individual households would still fall outside the scope of the subsidy

regulations. All these financial benefits are applicable
only to investments in approved equipment, i.e., to
technology and products that have been tested and certified by the standard-setting organisation in Israel.

The regulation of solar energy use. Two sets of
regulations promoting the use of solar energy are integral parts of the national building code. It had already
been the practice for several years to install solar hot
water systems in all public buildings when in April 1978
a law became effective requiring that all public buildings, including residential housing put up under government direction, should be equipped in this way. Administered by the Ministry of Energy in cooperation with the
Ministry of Housing, this law has direct and indirect
effects on the use of solar energy. The direct effect is
that at least 20.000 new apartments put up annually by
the Ministry of Housing for immigrants are equipped with
solar hot water equipment. This corresponds to approximately 50 percent of all new apartments built every year.
The equipment is collective, providing all apartments in
a building with hot water.

The law indirectly affects the plans of private contractors and property companies. For them the law signals
the seriousness of the country's energy situation. It
indicates the government's positive judgment of the
effectiveness and quality of the equipment available and
which it buys. Officials in the Ministry of Energy argue
that since the implementation of the law only a small
number of apartment buildings are built without a solar
hot water system.

Another law was passed in 1978 to remove barriers
faced by people living in older rented apartments who
want to install an individual solar hot water system.
Tennants always had the right to install the waterpipes
linking the system on the roof with their apartment. The
pipes, however, had to be installed on the outside of the
buildings for obvious cost reasons. This sometimes
caused protests from and conflicts with neighbors, and
installation plans often came to nought. The new law
forces builders of apartment buildings to integrate the
pipes linking the roof to the apartments from the beginning even if no collective system is installed.
Officials in the Ministry of Energy also planned to make
the installation of solar hot water systems compulsory.
However, this would have required the introduction of a
financial support scheme designed to support low income
groups of consumers.[12]

Other government measures in favour of solar energy
include:
(1) The reduction of the sales tax on solar energy
equipment.
(2) The organisation and financing of campaigns to inform

the population about the types of solar energy equipment
available and their possible uses.
(3) The organisation of continuing education and re-
orientation courses for engineers, technicians, and
craftsmen to upgrade their knowledge and skills with
respect to solar energy technologies and equipments.

However, not all regulatory measures passed by the
government were in support of the spreading of solar
energy equipment. A law had been passed very early in the
history of solar energy development which allowed municipalities to prevent for aesthetical reasons the installation of solar equipment. The oil crisis in 1973/74
induced a pragmatic policy shift inciting the public and
the municipal authorities to reduce the number of objections. This alleviated some of the effects of the law
although it has never been repealed.

The organisation of solar energy research with its
cooperation between university researchers and equipment
producers may have stressed short-term results to the
benefit of the equipment producers, but to the disadvantage of gaining more fundamental, theoretical insights
with long-term benefits.

Finally, other energy policies, often unintendedly,
reduced the attractiveness of solar energy equipment. The
prevailing electricity price structure provides industry
with subsidized energy and overcharges households. This
has retarded industrial investment in energy-conserving
solar technology equipment. It might have speeded up
conversion by households though. The bias in the subsidy structure for the introduction of solar energy
equipment in favor of industry almost suggests that the
subsidies for industry are a corrective response to compensate for the dysfunctional electricity rate structure.

The administration of the various support programs
on the national level seems to be satisfactory. Certainly
no criticism of the administration of the research support program has been voiced during all the years since
the program's inception in 1974. Project selection is
deemed to follow objective criteria. Administrative
decision-making does not seem to suffer from undue delays. The subsidy program for energy conservation was
still too new when we were in Israel to have already
generated noticable complaints.

. However, the effective use of the subsidies de-
pends crucially on the capability of the"Profession's
Energy Council" who vets the subsidy applications before
recommending support to the Ministry of Energy. The
problem arises because the Ministry of Energy pays the
subsidy before execution of the energy savings measures.
Enterprises and consultants could therefore pad the
suggested list of measures and include overcharged prices.
Or enterprises could realize less than had been promised
in terms of energy-savings investments. It was impossible

to receive confirmation one way or another about these
aspects of the subsidy program.

The only noticable delay in the branch development
process due to administrative incompetence and infighting
occurred in connection with the formation of the Ministry
of Energy. Energy matters had been handled before 1974 by
the Ministries of Finance and of Industry. The proposal
by the opposition parties after the first oil crisis to
form a Ministry of Energy to strengthen government action
in the energy field failed to be adopted by the government. Yet, the government was compelled in 1975 to form
the National Energy Authority (NEA) to coordinate energy-
related decisions between the different ministries concerned. Unfortunately, the law setting up the NEA failed
to determine which of the two ministries, Finance or
Industry, would be responsible for the agency. The
resultant conflict lasted for months during which the introduction of measures to promote energy savings was
delayed. The new Begin government decided within half a
year upon coming to power that the NEA should be subordinate to a newly established Ministry of Energy. The
above mentioned energy savings measures were then launched shortly thereafter.

Local Administrations

Local administrative bodies have been only weakly
involved in the development of the solar energy branch.
The only clear task of the municipal authorities with
respect to solar is the administration of the law regulating the installation of collectors for aesthetical
reasons. This law is only little enforced since the
first oil crisis was shifting energy policy priorities.

The law requires the buyer of a solar collector
system to get a permit from the local administration
before actually installing the system. This permit de-
pends on statements from the neighbors that they do not
mind the installation. The applicant has to collect these
statements himself. Only a small number of buyers of
solar equipment followed this procedure by 1979. But
those that do receive their permits within hours as
municipal objections are extremely rare.
The majority of buyers do not comply with the law and
install their equipment without formal approval. Doing
so they avoid the fee which has to be paid in some
municipalities. It seems that these buyers simply consider the energy situation to be too serious to bother
with aesthetical values (which were a concern of the
1960s). Anyway, nobody seems really to care about the
issue anymore. Municipal authorities do not even always
react when neighbors complain to them about a 'wild' installation. If they do, they ask the owner of the con-
tended equipment that he provide the neighbors' state-

ments as required by law. Neighbors' objections are simply ignored if they occur under these circumstances as the law does not give them a veto. It is rare indeed that someone is asked to take down again his equipment. But most non-complying buyers tend to get informal permissions from their neighbors before buying and installing the equipment if only to avoid administrative complications.

It is therefore not surprising that municipal authorities in some parts of the country have simply stopped enforcing the law. This non-interference with the installation of solar equipment explains the judgement that local administrations have not hindered the growth of the solar branch.

The Israel Electric Company

The I.E.C. is state-owned and possesses the monopoly for the production, distribution and sale of electricity. We have already mentioned the company's decision in 1963 to reduce night time electricity rates but only for the electric heating of water. This action was therefore clearly designed to stop the further diffusion of solar heating equipment.

I.E.C. had two motives for trying to stop the further growth of solar. For one, the electricity rate structure was -- and still is -- skewed in favor of the commercial sector. Profits were all coming from electricity sales to the residential sector. In this sector, electricity was mainly used for water heating purposes. The spreading of solar water heating posed therefore a clear threat to the utility's profit base as long as it did not consider charging more for electricity deliveries to the commercial sector.

Secondly, I.E.C. felt that the expansion of solar energy use was accentuating its peak load problems. Solar water heating equipment is generally combined with an auxiliary electric water heater. Switching from all-electric to solar water heating, and expansion of water heating (but generally using solar) reduced base load or at least reduced base load growth, and potentially accentuated peak load demands. This development required increased investment in expensive production capacity without a guarantee that electricity charges could be adjusted accordingly.

The I.E.C.'s price offensive had just the opposite effect from the expected one, at least in the long-term: solar equipment sales stagnated only shortly but electric water heater sales did not increase significantly. The I.E.C. failed to reduce the market share of solar. It has not undertaken other actions since then, leaving solar branch development to itself.

Other Actors

Two actors are of special interest here, the Standard Institute of Israel (SII) and the mass media.

Standard Institute of Israel. The SII is an independent organisation which tests and evaluates materials and products and which sets quality standards. It has entered the solar branch development process in the mid 1970s due to an initiative from the solar equipment manufacturers. It has done research on efficiency measurement, corrosion and pressure resistance of solar equipment, and on safety questions. It has suggested measures to assure qualitatively satisfactory products and has designed a company-internal standard procedure for production quality control. Manufacturers receive a quality certificate if they meet these standards. They then are subject to continuous SII control. Refusal to heed SII´s suggestions can lead to withdrawal of the quality certificate.

Participation in this quality program is in principal voluntary. It is financed by the manufacturers. This increased cost and the resultant slightly higher prices have not led to falls in sales. To the contrary, an increasingly larger number of equipment buyers purchase certified equipment as knowledge about the SII program is spreading.[13] The higher equipment price is obviously less important than the gain in certainty about product quality for a relatively 'new' product about which customers cannot draw on a store of general know-how. The big buyers of solar equipment, such as the state and municipal authorities, acquire only certified equipment.

Fifteen producers had asked for and received certificates by May 1979, and many more had applied for joining the program. The positive effect of certification on market share has induced the over 200 non-participating producers to also pay increased attention to the quality of their products. It seems therefore that the SII's quality assurance program has had an overall positive effect on solar branch development because it is strenghtening general confidence in the equipment.

The mass media. Mass media have served as communication channels without taking an independent stand for or against solar energy. Newspapers have printed many debates about advantages and disadvantages. Television, radio and newspapers have used features to highlight the solar energy option and to inform about new products and about research progress.

The mass media however has been effective in the late 1970s in supporting the government's propaganda campaign in favor of solar.

Interest organizations. Such organizations have not become involved in solar branch development. Commercial activity on the part of the producers and the effective spreading of information among buyers, actual and potential, have created the solar equipment market. The only outside intervention with some consequence has of course been the I.E.C.'s propaganda and price campaign in favor of electric water heaters and the government's propaganda campaign for solar.

CONCLUSION: GROWTH PROMOTING AND BLOCKING FACTORS

Two contextual factors outside of Israeli control have set a 'favorable' background for the development of solar energy in Israel: The sunny climate, and the conflict opposing Israel and the Arab countries (including the world's dominant oil producers and exporters). Domestically, promoting factors existed or continue to exist in four spheres of social life: the political, the organisation-institutional, the economic, and the cultural.

Blocking factors have been entirely domestic and have been concentrated in the first three of the four spheres listed above.

Contextual Promoting Factors

The sunny climate. The climate provided the opportunity to exploit the alternative energy source of solar. A slightly less favorable climate might well have delayed the emergence and the growth of the branch. Solar collectors which are able to operate effectively under diffuse light conditions are only now leaving the research and entering the development stage. It is unlikely that the development of the diffuse light collector would have gone as far as it did if the traditional solar collector had not existed to provide a market and hence to generate profits with which to finance further research. And this depended on good solar condition.[14]

Similar factors are underpinning the solar pond development and the development of solar air-conditioning technology. The hot climate creates the demand for air-conditioning equipment. Solar might be the solution given the high electricity prices. Solar ponds, to be effective, require lots of sunshine and the price paid for clean, salt-free water is an added benefit which might just be required to make this option profitable.

The international struggle and precarious oil supplies. The difficult situation in which Israel is finding itself, and its effect on the insecurity of oil supplies, might of course in any case have pushed Israel into the direction of solar energy use. But the developments throughout the 1960s and early 1970s suggest otherwise. During that time Israel shifted its source of oil supply increasingly to Iran, and it expanded its oil production from fields lying in the occupied Sinai.[15] The failed OPEC oil boycott of 1967 and the successful one after 1973 did not really change this situation, although the latter introduced an economic problem due to high oil prices. Official government support for solar energy development was accordingly low. Research funds were cut in the mid 1960s. Subsidies to buyers did not exist. Sales stagnated or grew only slowly.

Only the Iranian crisis really shocked the government into action with respect to solar energy. Iran supplied about 60 percent of Israel's energy needs when the revolution occurred in 1978 and 1979. The second oil price shock made the problem only more urgent especially as Israel had difficulties to find other, reliable long-term sources of oil supply and had to rely almost exclusively on spot market purchases.

Domestic Promoting Factors

Political Support. With hindsight it is now clear that the support of the then Prime Minister Ben Gurion has been decisive for all subsequent solar development. Ben Gurion's support for solar energy research, and the work of Tabor's group in particular, had led to the allocation of government research funds for fundamental work which is now beginning to pay off.

Tabor's work on selective surfaces during the 1950s led to theoretical and practical knowledge which has become fundamental for solar collector development in the late 1970s and the 1980s. It makes possible the building of collectors which can economically operate even under diffuse light conditions, thus extending the period when solar collectors can provide all the energy needed for water heating and now increasingly also for air-conditioning.

The work by Tabor and his associates, supported by Ben Gurion, had also led to the solar pond concept and the development of the Rankine cycle turbine and early experimentation with both of them when the government decided to cut back support in the 1960s. Yet the work had progressed far enough to allow for an emergency restart in 1979 when the energy price and supply conditions had taken several turns to the worse. The pond and turbine work opens the way to a large-scale use of solar energy.

General political support for solar energy development has reemerged since 1973. It has led to a number of government actions--research support, equipment subsidies, regulatory changes--which have definitely had a positive influence on the diffusion of solar energy use. Political support is widely spread through all political parties. No single party or politician is known as a particularly strong supporter of solar energy development. Support for solar seems to be based on a pragmatic feeling that it is good for lessening energy dependence and is helping to reduce the severe balance-of-payments impact of high oil prices. Of course, this same pragmatism had induced the government in the 1960s to cut research funding for solar energy development, thus delaying in particular development of solar pond and low temperature turbine technologies.

Luckily, energy price developments, above all those for electricity, helped to compensate a little bit for the effect of political non-support up to the later 1970s. The differentiated electricity pricing in favor of commercial users of electricity--although in no way intended to support solar--had the unintended effect of making solar water heaters an attractive option for residential energy consumers even when oil prices were falling in real terms.[16] This electricity price structure unfortunately ruled out the adoption of solar for commercial and industrial enterprises until at least 1978. Electricity price increases since then have made solar a competitive option to electricity for water heating purposes even in these sectors and despite rates which are still 12 percent below those for residential users. Politicians in Israel as in other countries have been slow and reluctant to intervene in electricity rate setting procedures in order to support alternative energy developments, especially if it meant changing the structure of rates and not just their levels.

Organizational-institutional factors. Of particular importance here has been the way research is funded and carried out in Israel. The need for university researchers to combine state funding with funds coming from enterprises has been certainly helpful in orienting research towards products and applications with a commercial potential. It also has speeded up the transfer of knowledge from the laboratory to the enterprises and into their products and production processes.

This system of research and development has also induced enterprises to work together informally although they might be competing commercially. It was this informal cooperation which helped convince the political system to eliminate the tariffs on imports of raw materials used in solar collector manufacturing. Price falls of 15 percent made possible by this tariff reduction was substantial enough to widen the market.

The work of SII in setting quality standards, in

pushing for better production processes, and in issuing quality certificates for products and manufacturers has also been important in widening the market. The existence of such an organisation and the wide acceptance of the institution of quality certificates made it of course much easier to submit solar products and solar manufacturers to such a regime.

Finally, all our information points to the important role played by the Office of the Chief Scientist at the Ministry of Industry as of the mid 1970s in speeding up the allocation of research funds. The office apparently made sure that solar research applications were treated more rapidly than other research applications by the relevant ministerial instances, thus accelerating research and development work in solar energy.

Economic factors. It is not clear if it was strictly profitable during the 1960s to use solar energy for water heating purposes before the first oil price crisis. The popularity of solar water heaters throughout the 1950s and 1960s and the result of the price competition initiated by I.E.C. in 1963 would however suggest that it was, at least in the mind of the buyers. The oil price developments throughout the 1970s have however made sure that solar is competitive today. In addition solar water heaters provided a more frequent availability of hot water and this might have settled the economic issue.

Oil price increases fed regularly through to electricity price increases, at least until recently and as long as the I.E.C. was relying on oil to produce electricity. Of course, solar equipment increased in price due to inflation, but so did electricity. The latter being energy intensive, and the former labor intensive meant, however, that solar equipment became relatively cheaper over the years.

The quality of solar equipment improved steadily over time, both in terms of efficiency and durability. The quality standards set and enforced by the SII played an important role here. This development also improved the economics of solar because it provided a greater energy output at relatively lower capital costs. Solar equipment produced in 1979 has reached an expected life time of fifteen to twenty years. It is estimated to have a pay-back period of between three and eight years which certainly makes them competitive with electric water heaters.

Macro-economic consequences of solar have apparently helped to convince the political leadership and the central administration that public support of solar has important social benefits. Oil dependency is decreased. Not only does this lessen the problem of finding sufficient and secure sources of supply. It helps in reducing the balance-of-payments deficit and it increases national control over the pricing of energy.

Long-term consequences in terms of employment and industrial activity might be even more important than the positive short-term benefits. This is especially so if the export potential of solar equipment is finally realized, something that has now begun to happen after the second oil price shock and the development of new types of equipment and new solar technologies.

Cultural factors. Solar energy use is today a part of Israel's culture: it is a custom if not an institution to use solar for water heating purposes. This outcome is the result of a fortuitous coincidence: the introduction of solar energy use and the early development and diffusion of solar coincided with the formation of an Israeli culture. Immigrants coming from a way of life and a climate quite inadapted to Israeli conditions could without difficulties adopt solar while they were also forced to change their whole way of life.

A number of other factors seems to have facilitated this assimilation of solar energy use into the emerging Israeli culture. The historical experience of the Jewish people has taught them to be adaptable to local circumstances. Even immigrants from highly developed, industrialized countries quickly accepted and learned to use hot water when solar energy was available. It is now part of individual behavior to postpone doing the laundry, for example, until sunny days are here again instead of going ahead and use the auxiliary electric water heater--integrated into most solar collector systems.

Reliance on national resources, even if it involves some inconvenience, is an accepted national goal because it strengthens national independence. And national independence is highly valued given the historical experience of large parts of the Israeli people.

Israelis have a high level of education and of natural science and engineering knowledge. This factor has facilitated the building up of a national solar energy development program involving quite substantial basic research.

Being a developing country, subject to great threats to national independence has so far made pragmatic values prevail. The visual pollution from solar collectors has therefore been widely tolerated--and the haphazard way of enforcing the law requiring permits for solar collectors only illustrates the point.

Our informants from the solar energy branch believe that these factors have been important for supporting the development of the branch. This view seems resonable when considering that up to 200,000 solar water heaters have been sold up to the first oil crisis in 1973 and 1974 and this despite sometimes questionable economic benefits and lack of government support.

Blocking Factors

Political factors. Inconsistent and weak political
steering of solar energy development has certainly
slowed down the exploitation of this resource. The three
most damaging instances here were the interruption of
research support in the 1960s, letting the I.E.C. try to
expand the use of electricity for water heating purposes
in 1963, and the delayed formation of the Ministry of
Energy and in this connection the preceding vacillation
about the National Energy Authority. Yet the need for
coordination of national energy policies was quite
obvious even before the first oil crisis.
The partial attempts at solving the coordination
problem were just that. Placing responsibility for solar
energy research with the research department of the
Ministry for Industry helped in giving higher priority
to solar energy research after 1973/74. But this department simply was unable to take new research initiatives
which had to wait until the problem with the NEA and
the formation of the Ministry of Energy was resolved in
1977.
The law passed in the 1960s giving local authorities
the right to regulate the installation of solar collectors is an other instance of this uncoordinated political decision making. Luckily it was never really enforced, especially not after the initial oil crisis. Yet
it might well have dissuaded some buyers to go ahead and
buy a solar water heating system. Licence fees and
bureaucratic hurdles simply did not help making the buying decision.
We have already pointed out how the electricity rate
structure slowed down the introduction of solar energy
equipment in the commercial and industrial sectors. Of
course it accelerated it in the residential sector. The
overall effect might therefore well have been neutral
with respect to the speed of branch development.

Organizational-administrative factors. The lack of
strong interest organizations (producers, researchers,
ecologists, etc.) prevented a more rapid development of
solar energy use. Popular mobilization could have been
faster because these organizations could have organized
the information spreading process. They could also have
lobbied more effectively with the state to maintain research support, speed up tariff reductions, and demand
financial incentives and other positive regulatory
measures.

Economic factors. The main blocking factor has been
the stable energy price level from 1950 to 1972, while
at the same time inflation pushed up the prices for solar
energy equipment. But such an energy price policy was not

only Israel's fault, nor was it then seen nor is it quite clear today, if another price strategy would have been much better over all.

ABBREVIATIONS

I.E.C.   Israel Electric Company

NEA   National Energy Authority

SII   Standard Institute of Israel

NOTES

1. Data and information used in this paper come from interviews of the author with participants in the solar energy branch development unless indicated otherwise.
2. Chapter 4 mentions the migration of solar technology from California to Florida during the 1920s when cheap oil and gas were making solar uncompetitive in California. Solar collector use was still widespread in Florida in the 1940s until cheap oil and gas also became available in this region.
3. Sobotka (1966:9-12) presents in detail hot water consumption patterns, rationing rules, and hot water heater cost comparisons. To illustrate the seriousness of the Israeli electricity shortage in the 1950s it is sufficient to point out that in 1955 total per capita electricity production was a low 720 kWh (and only 286 kWh went for residential consumption). This compares to a per capita world average in 1975 of 1'623 kWh with Norway, the leader, producing a high 19'336 kWh.
4. The reduction in collector size due to the use of thinner piping did lessen space requirements. This development has increased the number of individual collectors that can be mounted on rooftops.
5. Ben Gurion's roots in a Kibbutz in the Negev explain maybe part of this interest.
6. Tabor (1966).
7. Geopolitical realities make the realization of this scheme rather questionable. Large-scale intervention in and around the Dead Sea raises the problem of ecological consequences, among them changes in sea level and currents. Israeli territory covers only part of the Dead Sea. Unilateral Israeli action would generate serious political conflicts with Jordania. Cooperative exploitation of the energy potential of the Dead Sea is unlikely unless the Middle East conflict is lastingly resolved.

52

8. The attempted but failed oil boycott by OPEC during and after the 1967 war in the Middle East may have convinced the government that there was no danger involved in Israel's energy import dependence.
9. Sobotka (1966:11).
10. Schmookler (1966) especially has pointed out how the speed of technical innovation is essentially a function of the rate of market expansion and therefore of the profit potential involved.
11. High risk research projects can get government financing for up to 80 percent of costs. The projects developing solar air conditioning technology and solar ponds have benefited from this higher support level.
12. The price for a typical solar hot water heater for a family of four varied in August 1981 between 6'000 and 7'000 shekels (about $ 490 to $ 570).
13. All fifteen producers of solar equipment certified by May 1979 experienced increasing sales (both absolutely and in terms of market share) after having received the quality certificate.
14. Israel has about 3'500 annual sunshine hours, compared to 2'800 for Portugal. Maximum insolation during June and July (7'500 kcal/square meter/day) is about three times the December rate (Sobotka, 1966:11-12). There exists therefore an incentive to develop diffuse light collectors.
15. The Gulf of Suez and Sinai oil sources provided about 50 percent of Israel's oil needs until the former were returned to Egypt in 1975. The Sinai fields were still able to cover 25 percent. Their return to Egypt reduced Israel's oil self-sufficiency to 4 percent.
16. Even in 1965, solar water heaters remained competitive with electric ones when disregarding the imputed interest costs on the investment (something that most buyers of household appliances do) (Sobotka, 1966: 10).

BIBLIOGRAPHY

Schmookler, I. 1966 Invention and Economic Growth. Cambridge: Harvard University Press.
Sobotka, R. 1966 "Economic Aspects of Commercially Produced Solar Water Heaters." Solar Energy, Nr. 1.
Tabor, H.Z. 1966 "Solar Ponds." Science Journal, (June): 66-71.
United Nations 1981 National Report by Israel to the UN Conference on New and Renewable Sources of Energy. New York: A/Conf. 100/Nr/19.

4
Solar Water Heating in California: Policy Evolution and Industry Development

James Ward

This report describes the evolution of the solar industry in California through the late 1970s. Although the emergence of the solar industry is a national phenomena, California is generally acknowledged to be the leading 'solar state' in terms of regulatory policy, industry development and market penetration. For these reasons this report has focused on developments within California generally excluding policy and industry developments in other states and at the national or federal level.

California has led the nation in utilizing solar energy for water heating applications. California's leadership is often attributed to the state's especially sunny climate, but this study has instead found California's regulatory environment to be the major facilitating factor. Solar systems operate perhaps 10 percent more effectively in California than they do in most other states.[1] This slight advantage appears insufficient to explain California's relative success with solar. This report therefore deemphasizes climatic conditions and instead focuses on the evolution and current status of California's solar policy and solar industry.

Interest in solar among California public officials emerged from the national concern over energy following the 1973 oil embargo. California was becoming less energy self-sufficient and relied heavily on fossil fuels. Solar had flourished in California in the 1900-1930 period and was a simple, proven technology. Governor Brown became a strong solar advocate, supporting solar

James Ward has an MA in economics and has completed work towards a Ph.D. at Stanford University. He has also worked in the Norwegian oil industry.

legislation and using his authority to appoint pro-solar officials to the California Energy Commission (CEC). Governor Brown also established the Solarcal Council, an advisory group, to pursue solar commercialization.

The solar office within the CEC grew to a staff of about 35, providing research support for solar legislation and initiating programs to disseminate solar information. Additionally the solar office took administrative responsibility for the solar tax credit and for providing consumers with standards for solar systems through the TIPSE and CALSEAL programs.

Solarcal Council provided a forum for solar commercialization because it included a broad range of interest groups. Representatives were drawn from labor unions, banks, local governments, universities, groups advocating social change and appropriate technologies, small solar companies, public utilities, and multinationals. While the council had only advisory status, the council's recommendations incorporated the diverse and often conflicting interests of groups promoting solar commercialization.

With support from these two groups, California has since 1975 put together the strongest package of solar legislation and policies in the United States. Most important among these has been the 55 percent tax credit which can reduce the cost of solar systems by over 50 percent.

Despite California's efforts to remove financial and institutional barriers to solar, sales of solar systems have not met the expectations of California officials or of solar manufacturers. The primary reason appears to be a lack of consumer acceptance. Initial sales of solar systems have been concentrated among consumers with technical or mechanical interests or people associating solar with lifestyle preferences. This latter group may stress the environmental benefits of solar or may see solar as a step away from a high-technology, highly centralized society. However, private investment in a residential energy production system has not been widely accepted beyond these groups.

The issue of utility involvement in solar has been controversial. Opponents fear a utility monopoly on solar, a view contrasted by those seeing utility involvement as a method to utilize existing institutions to accelerate solar deployment. A compromise proposal, introduced in early 1980, requires California's utilities to provide interest-free loans for 175'000 solar hot water systems over the next three years. This additional incentive for consumers will bring solar sales up to the goals set by the CEC.

CALIFORNIA'S ENERGY SITUATION

California is one of the largest economies in the world, with an energy consumption almost equivalent to the one of Canada. The state's public and private interest in solar energy is an out-growth of concern over recent trends in California's energy supply and demand situation characterized by: (1) rising energy consumption levels; (2) a dependence on imported fossil fuels; and (3) a highly concentrated energy supply industry.

The utilization of solar energy has been viewed as having the potential to significantly contribute to reversing these trends.

Energy Consumption

Energy use in California on a per capita basis is about 15 percent below the national average. This results in part from the state's industrial structure and, perhaps more importantly, from California's warm climate. The average California resident used 281 million Btu. per year in 1975 compared to a national average of 330 million Btu. Residential, commercial and industrial energy consumption were below national averages while energy use for transportation exceeded the national mean.

Growth rates for electricity sales have slowed since the 1973 oil crisis. For the 1963-68 period electricity sales grew by 8.7 percent annually. This figure dropped to 6.3 percent for the 1968-73 period and 1.2 percent for 1973-78. Despite the recent slowdown, the utilities are estimating annual growth rates in electricity sales of 3 to 4 percent for 1978-2000. Over the same period natural gas sales are expected to rise about one percent per year.

Dependence on Imported Fossil Fuels

As indicated in Table 4.1, the relative components of energy supply have not changed dramatically over the 1960-75 period. 80 to 90 percent of California's energy in 1975 came from fossil fuel sources, largely oil and natural gas. Both nuclear and geothermal facilities have been added during the period, but remain relatively insignificant in the total supply picture.

Prospects for future oil and gas discoveries in California are uncertain and further increases in the state's fossil fuel consumption would be likely to lower California's self-sufficiency ratio. In 1960, 63 percent of California's total energy supply was produced in-state, but this figure has since fallen to 55 percent in 1970 and 42 percent in 1975.

TABLE 4.1
Sources of Primary Energy in California, 1960-1975 (in percent)

Energy Source	1960	1965	1970	1975
Petroleum	56	50	49	52
Natural Gas	37	41	39	32
Hydroelectricity	5	7	8	11
Geothermal Electricity	-	0	0	0
Nuclear Electricity	-	0	1	1
Liquid Petroleum Gas (LPG)	1	1	1	1
Coal	1	1	2	3
Total Supply (in 10^{12} BTU)	3'932	4'756	5'982	6'117

Source: Statistical Yearbooks

Concentrated Energy Supply Industry

Excluding the petroleum transportation sector,
California's energy supply is concentrated in the hands
of a small number of large companies. Twenty-one power
companies operate in the state, but 95 percent of all
electrical energy is delivered by three public utilities, Pacific Gas and Electric (PG&E), Southern California Edison (SCE) and San Diego Gas and Electric
(SDG&E). PG&E is the largest of these with almost 25'000
employees and sales in 1976 of $2.65 billion. In compa-
rison, SCE's 1976 sales totaled $1.8 billion and SDG&E
had 1976 revenues of $448 million.
In addition to publicly held utilities, California
has municipal utilities, owned by governmental agencies.
The largest of these are the Sacramento Municipal Utilities District and the Los Angeles Department of Water
and Power.

Solar's Potential Role

The CEC has estimated that an accelerated active
solar program could displace 118'000 billion Btu by
2000. An additional 29 billion Btu could be saved
through passive solar. Combined, this would only amount
to 1 to 2 percent of California's energy requirements in
2000, but would cover 15 to 20 percent of projected demand increase for the 1978-2000 period. At the same
time, solar would not contribute to fossil fuel or import dependencies nor further promote centralization in
the energy industry.

CALIFORNIA SOLAR ENERGY LEGISLATION

Since the middle of the 1970s there has been a general consensus among California legislators that increased utilization of solar energy was a desirable goal
for the state. To this end, the California legislature
has enacted numerous bills effectively subsidizing consumer purchases of solar equipment.
Supporters of state subsidies argue that the relative price of solar energy vis-a-vis other energy sources
has been distorted by the large subsidies granted to oil
and gas producers and to the nuclear industry. In addition, they argue that the average cost pricing principle
used by the utilities distorts the true relative social
costs. Subsidies for solar would tend to lessen this
distortion.
A second argument advanced in support of solar subsidies is that prices for fossil fuels and nuclear power
do not reflect the externalities of pollution and of
radioactive waste. The market prices of these energy
resources are therefore below their true social cost. As
solar proponents view solar as being free from such externalities, they argue solar is overpriced in the market relative to fossil fuels when externality considerations are included.
A final argument, which was especially influential
in the California solar debate, is that there are intangible social benefits associated with solar energy.
This view, an offshoot of the 'Small is Beautiful' philosophy, argues that decentralization of energy production
provides increased personal freedom and a dispersion of
political and economic power away from large institutions, and toward individuals.
Counterarguments exist for each of these views. But
these arguments have been persuasive enough to lead to
the passage of legislation both encouraging and mandat-
ing solar utilization in California. This chapter outlines the evolution of California's solar policy. It
begins with a discussion of proposed and enacted solar
legislation through 1977 followed by a discussion of the
state warranty program, the tax credit bill, the establishment of the Solarcal Council, and solar initiatives
at the local level.

Legislative Activity, 1970-1977

Interest in solar energy in California was only
renewed after real energy prices stopped falling in the
early 1970s. The quadrupling of oil prices and related
price increases for other forms of energy demonstrated
the need for government energy planning.
In 1973, a bill was introduced to create the CEC.
The CEC was charged with certification of power sites

and with drafting a program for research on and development of energy supply, consumption, and conservation. The bill also required the commission to develop plans to deal with possible shortages and it levied a surcharge on electricity to finance the provisions of the bill.

While public discussions in 1974 and 1975 debated whether the energy crisis was real or artificial, temporary or chronic, very little was achieved in the public sector in support of solar development. But a small solar sector was developing nonetheless, largely as an outgrowth of the plumbing, heating and air conditioning industry. A need to guide the industry and to offer support was recognized by some politicians, but six solar bills died in the legislature in 1975 after being introduced. These were:

1. A bill requiring the CEC to submit recommendations for standards for solar energy equipment, and to develop and fund the construction of prototype solar housing.
2. A bill to appropriate $10 million for demonstration projects for solar heating and cooling and for insulation throughout California.
3. A bill to permit a deduction from taxable income for the total cost of purchasing and installing solar energy systems.
4. An amendment to the state constitution to allow property used to generate energy by utilizing renewable sources to be exempt from property taxes.
5. A bill that would have prohibited any government agency from constructing any buildings over 35'000 square feet without conducting a cost analysis of solar versus conventional systems.
6. A bill to exempt property from taxation if used as part of a solar energy system.

However, in 1975, one significant bill was passed. Senator Alquist introduced a bill to allow any taxpayer a personal income tax credit equal to 10 percent or $1'000, whichever is less, of the cost of a solar energy system.

About the same time Jerry Brown, Governor of California, became a strong supporter of the 'Small is Beautiful' philosophy which proposed small-scale 'appropriate technology' solutions for contemporary economic problems. Brown increasingly advocated solar and a number of small organizations became active lobbyists for solar.

While solar received increasing public attention, legislative action during 1976 was weak. Of the eight solar related bills that were proposed, only three were enacted:

1. AB 338 (introduced by Kapiloff) would have directed the CEC to select sites and construct projects for the generation of electricity from
windmills, saline ponds, geothermal and solar
systems. It died in the assembly.
2. AB 2740 (Kapiloff) authorizes any city or county
to require that new buildings, subject to the
state housing law, be constructed to permit installation of solar energy devices. It was signed
into law in 1976 by the governor.
3. AB 3044 (Suitt) would have authorized any tax
payer subject to personal income tax to deduct
the cost of purchasing and installing any device
for the generation of energy from solar or wind
sources. It died in the assembly.
4. AB 3833 (Suitt) authorizes participation of the
CEC in large scale demonstrations of alternative
energy systems. Not more than one-half of the
commission's funds can be used for these demonstrations. The governor signed the measure in
1976.
5. AB 4054 (Fazio) would have enacted the 'Alternative Energy Source Bond Law of 1976' which authorized the issue of $250 million in bonds to
provide money for CEC approved projects that develop and use alternative energy sources. It
died in the assembly.
6. ACR 159 (Suitt) requests funds from the Federal
Government to begin construction of a solar
heating and cooling system for the Palm Desert
Middle School. It was passed.
7. SB 1524 (Smith) would have authorized the CEC to
write and administer a program to loan money to
finance residential installations of solar energy
systems. This bill also provided for the issue
of state bonds of up to $25 million to fund the
loan program. It was defeated in the statewide
referendum in November 1976.
8. SCA 45 (Smith) would have allowed the legislature to pass laws establishing loan programs for
the installation of energy insulation or solar
heating or cooling systems in residential structures. These loans could bear interest at less
than prevailing market rates. It too was defeated in the statewide referendum in November
1976.

The debate in the legislature on these bills involved financial concerns rather than the issue of solar/
anti-solar. Opposition to the solar bills came from conservative elements, but it focused on the fiscal impact
such bills would have on the California state budget
with respect to increased cash outlays or reduced state

tax revenues. The bills which were enacted demonstrated legislative support for solar as long as policies did not require substantial state expenditures.

With the continuous increases in energy prices, solar water heating became more cost effective vis-a-vis conventional energy sources. However, solar still suffered from public scepticism, lack of state financial support and the absence of coordinated state solar programs. During 1977, support for stronger solar legislation began to appear from numerous groups:

1. The California Solar Energy Industries Association (CAL-SEIA), the association of the solar industry, grew in size and became an active, efficient organization to coordinate interests of solar manufactures, contractors, and installers.

2. SUNRAE, an outgrowth of the anti-nuclear movement, began to coordinate efforts of diverse groups and to actively lobby in the state capital for solar legislation. SUNRAE's funding came from private contributions and the profitable operation of a recycling center in Southern California.

3. Governor Brown's influence over the appointees to the CEC resulted in a highly competent pro-solar group within the state bureaucracy.

4. Environmental organizations and groups promoting social change saw solar as a viable solution to California's energy dilemma. Environmental groups enjoy high visibility in California. They promoted solar as an environmentally benign energy solution. Building on Schumacher's and Lovins' ideas, groups such as the Council for Economic Democracy (CED) saw solar as a method to decentralize energy production and reverse the trend toward energy (and power) monopolies.

As these organizations became more cohesive, defined their roles, and received public exposure, the solar lobby became increasingly influential.

State Testing and Labelling Programs

A significant infrastructure problem for the industry was addressed in early 1977. A bill (AB 1512) was proposed that allowed the CEC to develop testing standards for solar energy equipment, and to produce a manual of designs, costs, performance and evaluation procedures for passive solar systems. At that time, the solar industry was largely composed of small businesses: manufacturers of collectors, contractors, and installers selling a wide variety of components and systems. Warranties, when given, varied considerably. Consumers had little to protect them from contractors selling inefficient devices. The legislature recognized these infrastructure problems and empowered the CEC to begin work on a solar standards program through passage of the bill in September 1977.

In response to this action, two types of testing and certification programs have developed. The Testing and Inspection Program for Solar Equipment (TIPSE), administered by the CEC, provides comparable performance data on solar collectors. CAL-SEAL, a joint program administered by CEC and CAL-SEIA, was designed largely to certify collectors for the state tax credit.

TIPSE is a voluntary program through which manufacturers can have their glazed flat plate collectors subjected to testing. The tests, which are performed by independent laboratories, are carried out under equivalent conditions for all collectors. As of April 1979, 26 manufacturers with 54 models of solar collectors had been certified under the program. By 1981 these had grown to 71 manufacturers and 167 models of solar collectors.

In the TIPSE program, the following tests are performed on a flat plate collector taken at random from a manufacturer's production line:

1. 30-Day Stagnation Test: The collector, with no fluid flowing through it, is exposed to the sun for a period of 30 days. When no fluid passes through a collector to carry away the heat, temperatures of 300 to 400°F (150 to 200°C) are not uncommon. The collector must withstand these high temperatures without significant reduction in performance.

2. Thermal Shock and Water Spray Test: The shock of cold rain hitting the glazing of a heated collector is simulated to see if stress defects appear in materials or construction.

3. Thermal Shock and Cold Fill Test: The heated collector is filled with cold fluid to see if it suffers stress-related damage.

4. Static-Pressure Leakage Test: The collector is pressurized to at least 125 percent of its rated maximum pressure to determine if any of the previous tests have caused serious damage.

5. Thermal Performance (Efficiency) Test: This final test measures the collector's efficiency, which is the ratio of useful heat output from the collector to the solar energy input.

The TIPSE label includes the thermal performances data and is affixed to all production-line assemblies of collector models that successfully completed the testing procedures. An important benefit to consumers is that they can now use independent test data (instead of just the manufacrurer's data) to compare collector efficiencies.

A CAL-SEAL label affixed to a solar energy system

indicates that both CAL-SEIA and the CEC have found that
the system meets the technical requirements for the California solar tax credit according to the CEC's regula--
tions; however, the final decision of taxpayer eligibility can only be made by the Franchise Tax Board. CAL-SEAL
labels are issued for solar energy systems installed by
properly licensed contractors or by owner-installers.
The program also assists owners of labeled systems who
have complaints regarding system operation by providing
trained,neutral field inspectors and by mediating consumer disputes. If manufacturers do not respond to valid
consumer complaints, the right to issue CAL-SEAL labels
may be revoked. The procedure for processing complaints
is illustrated in figure 4.1.
    One problem with the industry's self-regulation sur-
faced in early 1981. A small solar manufacturer was denied certification by CAL-SEAL. He subsequently filed a
$10 million suit against CAL-SEIA and the firms whose re-
presentatives form CAL-SEIA's board of directors. The
suit charged unfair competition and conspiracy to interfere with the plaintiff's business by wrongfully with-
holding CAL-SEAL labels. The suit's outcome has yet to
be determined. But the suit is already raising important
questions concerning the appropriateness of CAL-SEIA's
involvement in product certification.

The 55 Percent Tax Credit

    The most significant legislation enacted to date
was the one proposed by Assemblyman Gary Hart in April,
1977. Hart's bill would have allowed a 50 percent tax
credit to replace the 10 percent tax credit of 1975. Conservative, fiscalist legislators questioned the need for
such a tax credit and were concerned over its impact
on the state budget. The Revenue and Taxation Committee
proposed a compromise: if a federal tax credit was enacted, the combined total could not exceed 50 percent.
The bill so amended was sent to the legislature. For
publicity, SUNRAE set up solar exhibits on the state
capitol grounds and Governor Brown appeared at a press
conference, examining the SUNRAE exhibit and endorsing
the bill. The CEC and the Public Utilities Commission
(PUC) also voiced their support.
    Surprising opposition to the bill came from liberal
legislators, claiming tax credits benefit only the
wealthy. Another compromise was achieved and the final
bill was enacted allowing for a 55 percent credit up to
$3'000. The key components of the bill are as follows:

    1. Time Frame: Good for any system installed be-
tween January 1, 1977 and January 1, 1981.
    2. Amount: For any system under $6'000 the credit
is 55 percent or $3'000, whichever is less. For systems

63

FIGURE 4.1
CAL-SEIA Complaint and Rectification Procedure for Buyers of Solar Water Heaters in the PG&E Area.

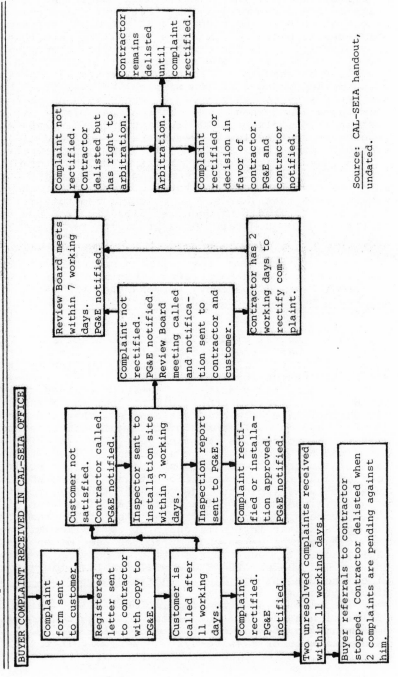

Source: CAL-SEIA handout, undated.

installed on other than single-family dwellings (e.g.,
apartments and commercial installations) which cost in
excess of $6'000, the credit is $3'000 or 25 percent,
whichever is more. For builders installing more than one
single-family unit, the credit is 55 percent up to $3'000
per system installed. The amount covers acquisition and
installation charges and also energy conversation techniques applied in conjunction with the solar system. For
hot water systems, this includes measures such as low-
flow faucets and insulating the tank and pipes. For space
systems this includes wall, ceiling and floor insulation
in excess of state law requirements. The credit will also
probably cover the installing of swimming pool covers.

3. Credit Carry-over: For taxpayers whose credit ex-
ceeds their tax bill, the remaining credit can be carried
into the next tax year and taken off what the taxpayer
would owe in that year and so on until the full credit
is taken. The credit is deducted directly from any amount
of tax owed to the state. This provision remains in effect past 1981.[2]

4. Federal and State Interaction: If any federal
solar credit is passed, the combined state and federal
credit cannot exceed 55 percent. This means, if a federal credit is 30 percent, for example, the state credit would only be 25 percent, to bring the combined total
to 55 percent.

While the tax credit itself was conceptually
straight forward, the success of the bill was in part a
result of the pro-solar resolution of the issue of administrative responsibility.

The solar tax credit legislation contained several
definitional problems and it did not name an administer-
ing agency. After the bill was enacted, the decision as
to which agency would issue precise guidelines and administer the program was not clear-cut. The Franchise Tax
Board was the logical choice since the bill dealt with
taxes. However, it was apparent to a number of solar advocates that the tax board did not have the capabilities
to effectively implement the goals of the tax credit
scheme; it had no expertise in the technical side of
solar systems. Advocates of solar also argued that the
tax board had an institutional bias toward maximizing
tax revenues which ran counter to the goal of encouraging solar through tax reduction. A compromise solution
was reached whereby the CEC would establish the guidelines and the tax board would administer the tax aspects
of the program.

The task of drafting regulations fell to the Solar
Office within the CEC. One of the initial problems was
determination of what constituted a solar system. A key
issue was whether passive systems were within the scope
of the bill. After considerable staff disagreement, the

Solar Office issued regulations allowing eligibility, under certain circumstances, for passive systems.

The Solar Office also felt that no tax credit should be given unless solar systems were installed in conjunction with other energy conservation measures. Although the tax credit bill appeared to allow no more than the cost of cursory conservation measures to be included in the cost of the eligible solar system, the Solar Office proposed regulations that certain conservation measures be required in order to qualify for the tax credit. The logic was that the state should not extend credits for solar systems when more cost-effective steps to conserve energy were not simultaneously being taken. The problem was that the Solar Office went beyond the scope of the legislature's intent and the requirement for conservation was ruled invalid.

The same criticism was raised with respect to the Solar Office's inclusion of passive devices as the legislation did not clearly encompass passive systems. However, on this point the bill was sufficiently unclear to allow the Solar Office's guidelines to stand.

A third gap in the bill was whether one taxpayer could claim credits for more than one system. If so, a taxpayer could claim a $3'000 credit for a hot water system, another for a space heating system, and a third for a pool heating system. The Solar Office ruled that the credit could be taken for each system.

The split administration of the tax credit program promoted friction between the tax board and the CEC. The tax board felt the CEC interpretation of the act was too expansive. In the end, the tax board incorporated the Solar Office's regulations as proposed. By ultimately choosing the CEC to administer the program, the legislature was assured of an enthusiastic and expansive administration of the bill. If the tax board had been charged with sole administrative responsibilities, the tax credit would most likely have been interpreted and administered more restrictively.

The 1977 Solar Tax Credit Returns[3]

Out of 9 million tax returns filed in 1977, 13'500 claimed the solar tax credit. This was about 250 percent more than the number who filed for the 10 percent credit offered in 1976. Of the 13'500 returns claiming the credit, 99.7 percent were credits on personal income, while 0.3 percent were claimed by corporations. Of the personal income tax credits, 89 percent were for single family housing, while only 22 percent of the bank and corporation tax credits were claimed for this category. The data substantiates the view that the initial market penetration for solar systems has been single family housing and that the corporate sector has not signifi-

cantly utilized solar. Of the 36 returns filed by corporations, the real estate, sales and construction industries accounted for 27 returns, while manufacturing industries filed less than three.

Of the 13'500 systems installed in 1977, 72 percent
were for active swimming pool heating systems or pool
covers. Only 2'000 solar hot water systems and 700 active
space heating or cooling systems were installed. The
reasons for the large number of swimming pool credits may
be related to the fact that the PUC has established lifeline rates which render pool covers and solar pool heaters especially cost effective. The lifeline rate provides a low-cost initial block of electricity (or gas) to
residential consumers to cover essential household needs.

The returns for 1977 lend some credence to the criticism levied at the equity implications of the 55 percent tax credit. The median income of individuals claiming the solar tax credit was $30'581 which was almost
$9'000 above the average for those not claiming the
credit. Moreover, 31 percent of the total amount of credits went to taxpayers with incomes over $50'000 while
only 1.6 percent went to those with incomes below
$15'000. These results are not surprising as higher in-
come families tend to own homes and pools and can more
easily finance the initial capital outlay required for
a solar purchase.

Further Legislative Breakthroughs

Passage of the Hart tax credit bill had a snowball
effect on solar legislation. During the remainder of the
1977 legislative session, the following bills were proposed:

1. AB 2056 (Dannemeyer) would have directed the
   CEC to develop and disseminate a reading list
   on energy to libraries throughout the state.
   It died in the assembly.
2. SB 146 (Alquist) would have exempted property
   from taxation if part of an alternative energy
   system. Although signed by the governor, it died
   with the defeat of SCA 15 (see Point 5 below).
3. SB 150 (Alquist) requires all new state buildings to use solar water heating systems and demands that the CEC prepare a manual showing how
   to evaluate cost-effectiveness of solar compared
   to conventional energy systems. This measure was
   signed by the governor in 1974.
4. SB 373 (Rains) provides $2'000 no-interest loans
   for residential installations of solar space
   systems to owners of dwellings damaged or destroyed in state-declared disaster areas occurring between July, 1977 and December, 1980. It

was signed by the governor in 1978.
5. SCA 15 (Alquist) would have amended the State
Constitution to exempt property from taxation
if part of an alternative energy system. Voters
defeated the measure in the referendum of November 1978.

Tom Hayden's CED drafted a plan for a Solar Council
to advise the state in solar policy.[4] The plan was officially adopted on May 3, 1978 (Sun Day). While Hayden
was named Solarcal Chairman, the council included representatives from diverse segments of business and government.[5] The initial responsibility of the council was to
provide a focal point within state government to serve
as a catalyst and coordinator for solar commercialization.

The official purpose of the council, as stated by the
governor, was to advise him "on the means to achieve rapid
development of solar energy in the State."[6] The council
was charged with developing administration policies and
plans for maximum feasible solar commercialization, for
making information available to the public about the use
and benefits of solar energy and for promoting cooperation in solar energy development in California with the
federal government as well as public and private interests.

The council was also a device to bring outside critics into the administration framework, shifting the
pressure to produce results from the administration to
the critics. The council had only advisory status. But
its recommendations had weight because they incorporated
the diverse and often conflicting interests of groups
promoting solar commercialization.

As adopted, the Solarcal Council was a weaker organization than originally envisioned by the CED. The initial proposal was to create a type of public corporation
with centralized authority to promote solar energy. This
Solarcal Corporation would have designed solar education
programs, certified solar equipment, engaged in solar
lobbying and initiated a $500 million solar loan program.
It seems to have been the intention of the sponsors of
the initial proposal to use Solarcal Corporation to compete with and ultimately squeeze out the other organizations involved with solar, such as CAL-SEAL (with its
certification program) and SUNRAE (with its lobbying
activities), which were weakly developed at the time.

Solar Initiatives at the Local Level

Since the establishment of the Solarcal Council in
1978, the most significant legislative actions have occurred at the local level. The CEC in conjunction with
the Solarcal Council has urged local governments to en-

act appropriate local policies to promote solar usage
and energy conservation. Given California's demographic
and climatic diversity, appropriate policies may vary
significantly from region to region within the state. At
least five significant ordinances had been passed by
late 1979 at the community level.

Solar Water Heating Ordinance. By unanimous vote,
the San Diego County Board of Supervisors adopted the
nation's first solar water heating ordinance. As of
October 1979, all new subdivisions where natural gas was
not available,were required to install solar water heating systems. The ordinance takes a stronger position as
of October 1980, when all new residential construction
will be required to include solar systems for water
heating. The board's rationale for the ordinance was
based on a 1978 solar feasibility study which demonstrated solar's cost effectiveness and on the board's
feeling that the ordinance would boost local employment.
The action is expected to save 12.5 billion cubic feet
of natural gas per year in the San Diego area.

While many local solar businesses saw the bill as
the beginning of a San Diego solar boom, CAL-SEIA, the
statewide association of solar businesses, opposed the
bill. CAL-SEIA has generally taken positions against
mandatory solar, favoring a reliance on free markets
and minimal government involvement in the economy.
SUNRAE supported the bill citing the subsidies currently
provided to other competing energy sources.

Priority solar processing. In early 1979, San Diego
county adopted 'a last in-first out' priority processing
for solar developments. In return for a builder's pledge
for utilizing solar in building construction the county
or city planning department gave priority in processing
the subdivision maps. It is estimated that this saved
contractor two weeks, generating financial savings
which can be invested in solar. The policy expired in
October 1980, as from then on all new construction had
to include solar to receive permits (see preceding item).

Solar Swimming Pool Ordinance. The County of Santa
Barbara has enacted an ordinance requiring all new swimming pools to be furnished with an active solar system
which will maintain a pool temperature of 78°F (25°C).
The ordinance is based on studies demonstrating a pay-
back period of one to five years for solar pool systems.
Opposition to the bill from two conservative board members reflected the question why there was a need to
mandate solar if it is so economical anyway. Swimming
pool manufacturers also opposed the bill citing the
higher initial costs involved.

Energy audit and conservation measures. The County
of Santa Clara proposed in 1979 as a first in the U.S.
an ordinance to require a property owner to retrofit conservation measures and to have homes energy audited before their sale. The Santa Clara County Energy Task Force
found energy costs to be a significant county-wide problem and estimated that gas and electricity prices would
increase 14 percent and 11 percent per year over the
next decade. Since new housing fell under state insulation requirements, the largest potential savings lies
in the retrofit of existing houses. The ordinance set
minimum standards for attic insulation, weather strip-
ping and water heating system insulation. The energy
audit would certify these standards and could be conducted free by PG&E or a private energy audit service.[7]

Sun rights. California's local governments were
given the authority to guarantee a solar system owner's
rights to sunlight through the Solar Rights Act and the
Solar Shade Control Act. In both cases the drafting of
ordinances will occur at the local level with CEC personnel and support available if needed. These two state
bills provide the general framework that local officials
may follow in defining solar rights or solar access.

A significant feature of the Solar Rights Act is
that it allows local governments to adopt an ordinance
requiring the dedication of easements for solar access
as a condition of subdivision map approval. Solar easements were recognized in California law through this act
which provides that the right of receiving sunlight upon
and over land may be attached to other land as an ease-
ment.

Neither act requires specific legislation or action
by local governments. Instead the bills can be used to
support locally-developed solar energy policies.

THE CALIFORNIA SOLAR INDUSTRY

California had a flourishing solar industry in the
early 1900s. Although the industry died out during the
1930s, the basic design principles became established
and were the cornerstone for solar's reemergence in
the 1970s.

This part outlines the evolution of solar technology in the early 1900s and presents an overview of the
solar industry in California today.

The First Solar Boom, 1890-1940[8]

The first commercial solar water heater was patented
by Clarence M. Kemp of Baltimore in 1891. The invention
consisted of a water tank or series of tanks inside a

white pine box insulated with felt paper and covered by
a glass top. The tanks were connected by tubing and were
installed on the roof of a house. Cold water entered the
bottom of the tank and hot water heated by sunlight
flowed from the top of the tank when the faucet was turned on.

Kemp's invention was not overly successful and he
sold the exclusive rights to his solar heater, called
the Climax, to two Pasadena, California,businessmen in
1895.

The Climax cost about $25 and saved its owner about
$9 worth of coal annually and was cleaner and more con-
venient than the coal heaters in widespread use at the
time. Sales expanded from the Pasadena area to the entire Southern California region. By 1900, 1600 Climax
heaters had been installed.

In 1898, Frank Walker invented an improved design.
Walker's system had tanks enclosed in a glass covered
box set so that the glass top was flush with the roof.
Walker's design included a metal reflector under the
tank to reflect sunlight into it. The Walker heater
could be linked to a gas or coal heating system if desired.

Both the Walker and Climax heaters saw improvements
in subsequent years, but continued to suffer from the
major problem of having badly insulated tanks. Water
seldom retained its heat overnight. This problem was
overcome by William Bailey in 1909 with a design that
created the configuration still in use today. Bailey,
an engineer employed by Carnegie Steel to upgrade manufacturing processes, rented a home in L.A. with a tank
solar heater and applied his skills to upgrading the
device. He divided the system into the collector and
the water storage unit. The collector was more efficient because the coiled tubing offered a larger surface
area of exposure to the sun and a smaller quantity of
water was heated at a time. The tank was heavily insulated keeping temperature losses to 1°F per hour during
the night. The tank was placed above the collector, eliminating the need for pumps.

Bailey called this system the 'Day and Night Solar
Heater'. It had a 40 gallon tank and sold for about
$100 installed. It saved the consumer about $25 annually.
Depending on the system and on whether they replaced
coal, gas or electricity, the Day and Night systems had
a two to four year pay-back period.

The solar industry's first crisis occurred in 1913
when an unprecedented freeze hit Southern California.
The water in the tubes froze and the tubes split.
Ceilings flooded and entire systems were ruined, sending
Bailey back to design a non-freezing solar heater. He
made the collector's circulation system independent of
the storage unit's water supply. A non-freezing solution

passed through the collector coils and then through a
heat exchanger in the water tank.
    With the freezing problem resolved, Day and Night
expanded its sales to Northern California, Arizona and
Hawaii. By the end of World War I sales were about 1000
per year for the Day and Night heater.
    In the early 1920 natural gas was discovered in the
Los Angeles Basin. This marked the beginning of a gradu-
al erosion of the solar market. In 1900, natural gas cost
$3.20 per thousand cubic feet (TCF), while in 1927 the
price had dropped to $.90 per TCF. By 1926, Day and
Night's sales had fallen to 350 annually and in 1930
only 40 were sold.
    Bailey sold the patent rights to a Florida entre-
preneur during the 1920s where a solar industry began
to flourish. In California, however, the industry continued to contract until all production stopped just
prior to World War II.

The Solar Industry Today

    Starting in the early 1970s, a number of individu-
als began rediscovering solar energy. The driving force
behind the renewed interest was the dramatic increase
in fossil fuel prices. By 1975 California had over 300
firms involved in some aspect of solar. Five years later,
the number had grown to almost 1200, leading to increased
specialization. Today the industry is made up of the
distinct subgroups of the equipment manufacturers, the
distributors and installers, and the builders.

    Equipment manufacturers. They produce the key com-
ponents of the solar water heating system, the collectors, heat exchangers, storage tanks, and pumps. Below
we discuss the structure of the manufacturing group, the
collector technology, employment, sales growth and profitability, and financing aspects.
    1. Structure: The manufacturing segment of the in-
dustry in California is composed of about 225 firms.[9]
Most of them face highly competitive markets. Most of
them are independent firms often solely engaged in solar.
FAFCO, the largest of them, is a typical example of this
group of branch participants. These firms were typically
started with personal and family funds. They survive because they have developed product and locational niches
within the industry.
    A second group of firms are those who supply stock
components such as pumps and storage tanks to the industry. For those companies solar is one of many markets
for their products. As the solar industry developed, a
new market for already existing products emerged.
Grundfos Pump Corporation is an example. Grundfos, a

subsidiary of a Danish multinational corporation, had
sales of solar system pumps of about $2 million. This
gave them a market share of 75 percent of the U.S. solar
market. In 1981, sales reached about $4 million al-
though they still make up only a small percent (about 5
percent) of total sales. Market share in 1981 is anywhere between 85 to 95 percent.

The third group consists of large corporations that
have become involved in solar manufacturing. In most
instances, they are involved in an industry that complements solar manufacturing. Olin Brass, PPG and Revere
produce copper or glass products and have viewed solar
as a new market for their materials manufacturing expertise. Energy companies such as Exxon and Arco see
solar as a natural extension of their current energy
involvement. Others such as General Electric and Grumman
felt solar fitted with their product development or
engineering expertise. Entry into the industry has come
both from in-house product development, and acquisitions.

2. Collector technology: Easy entry into the industry is in large part due to the simple nature of the
technology. Conceptually the technology is the one developed in the early 1900s. Over the last ten years design
improvements and new materials have been added, but the
basic product remains the flat plate collector.

A typical residential collector of 22 square feet
(2 square meters) weighs about 122 lbs (55 kg) and consists of glass (46 percent), steel (27 percent), copper
(23 percent), and fiberglass (4 percent). Two such collectors are usually required for an average household's
water heating requirements. Cost range from $8 to $22
per square foot ($90 to $240 per square meter). Collectors made from steel are cheapest but they corrode.
Expensive collectors are made from copper or aluminum.
The average size of installed systems is 57 square feet
(5 square meters); 57 percent of all the systems sold
measured between 45 and 60 square feet (4 and 5.5
square meters).

One of the major innovations over the last decade
has been in materials. FAFCO is a leading example.
FAFCO was established in 1972 and spent four years developing a polymer flat plate collector. By 1976 they
had developed a new patented type of polymer as well as
a thermoforming manufacturing process for collectors.
These innovations have allowed FAFCO to market a relatively low cost collector with the durability of those
constructed from traditional materials.

3. Employment:[10] About 50 percent of the industry's
employment of 3'000 to 5'000 is directly involved in
manufacturing and installing. The other 50 percent are
engaged in sales, collector design, administration,
and other support functions.

The California Public Policy Center (CPPC) has estimated that the average production time for collector manufacturing is 0.103 employee hours per square foot (1.1 hours per square meter) of collector manufactured. This estimate compares almost identically with Grumman's manufacturing projections for their California facility. In contrast, the Jet Propulsion Laboratory (JPL) estimates that 0.33 employee hours are required per square foot (3.6 hours per square meter) of collector manufactured. This discrepancy can be accounted for by the fact that the JPL study only includes employees in the final stages of collector manufacturing while CPPC includes sub-assembly work. Given the close correlation between the CPPC estimates and Grumman's projections, the CPPC number appears reasonable.

In addition to collectors, production of controls, pumps, storage tanks along with installation work directly create employment. Including these along with directly induced jobs, CPPC estimates that for retrofits 0.429 employee hours are required per collector foot manufactured (4.6 hours per square meter). For new residences the figure would be 0.32 (3.4). Using CPPC's estimates and the CEC's data indicating an average installation size of 57 sq ft. for residential applications, the production and installation of one solar system would create almost four man-days of employment.

In comparing solar employment with other energy employment figures, solar appears to be more labor intensive and to create more jobs per energy output. It has been estimated that the controversial Sundesert nuclear power plant would create 36,268 job years while an equivalent amount of solar energy production would create over 240,000 jobs.

Manufacturing of reliable collectors and solar components requires precise workmanship, but the process need not involve highly skilled or educated labor. Grumman's plant in Corchran, California is manned primarily with unskilled labor. Each collector is individually constructed using simple tools and finally subjected to numerous quality control tests. Through on-the-job experience, workers have advanced to the point where constructive design and production suggestions have originated on the plant floor. Other firms appear to share Grumman's experience.

4. Sales growth and profitability: Despite the strong sales growth during the late 1970s and 1980 (see Table 4.2), industry growth has not met expectations. The drop in sales during the second half of 1978 has been attributed to lack of publicity concerning California tax credits and uncertainty about federal policies. Apparently many consumers postponed purchases until they had clear guidelines on the state and federal tax credits. By 1979 manufacturers had incorporated tax

TABLE 4.2
Solar Collector Sales in California (in thousands of square feet)

| Period | Sales | Growth Rate (in Percent) | | |
		on preceding period	on a year ago Sem. I	Sem.II
1977 (July-Dec)	2'112	–	–	–
1978 (Jan-June)	2'644	+25	–	–
1978 (July-Dec)	1'953	–26	–	– 8
1979 (Jan-June)	3'545	+82	+34	
1979 (July-Dec)	3'547	0	–	+82
1980 (Jan-July)	4'889	+38	+38	–
1980 (July-Dec)	5'702	+17	–	+61

Source: U.S Department of Energy (1981).

Note: Total sales during the period were 24'392'000 square feet. Sales in Semester II, 1980 were 170 percent higher than sales in Semester II in 1977.

incentives into their marketing promotions. This along with the substantial increase in fossil fuel prices that occurred in 1979-80 led to a threefold increase in collector sales over a two year span.

The growth surge in the first half of every year is mostly accounted for by the fact that solar systems for heating swimming pools, the dominant solar product, are sold in the early months of the year in anticipation of the swimming season.

While the sales increases shown above are impressive, they fall below expectations of state policymakers and industry leaders. In early 1981 Exxon pulled out of the solar heating industry by disposing of its Daystar subsidiary. Daystar's revenues had grown more slowly than the company expected so it was sold to American Solar King, a small solar manufacturer.

A related problem for solar manufacturers has been the industry's lack of profitability. Under Exxon, Daystar never had a profitable year. Grumman, one of California's largest solar manufacturers, has had a similar experience with its solar unit. A contributing factor to this low profitability has been the ease with which a new firm could enter the industry. Between 1977 and 1979, 580 new firms entered the solar industry in California. Bankrupties and exits have reportedly remained low durina this period.

One company that has countered this trend is FAFCO. They have concentrated on the swimming pool heating

market while most larger companies focused on household
hot water heating systems. By yearend 1980 FAFCO had
accumulated profits (retained earnings) of over $1.8
million. In 1981 FAFCO plans to begin marketing a household water heating system to complement their pool heating business.

The contrasting experience of FAFCO and companies
such as Exxon and Grumman is related to the large share
of pool heating systems in the total solar market. In
1978, 80 percent of solar collector sales went to pool
heating systems. Companies like FAFCO which have focused
on this market have done well. Most companies however,
have looked to household hot water systems as their
large potential market, a market that has not developed
in line with expectations.

5. Enterprise Finances: A critical problem for any
new industry is the financing of a new venture. The
California state government has not funded equipment
manufacturers, but has concentrated efforts on creating
demand. Manufacturers have received some federal assistance through the Small Business Administration and
through federal contracts for R&D and demonstration
projects.

The largest source of fund for the industry has
been personal resources and loans or equity funds provided by friends of the entrepreneur. Commercial banks
have tended to view the solar industry as high risk and
have generally only provided loans to established manufacturers.

About 150 solar companies have received venture capital financing. Details of these financings are not
widely publicized, but involve the placement of equity
or convertable debt. Venture capital financing fills
the gap between private funds utilized for a start-up
and commercial bank loans or stock sales for a well
established firm. Members of venture capital firms
often sit on the board of companies they finance and
provide management advice.

Distributors and installers. Some manufacturers
distribute their own products. But most solar systems
are marketed at the local level through installation
firms. Aggee James, director of CAL-SEIA, indicated
that installation firms are the most profitable segment
of the industry. These are generally small firms or
partnerships with previous experience in the plumbing
industry, employing between two and twenty-five people.

Distributors, on the other hand, have been squeezed
between the manufacturers and the installers. San Diego's largest distribution company, Great Western Solar
(GWS), went out of business in 1978. The company president stated that the small manufacturers he used could
not stand behind their products due to insufficient

profit margins, leaving GWS liable for product service
and warranties.

On the other side, GWS had problems with government
regulation and labor unions. Each job cost them about
$300 in filing building and other required permits. Of
GWS's 100 employees, four people were employed to handle
government-required paperwork. Fighting unionization
allegedly cost GWS $120'000 during their last year of
operation. Due to its size and visibility, GWS was a
prime target of the plumbers and pipefitters union's
attempt to unionize solar.

Builders. A major cornerstone of the solar industry is contractors and builders. They are not primarily
in business to install solar systems. Instead, they view
solar systems as one of several alternative methods to
heat or cool homes, or heat water. Contractors and
builders have considerable leverage and generally are
not interested in adding solar equipment if it means
additional costs, construction delays, or consumer
resistance. Solar is unpopular with builders because:

1. Builders prefer to wait until a market is
   established by consumer demand before implementing a new technology. So far they are uncertain
   that homes with solar equipment will sell.
2. Builders are interested in the package price of
   their homes and an additional incremental cost
   of $1'700 to $1'800 for solar hot water dis-
   courages their involvement.
3. Some contractors are hesitant to involve themselves with solar energy because it is perceived
   as a cottage-type industry.

The California Builders' Council (CBC) proposed in
1979 a cooperative venture involving CEC and CBC. Under
the implemented plan, a special five member group representing each of the regional areas of the CBC serves
as an information source for and advisory body to the
CEC. This network is supposed to help create a better
understanding by the CEC of the problems and barriers
faced by builders who want to install solar. It also
provides builders with reliable solar information. The
CEC has begun solar seminars statewide to reach builders
and contractors on an individual basis.

Two types of seminars are organized. One focuses on
marketing and selling the energy efficient home; the
other provides a solar overview for builders. The seminars are co-sponsored by the local building associations.
Seminars cover installation, solar land planning, building codes, marketing builder incentives, warranties, and
tax credits.

The government's recent strong emphasis on educating

builders stems from the fact that builders and developers decide what appliances and heating systems are
to be installed in new housing. Given the current strong
demand for housing in California, builders can sell any
house they construct. Thus, little incentive has existed
to alter designs and increase construction and borrowing
costs. The 55 percent tax credit is now available to
builders and the CEC's information program is geared toward using this to generate involvement by builders and
developers in solar.

USERS OF SOLAR EQUIPMENT

Purchasers of solar systems tend to fall into three
broad categories: people with energy and ecological concerns; people who enjoy building and working with their
solar system; and thirdly, those people who buy solar
primarily to save money. As with other consumer goods
such as cars, economic considerations have not always
been the primary determinant in the decision to go solar;
few solar owners have accurate estimates of their
system's payback period, although many seem to have
rough guesses.
Perhaps as important a consideration as system
economics has been compatibility with values or lifestyles. Numerous owners interviewed indicated that they
would have purchased their systems regardless of system
payback concerns. They based their decision to buy on
solar's environmental benefits, harmony with nature, and
the desire for self-sufficiency. These people also seem
aware that they are innovators and appear to derive status benefits from solar ownership.
'Do-it-your-selfers' are another important consumer
category. By word of mouth, friends and periodicals such
as Popular Mechanics, technical information was available on simple solar systems. With the advent of mass
produced solar systems, this group has declined in relative importance to the total market.
The third group and potentially the largest, are
consumers who are primarily concerned with reducing
energy bills by installing solar. While some solar owners indicated that this had been their sole concern,
these 'pragmatic' owners seem still to be the exception
among today's owners of solar equipment.
In terms of the chronology of solar diffusion, the
do-it-your-selfers were generally in the first wave of
solar owners, followed by those with strong environmental
and lifestyle preferences. A large percentage of solar
owners who have emphasized system economics also share
the environmental and lifestyle concerns to some degree.
The large untapped market are those who detach solar
from social concerns and view the decision on a strict

payback basis.

Surveys taken of solar owners have found almost all of them to be satisfied with their systems. The systems have performed as expected, have required little maintenance, and have cut energy bills. Current owners also uniformly state that they would install solar equipment in a new home if they moved.

Consumer Financing of Solar[11]

Consumer purchases of solar energy equipment have been channeled through conventional consumer financing institutions. Banks and savings and loan associations (S&L) have responded to loan demand for solar systems in a mixed fashion. Through 1978, about 20 percent of California's banks had financed new subdivisions including solar, and about 25 to 30 percent had made loans for solar retrofits. However, in general, bankers feel there has not been a noticeable demand for solar loans.

Bankers appear optimistic as to future solar loan demand, and at least 10 percent of California's financial institutions have instituted special loan programs with preferential terms including lower interest rates and higher loan ratios. The optimistic outlook for solar by banks and S&L's is further confirmed by the fact that one third of California's banks have specific individuals responsible for keeping abreast of new developments in the solar field.

According to the CEC's survey, most institutions surveyed indicated the solar system's reliability as a major concern in granting a loan. The second most common concern was the system's life expectancy followed by methods of appraisal, cost-effectiveness, system maintenance and maintenance costs, and the secondary loan market for solar homes, in that order. Almost half of the institutions surveyed would consider an explicit solar loan program to be an attractive business feature that would enhance present lending programs. Bank of America, California's largest bank, does not have such a program but has given support to solar development by prequalifying more than 40 solar water heating and pool systems, and has made several hundred home improvement loans for solar equipment.[12]

Solar Economics

Purchase of a solar hot water heater can be viewed as an investment in a residential energy production system. The economics of solar are therefore similar to the economics of any investment decision. Costs and benefits in the form of expected energy savings must be estimated over the life of the system. Most estimates have shown solar to be cost-effective vis-a-vis conventional fuels for most California homes. These estimates, however, contain a high degree of uncertainty, being based on assumed values for the following key variables: (1) Inflation and discount rates; (2) solar system lifespans; (3) conventional fuel escalation rates; and (4) percent of conventional fuel displaced by solar. Reasonable projected values for these parameters confirm solar's cost effectiveness. However, 'worst case' assumptions show solar to be a poor investment decision with a 30-40 year payback period.

The economic decision to buy solar is a function of lifecycle costing. The consumer must decide if the initial outlay for the system and interest payments will be offset by the stream of reduced gas or electric bills over the life of the system. At high rates of inflation and interest, the present value of savings in the future drops sharply. For example, the present value of a $100 savings after five years of 16 percent inflations is only $42.[13] But consumers are not assured of constant inflation rates and must make assumptions of higher, lower, or stable rates which are critical inputs into discounted cash flow projections.

Most manufacturers estimate a system lifespan of 20 years, but in fact its useful life is unknown. If high levels of inflation are projected, the lifespan of the system becomes a less important factor, especially the decision to choose a 20 or 30 year assumed system life. Present value savings on energy bills after the 20th year would be insignificant.

Another major uncertainty consumers must deal with is the future escalation rate of energy prices. Assumptions of continuing rapid escalation in conventional fuels can dramatically improve the economics of solar alternatives.

Finally, consumers must evaluate their energy use patterns and local climatic conditions to estimate the degree to which solar will displace other fuels. For a water heating system, a household using the dishwasher, clothes washer, and taking showers during the morning may require more conventional backup and utilize less solar than a household spreading hot water usage out over the day. This consideration points to the importance of behavior modification for the validation of solar.

The CEC has studied solar economics in Santa Barbara County for single family dwellings, multifamily dwellings and pool heating. The commission concluded that "when compared with the marginal cost of conventional fuels, solar is dramatically and universally less expensive."[14] The study assumes 10 to 12 percent annual escalation in natural gas and electricity prices, an inflation rate of 8 percent and 70 percent of conventional fuel displaced by solar. Based on these assumptions the CEC found solar to be cost-effective

for each dwelling and pool case vis-a-vis natural gas
and electricity. Their results are shown in Table 4.3.[15]

TABLE 4.3
Twenty-Year Life Cycle Costs of Alternative Heating Systems in Santa
Barbara County, California (in US $).

Heating System	Single Family Homes	Multi-Family Homes (Per Unit)	Pool Heating
Natural Gas only	1'900	1'048	12'228
With Solar	1'758	647	9'247
Savings with Solar	142	401	2'981
Electricity only	2'989	1'772	
With Solar	2'084	864	na
Savings with Solar	905	908	

Source: California Energy Commission (1978).

Note: Assumptions are an annual inflation rate of 8 percent, energy
price increases annually between 10 and 12 percent, and a 70 percent
displacement of conventional with solar energy.

The CEC has done further studies for other areas
of California and has confirmed the cost-effectiveness
of solar statewide. Nonetheless, the average California
consumer doubts solar's cost effectiveness, a fact that
has been reflected in sales of household solar systems.
    A consumer must be personally convinced
of the benefits of solar in his own particular situation. The comparative cost calculation of solar versus
gas or electricity given below is as simple as it can
be made given the rather complex utility rate structures
in California. It avoids the use of discounting to calculate present values. But the error introduced in this
way is probably not too serious when one considers the
variation in energy savings expenditures resulting from
assumptions one has to make about the share of solar in
total gas or electricity consumption.
    The consumer has to start with an estimate of his
sanitary hot water use. Metered water consumption figures include both hot and cold water uses. A typical
household might thus arrive at a use of about 386
gallons (1460 l) per week.[16]
    Heating this water from 50°F (10°C) to 140°F (60°C)
and keeping it at this temperature requires an annual
energy input of about 5'900 kWh for an electrically
heated system, and of 293 therms for a gas-burning
system.[17]
    The calculation of energy expenditures implied in

this energy need is complex given California's Lifeline
Rate structures for gas and electricity. There exist
three different prices under this lifeline rate structure. The basic rate is applied to a minimum if energy
consumption, reflecting basic energy needs of a household. A typical monthly limit in the San Francisco area
is 240 kWh during the winter months, somewhat lower in
the summer in order to account for the winter heating
needs. The next block of monthly electricity consumption
--typically another 50 kWh-- is charged at a rate about
30 percent above the 'basic needs' rate. All electricity
consumption above the first two blocks is charged at an
even higher 'excess' rate which is more than double the
'basic needs' rate. Gas rates follow a similar pricing
principle.[18]
    The lifeline rate structure prevents an easy cal-
culation of the energy expenditures implied by a given
volume of hot water consumption because energy used for
this purposes is added to energy used for cooking, etc.,
to determine total electricity and gas consumption, and
therefore the marginal rate which will be charged. An
energy conserving household may be purchasing all energy
at the basic needs rate, while another consumer may use
more than the allotted energy for basic and secondary
needs, requiring large energy purchases at the highest
or excess rate.
    Average energy prices paid are therefore a function
of energy consumption, and so are energy expenditure
savings when evaluating solar compared to electricity
or gas. The analysis therefore uses three different consumption levels. The low consumption profile assumes
that the consumer pays all his energy at the 'basic
needs' rate (i.e., that his overall electricity consumption per month is below 240 kWh in wintertime). The
average consumption profile assumes that the energy use
to heat 286 gallons of water a weak is pushing the
household into the 'secondary use' electricity or gas
rate. The high consumption profile in contrast assumes
that the consumer is paying the 'excess rate' for all
his hot water consumption. Figure 4.2 shows the hot
water energy expenditure costs for these three consumption profiles for both electricity and gas use.
    These energy costs must be measured against the
annual costs of a solar system. Prices in 1981 for an
average system in California run from about $2'000 to
$3'500. For our typical household assume a system cost
of $2'600. Subtracting the 55 percent tax credit leaves
a net installed cost of $1'170 or an annualized cost
of $59.50. Adding to this an annual expense of $50
for maintenance and repair gives an annual operating
cost of $109.50 (as indicated in Figure 4.2 in each
column's left-hand sub-column).

Figure 4.2
Comparative Heating Expenditures for Gas, Electricity,
and Solar (in San Francisco Area).

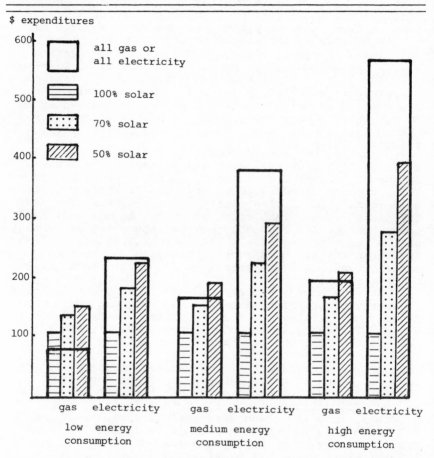

$ expenditures

□ all gas or
  all electricity

▤ 100% solar

▦ 70% solar

▨ 50% solar

gas   electricity   gas   electricity   gas   electricity

low   energy   medium energy   high energy
consumption   consumption   consumption

Note: Energy for the low consumption scenario purchased
at 'basic needs' rate. In high consumption scenario, energy needed for hot water production is purchased at 'excess consumption' rate.

If solar could provide 100 percent of the energy
needed to satisfy the household's hot water needs, solar
would be cost effective except for the low energy consumer using gas (as indicated in Figure 4.2). However
solar will usually only provide 50 to 70 percent of a
household's water heating requirements. If the usual
70 percent figure is used, the household will have annual

solar expenses of $109.50 plus annual back-up fuel expenses equivalent to 30 percent of the energy costs using conventional fuels. Figure 4.2 shows that solar is still not cost-effective for the low gas consumer. But the high electricity consumer realizes savings of more than 50 percent.

The sensitivity of these estimates can be illustrated by comparing this situation with a solar system providing only 50 percent of the households water heating needs. Solar cannot any longer replace gas and the benefits are even marginal for the low electricity consumer.

Obviously a shift in assumptions for one parameter alone can have significant effects on solar's cost-effectiveness. Given that consumers must estimate a number of key parameters, most solar cost-effectiveness studies will leave consumers in the fuzzy range of uncertainty.

Almost without exception, pool heating solar systems will replace 'excess' consumption under lifeline rates and would tend to be more cost effective than a household system which may replace 'basic' consumption. This, combined with the fact that pool owners with their higher incomes are more likely to utilize the tax credit, offers an explanation for the fact that 80 percent of solar system sales consist of pool heating systems.

THE INVOLVEMENT OF PUBLIC UTILITIES

The degree to which California's public utilities are involved in solar and the nature of their involvement has become an important issue in California. The utilities have been the traditional suppliers of energy and could potentially accelerate solar development with their support. Their peak load needs could also become affected by widespread solar use.

The Utilities' View of Solar

Currently, the utilities skeptically question whether the solar industry has demonstrated that solar systems are feasible or cost effective. Some utilities hold the view that solar is analogous to heat pumps in the early 1960s. The utilities promoted heat pumps but technical and installation problems were not adequately resolved before their promotion and heat pumps acquired a reputation of unreliability.[19] Demand did not develop as assumed and the utilities failed to recoup their investment in heat pump promotion. The utilities' view of solar might be best summarized by the following quote from a PG&E representative:[20]

There aren't enough people out there right now who know how to make solar water heaters with all the equipment. There aren't that many people out there who know how to install them. There aren't that many places out there, (where)...you can call to get someone to come fix it. This whole infrastructure could be extremely damaging if we don't make it work right.

These doubts about the maturity and reliability of both the technology and the industry, combined with the utilities' unpleasant experience with heat pumps, have generally led to a lack of enthusiasm among utilities for actively promoting the widespread use of solar. Nonetheless, California's major utilities have instituted solar water and space heating programs which vary significantly from one utility to another.

Possible Utility Roles in Solar

The solar industry and public regulators are divided on the issue of whether the utilities should play a major role in solar development. Some manufacturers see utility involvement as an opportunity to aggregate a large market for their products, while others fear a diminished level of competition with the utilities' potential monopoly power.

The two opposing views are illustrated by two bills proposed in 1978. AB2987 attempted to outlaw any utility involvement in the solar industry.The bill died in assembly. But AB3247, which required the PUC to investigate the feasibility of utilities and/or banks providing financing of solar, was enacted.

Those who oppose utility involvement in solar advocate solar energy as a way to gain independence from the large centralized utilities. A more specific concern held by legislators, bureaucrats, and solar manufacturers is that utility involvement will create a monopolistic market in what is now a highly competitive industry. An example quoted by Ron Doctor of the CEC is the recent solar project of SDG&E. When SDG&E's sales and leasing plan was proposed, they assured CAL-SEIA that they would involve a large number of qualifying manufacturers and installers. In actuality, out of the twenty-five installers who are operating in the San Diego area, only three qualified. Of the solar manufacturers, only one qualified. SDG&E's selective approach to the operation of the program simplified the project and probably kept the quality standards high. However, it illustrates the difficulty such a program has in promoting competition in the solar industry.

The argument for utility involvement focuses on

using established institutions to accelerate solar deployment. Utilities have greater access to capital markets than do small solar manufacturers or consumers. By raising capital and making it available to consumers, utilities could help overcome the first cost barrier associated with solar energy purchases. Additionally, consumers may more readily accept systems screened and provided by established institutions.

Most importantly, utilities could provide a price incentive. The price that consumers pay for electricity is an average of the utility's energy costs. The higher costs of newer energy sources are averaged with the lower costs of older supplies. To the consumer, solar systems are weighed against the average cost of the utilities' energy costs and may be uncompetitive. In contrast, the utility must weigh solar against competing high cost sources of new supplies. Essentially this means solar will be competitive for the utility at a higher cost than for the consumer. The utility could then average solar with lower costs of existing energy supplies, an option unavailable to the consumer.

Of the possible worries about the utilities' involvement in solar, ownership, sales or leasing of equipment seems to be the most controversial.

In February, 1980, the PUC issued their report on the feasibility of utility financing as required under AB3247. The PUC told the state's four largest utilities, PG&E, SCE, Southern California Gas, and SDG&E, to submit plans within 60 days to finance installation of 175'000 solar water heaters over the next three years. The PUC plan, which still requires public hearings and full PUC approval, is an attempt to utilize the advantages of utility involvement without allowing the utilities' monopoly power to influence the solar market.

Under the plan, the four utilities would raise close to $500 million to provide interest-free or low-interest loans to finance residential solar water heating systems. The costs of the subsidized loans would be passed on to the utilities' other consumers through general rate increases.

By both providing subsidies and eliminating the barrier of high initial cost, the PUC plans to increase the number of solar systems in California by 1'700 percent without involving utilities in solar ownership or leasing. Homeowners would repay loans over twenty years in monthly installments or in a lump-sum payment upon resale of the house. Gas utilities would be required to finance 2 percent of their hook-ups and the electric utilities 10 percent.

The Load Management Problem

The question of solar's impact on the utilities load management is not well researched and contracdictory views are offered. Some utilities hold the view that widespread solar use will cause a reduction in the utilities' revenue without a reduction in the utilities' peak capacity needs. The utility would lose sales during off-peak hours, when power is cheaper to provide. Yet on the peak day, for example the coldest day of the year when it is cloudy,the electric system would have to provide back-up for solar systems. On the other hand, if solar systems had adequate storage capabilities, they could reduce the utilities' peak capacity needs. Rate structures to encourage use of such solar systems have been proposed.

In any event both sides in the debate feel that solar will not have any significant impact on the utilities for at least five to fifteen years.

For hydro-based utilities, load management considerations are somewhat altered. Systems which are characterized by large hydroelectric plants and by a capability for pumped storage appear better matched with solar energy. These systems have ample peak generating capacity or can add additional turbines and let more water out of the reservoir. Instead their problem is the shortage of firm power. Water can be saved and more used over short periods, but maximum power output cannot be maintained over long periods due to insufficient water supply. Consequently the time (peak or off-peak) solar is used (and electricity saved) is less important for them than the length of time during which solar is making only a minor contribution to system supplies.

In short, it seems that the utilities do not have either an uniformly negative or positive attitude towards solar.

CONCLUSION

California's solar industry emerged in response to a market niche opened up by rising oil prices in the early 1970s. Both politicians and entrepreneurs recognized the need to develop cost-effective renewable sources of energy to replace fossil fuels. Under the guidance of Governor Brown, California established a legislative infrastructure which offered financial incentives to solar consumers and addressed potential barriers such as quality control and solar easements which could have stifled the widespread deployment of solar. At the same time, the solar industry evolved from a cottage industry in the early 1970s to an energy industry branch producing

sophisticated products using mass production techniques.
By most standards, the state's solar industry has
shown exceptional growth. However both industry representatives and state officials had expected a more significant market penetration for solar hot water heaters based
on solar's estimated cost-effectiveness. Solar has done
well in the swimming pool market and among consumers who
feel solar complements their lifestyle. But solar's largest potential market, pragmatic consumers who stress
cost-effectiveness, remains relatively untapped. As a
consequence of this slower than expected adoption of solar systems, the budget means made available in support
of the tax and subsidy schemes for solar have not been
exhausted.
Capturing this large potential market will probably
require a change in marketing strategies. Early advertising has typically focused on the lifestyle image of solar energy. What might be required instead is advertise-
ment which invites and teaches homeowners to calculate
solar's cost-effectiveness for their own specific circumstances. This is especially required for consumers requiring a solar retrofit.
Consumer acceptance of solar in new housing is more
widespread than in the retrofit market. By 1980 solar was
generally viewed by builders abd contractors as an attractive selling feature and solar housing developments had
become more common in California. The decline in new home
construction which followed upon the sharp deterioration
of the state's housing market in 1981 has, however, led
to a significant drop in the sale of solar systems.
The future of the solar industry in California will
therefore depend on the manufacturers' success in convincing consumers of solar's cost-effectiveness in the retrofit market. But its fortune will always remain closely
linked to housing cycles in the construction market for
new buidlings.

ABBREVIATIONS

AB   Assembly Bill
CAL-SEIA   California Solar Energy Industries Association
CBC   '   California Builders' Council
CEC   California Energy Commission
CED   Council for Economic Democracy
CPPC   California Public Policy Center
GWS   Great Western Solar Inc.
JPL   Jet Propulsion Laboratory
PG&E   Pacific Gas and Electric
PUC   Public Utilities Commission

SB	Senate Bill
SCE	Southern California Edison
SCR	Senate Constitutional Amendment
SDG&E	San Diego Gas and Electric
TCF	Thousand Cubic Feet
TIPSE	Testing and Inspection Program for Solar Equipment

NOTES

1. Average projected annual solar energy collection for thirty-two locations in North America between Winnipeg (Manitoba) in the north and Brownsville (Texas) in the south is 11 million BTU. Table 4.4 below gives the data for all of the 32 locations.

TABLE 4.4
Projected Annual Solar Energy Collection in Million BTU

Above Median		Below Median	
Location	Energy	Location	Energy
Albuquerque, New Mexico	12.1	Winnipeg, Montana	10.3
Phoenix, Arizona	11.9	St. Cloud, Minnesota	10.3
Ely, Nevada	11.9	Portland, Maine	10.3
Lander, Wyoming	11.3	Sayville (L.I.), New York	10.2
Los Angeles, California	11.1	Atlanta, Georgia	10.2
Glasgow, Montana	11.1	Lemont, Illinois	10.0
Boise, Idaho	11.0	Indianapolis, Indiana	10.0
Miami, Florida	10.9	Greensboro, North Carolina	9.9
Honolulu, Hawaii	10.9	Nashville, Tennessee	9.8
Bismark, North Dakota	10.8	Ottawa, Ontario	9.8
Columbia, Missouri	10.8	Madison, Wisconsin	9.7
Lincoln, Nebraska	10.7	Sault Ste. Marie, Michigan	9.7
Grand Lake, Colorado	10.6	Cleveland, Ohio	9.6
Brownsville, Texas	10.5	State College, Pennsylvania	9.4
Fort Worth, Texas	10.4	Boston, Massachusetts	9.2
Lake Charles, Louisiana	10.4	Seattle, Washington	8.6
High Average	11.0	Low Average	9.8

Source: Grumman Energy Systems, Handout, no date. Projected for Sunstream 60 Solar Domestic Hot Water System, measured with two collectors and 75 gallons of daily hot water use.

2. This carry-over privilege reduces the 55 percent

tax credit to an effective, discounted average cost reduction of 50 percent.

3. This section draws on CEC (1979).

4. Tom Hayden was a leading radical activist during
the late 1960s. He has now become a California politician
of the New Left. The CED is a research, information and
lobbying organization of the New Left which doubles as a
political support organization for Hayden's bids for political office.

5. Two state assemblymen and senators are ex-offi-
cio members. So are representatives from the PUC, the
Office of Appropriate Technology, the State and Consumer
Services Agency, the Office of Economic Planning, Policy
and Research, the Department of Industrial Relations, and
the Solar Business Office. Also represented are electric
and gas utilities, solar equipment producers, a trade
union, local officials including planners, solar interest
groups, academics, lawyers, and savings and mortgage
banks.

6. Solarcal Council (1979).

7. The ordinance was utlimately adopted although in
a weakened form. Ordinances of this type have since been
passed in many places in the U.S.

8. This section is based on Butti and Perlin (1980).

9. This and all other figures are only approximative.
Reporting enterprises apply different cut-off criteria
when defining themselves as manufacturers, distributors
and installers.

10. The data presented here is coming from CPPC
(1978) and from a conversation with a manufacturing manager from Grummen Energy Systems.

11. This section draws on Solarcal Office material
reporting on a CEC survey.

12. The survey furthermore indicates that in 1978 7
percent of California's financial institutions planned to
utilize solar energy systems in their own facilities in
the near future.

13. Inflation-compensating energy price increases
are likely to offset this savings erosion.

14. CEC (1978).

15. These estimates were done with SOLFIN, a compu-
ter program developed to analyze life-cycle costs of solar energy systems. The model includes seventy variables
which further illustrates the complexity of the solar
purchase decision (Johnson, 1979).

16. This figure is made up of the following weekly
water uses: bathing (14 times 15 gallons each); laundry
(5 times 20 gallons); dish washing (14 times 4 gallons);
and other uses (20 times 2 gallons).

17. The weekly BTU requirement has been calculated

by applying a factor of .75 and multiplying by 52. This results in an annual use of 20.05 million BTU of electricity or 22.55 million BTU of gas.

18. PG&E applied in 1981 the following lifeline rates in the San Francisco area (in $):

	Gas (therms)	Electric (kWh)
Basic Needs	.2969	.0403
Secondary Uses	.5806	.0657
Excess Consumption	.6824	.0976

19. See Chapter 6 with a similar development.
20. CEC (February 1978).

BIBLIOGRAPHY

Bainbridge, D. and M. Hunt 1978 "California's New Solar Tax Credit." Solar Age, June.
Butti, K. and J. Perlin 1980 A Golden Thread: 2500 Years of Solar Architecture and Technology. Palo Alto: Chesire Books.
California Energy Commission 1977 "Solar Tax Credit Regulations." Mimeo, June 17.
California Energy Commission 1978 "Solar Energy in California, Residential Thermal Applications." Draft, February.
California Energy Commission 1979 "California Energy Demand, 1978-2000." Staff Draft, August.
California Energy Commission 1979 "Toward an Alternative Energy Path for California." Staff Draft, August.
California Energy Commission 1979 "California's Solar Energy Tax Credit: An Analysis of Tax Returns for 1977." Staff Report, September.
California Energy Commission 1980 "Adopted California Local Government Solar Energy Ordinances." Staff Report, November.
California Public Policy Center 1978 "Jobs from the Sun." Report, February.
Johnson, D. 1979 "Users Guide to SOLFIN." California Energy Commission Report, September.
Solarcal Council 1979 "Toward a Solar California." Sacramento.
Solarcal Office No Date "Solar Energy and Consumer Lending." Bulletin.
Stasi, V. 1979 "A Survey of the California Solar Industry." California Solar Business Office, December.
U.S. Department of Energy 1978 "Psycho-economic Factors Affecting the Decision-Making of Consumers and the Technology Delivery System." Washington, D.C.
U.S. Department of Energy 1981 "Solar Collector Manufacturing Activity, 1980." Washington, D.C., March.

5
Wind Energy in Denmark

Halfdan Farstad and James Ward

In Denmark, supplementary electricity is increasingly produced with small windmills, erected and owned by
individuals and also some companies located in rural
areas. A technical break-through in the construction of
small windmills, achieved by an outsider, paved the way
for a new phase in the use of wind energy in Denmark. The
first mill was operational in 1975 after three years of
development. Two windmills were sold in 1976. Around
fifty windmills were erected in 1977 and more than 100 in
1978. Several hundred more were installed in 1979 and
1980. Sales in 1981 were estimated to have reached around
1'000 units although nobody really knows how many. units
are sold every year or are installed at this day.

Seventeen producers are presently offering small
windmills with a capacity of between 11 kW and 90 kW. The
government together with the electricity utilities is engaged in a research and development program for large
windmills. Plans to erect a first series of 200 mills
have however met with local resistances. This chapter
describes and analyzes this growth process, its facilitating and its constraining factors.

The first section describes briefly the Danish energy situation in the middle of the 1970s. A second section
provides an overview over the growth process of windmill
use for the small-scale production of electricity. We
analyze important actors and the roles they played as
driving or blocking forces in this process in the third
section. A final section discusses problems which might

Halfdan Farstad has an MA in sociology and is working for
Energy & Society at the University of Oslo on renewable
energy problems and the history of Norwegian oil developments. James Ward has an MA in economics and has completed work towards a Ph.D. at Stanford University. He has
worked previously in the Norwegian oil industry.

well already have slowed down the growth of the wind
energy branch or which might do so in the future if large
scale use is made of wind-generated electricity.

THE DANISH ENERGY SUPPLY SITUATION

Denmark, like any other industrialized country, experienced a rapid growth in energy consumption after
World War II. Energy use grew from 7.6 million tons of
oil equivalent (mtoe) in 1955 to 20.4 mtoe in 1977. In
this year, only 3.4 percent of this consumption was covered by domestic resources, and this was already an improvement over the half percent in 1973. Oil is still almost completely imported and its consumption fell only
slightly from 17.9 mtoe in 1973 to 16.7 mtoe in 1977.
Oil's share in energy supply is high although falling
from 90 percent in 1973 to 82 percent in 1977.[1] Before
the oil crisis, about 85 percent of Danish oil imports
were coming from the Middle East. And this oil provided
60 percent of the primary energy input into electricity
production. This share has now fallen to about 40 percent
in 1978 and should reach just 15 percent in 1985.[2]
The Danish government chose a dual strategy to try
to reduce this extreme dependency on energy supplies, oil
in particular, from politically very unstable areas. Oil
is to be substituted with coal and possibly nuclear (an
option which now has become uncertain). And suppliers
were to be diversified. In addition, the government finally consented to plan to use renewable energy resources
increasingly intensively in the coming decade.
Energy decision-making was taken out of the Ministry
of Commerce and concentrated in the newly formed Ministry
of Energy in 1979. The electricity system was left un-
changed where about 120 private and municipal utilities
make a quite independent energy policy with respect to
the utilization of windmills. Wind energy, for the moment
almost exclusively used for the generation of electricity, is only playing a marginal supply role today. The government expects a 4 percent contribution from renewable
energy resources to national energy supply in 1995. This
could rise as high as 10 percent under a scenario which
assumes rapidly rising energy prices and **further** significant technological improvements in windmill design.

THE HISTORY OF WIND ENERGY IN DENMARK

Alternative energy developments in most countries
can be divided into a period before the oil crisis and
the developments since then. This is also true for the
development of wind energy in Denmark although the revival of interest in wind energy predates the oil crisis by

a few years. Private, non-establishment actors made progress the cause of the small windmill at such an early
date. The state overcame its passivity only after the oil
crisis and then concentrated its support on the development of large windmills. There are almost no links between the spheres of the small and the large windmills.

Past Wind Energy Uses

Research on the generation of electricity with windmills started in Denmark before the turn of the century.
Poul La Cour, one of the pioneers, erected several windmills producing direct current (DC). The most famous of
his mills, the one erected in the town of Ascov, remained
in continuous operation from 1902 until 1960, only interrupted once in 1929 because of a fire.
About 30'000 windmills were in use during the 1920s
and the 1930s. Many of them were used for doing mechanical work such as pumping water and grinding wheat. The
mills producing electricity -still DC- had an installed
capacity of 100 MW. Most of these mills have since been
dismanteled.
Since then wind energy use has always been linked to
periods when the energy supply situation was problematical, or was perceived to be so. This was true for the
years during World War II and the second half of the
1950s in the wake of the Suez canal closures. Several
hundred windmills erected during those periods remain in
use today, mostly for the draining of soils and the pumping of water for the animals on the range. The 1956 Suez
crisis and the interruption in oil supplies from the
Middle East induced the Danske Elektricitetsværkers Fore-
ning (DEF - the Danish Association of Electricity Utilities) to build the well-known Gedser mill in South Zea-
land.
The Gedser mill has a capacity of 200 kW and was the
first to produce alternating current (AC) which was fed
into the electricity grid. The mill was planned to be a
pilot project. However, the mill was sold to SEAS, a utility, after a five year testing period and was used until
1967 for the commercial production of electricity. Suppo-
sedly high maintenance costs and the falling price for
oil led to the decision to stop the mill although it was
not dismanteled.[3]

The Wind Energy Revival

The discussion on the future of wind energy ended
together with the de-commissioning of the Gedser mill in
1967. This was just the time when the debates on nature
protection and resource scarcity became increasingly intense. These debates were the beginning of a revival in
the interest in the use of renewable energy resources,

wind energy among them. Idea formation and technological innovation were two initial phases of this revival. Actors outside the established political, economic and research milieus were driving forces in them as well as in the subsequent phase of small windmill commercialisation. The activation of government interest in wind energy development led to the emergence of two, almost independent systems of wind energy promotion: the private, alternative sector committed to small windmills, and the other sector where government, utilities and established companies and research milieus cooperate in the technological development of large windmills.

Social protest and idea formation. An increasingly strong and active environmental protection movement coalesced in 1973 in the Organisationen for Oplysning om Atomkraft (OOA - the Organisation for Information on Nuclear Power). The main goal of OOA was to prevent the introduction of nuclear power, then proposed by the electricity utilities and the government. OOA proposed as an alternative strategy the development of national, renewable energy resources including wind energy.

One of the initiators behind the formation of OOA was Bent Sørensen from the Niels Bohr Institute in Copenhagen. Already before the formation of OOA, he had begun to review all available technical reports on wind energy in order to determine the state of Danish wind energy technology. He concluded that it was possible to produce electricity with windmills, and this at a cost not prohibitively out of line with electricity costs when using oil-fired power stations. Sørensen, together with two economists, strove to analyze the costs and benefits of alternative energy systems within a wider political and macroeconomic framework.[4] In this view, the higher direct production costs of wind-generated electricity compared to electricity from fossil-fuel fired power stations are compensated by the greater supply certainty and the positive balance-of-payments effects. This argumentation was widely used in the debate on future energy supply developments which followed the oil crisis of 1973 and 1974.

Technological innovation. Simultaneously but not directly related to this theoretical, ideational and organisational development, a lone craftsman in Jutland did path-braking development work on a small electricity-generating windmill. Riisager, a carpenter by profession, had already built an electricity-producing watermill at his summer house when he and his wife decided in 1972 to develop their own windmill. The mill was finished in 1975 after three years of costly research and development work, all paid personally by the Riisagers. The search for a good rotor design had been especially time-consuming. A major technical break-through realized by

Riisager was the utilization of an asynchronous generator to produce 220 V AC. This enabled him to hook up the windmill to the electricity grid and to use it to control the operation of the windmill, automatically coupling and decoupling it according to wind-related performance.

The oil crisis of 1973 and 1974 and the developing debate on the wind energy alternative had by now given a different meaning to Riisager's work. Many Danes were beginning to look for individual solutions to future energy supply problems Riisager's mill, standing close to a heavily travelled road, attracted increasing attention from travellers who began to stop to request some information. This development changed Riisager's view on the commercial potential of his mill. He began to think about the commercial production of his mill and sold his first two units in 1976. These mills had a capacity of 22 kW.[5]

This technical development changed the character of the wind energy debate. Before it was a question of arguing that the construction of small windmills for generating electricity was technically feasible. Now such a small windmill was commercially available. It became now a problem of pushing people to adopt it.

Windmill commercialisation. The changing nature of the energy debate and Riisager's success stimulated other people to also experiment with the design and building of windmills. Some of these people simply desired to secure their own electricity supply. Others aimed at starting-up production of windmills for sale. Moral and ideological motives often mingled with more economic ones. For example, teachers at the experimental training school in Tvind decided to build their own windmill to reduce the increasingly onerous energy budget of their school. But they also embarked on this project of a 2'000 kW mill out of a spirit of self-reliance. The planning, building and testing of this mill during the years 1975 to 1979 was also a learning and educational experience for teachers and students alike.[6]

All this private research and product development work had been so far carried out without state support. New organisational development was in part designed to correct this situation and to accelerate windmill commercialisation through information gathering and spreading and educational activities. People from OOA and from other environmental groups formed the Organisationen for Vedvarende Energi (OVE - the Organisation for Renewable Energy) in 1975. OVE's goal is to promote the exploitation of domestic renewable energy resources. Wind energy is to be promoted through information spreading, education and consulting with potential buyers and producers of windmills. OVE has been a central actor in creating a public opinion in favor of the widespread use of wind energy as we will point out in more detail later on.

The wind energy committee of the Akademiet for de
Tekniske Vitenskaper (ATV - Academy for the Technical
Sciences) played also a very useful role in convincing
the public of the merits of wind energy. A first report
published in 1975 concluded that wind energy was an economically and technically satisfactory solution to the
energy problem.[7] The report stressed the positive balance-of-payment and employment effects of a domestic wind
energy program. It was extensively discussed in the mass
media. The electricity utilities distinguished themselves in this debate through their strong opposition to the
use of wind energy for the production of electricity.
This resistance backfired however because both OOA and
OVE pointed to the earlier uses of wind energy. The debate ended with the public opinion calling for increased
state support for wind energy development by, e.g., subsidizing research work.

This demand placed the government in a quandary. The
social-democratic government was apparently decided to
build out nuclear power. It did not think that wind energy could ever make a significant contribution to Danish
energy supply. Yet, it feared that a rapid expansion of
wind energy use might just be enough to force a further
postponement of the decision to go nuclear. Events in
other countries had by then suggested that the opposition
to nuclear power was more likely to grow with time. Yet,
disregarding the public's demand for an exploitation of
wind energy resources was likely to further weaken public
support for an already weak government.

The government started therefore to plan for some
development of wind energy as part of the general energy
plan which had been under preparation since the oil crisis. But before the government made any concrete decision,
the ATV published a second report in 1976 containing an
action program for the development of wind energy in Denmark.[8] Energy research tasks were listed in detail and it
was proposed to use public funds in their support. The
report contained also a time plan for the execution of
this research program and a proposal for the organisation
of the research effort. The report also discussed extensively the economic aspects of such a program.

The government's program on wind energy development,
published in 1976 shortly after the ATV report had appeared, followed in general the proposal made by ATV.
However, state funding was less than demanded by ATV and
the time horizon for completing the research work had been
prolonged. Management of the research program, exclusively
devoted to the development of large windmills, was given
to Danske Elektricitetsværkers Utredningsafdeling (DEFU),
the research and planning organisation of DEF. But both
DEF and DEFU had sofar mostly shown a negative attitude
towards the utilization of wind energy.

The government's energy plan, elaborated by the Mini-

stry of Trade, also introduced subsidies to households
to cover, initially, up to 40 percent of the total investment costs due to energy saving measures. Windmills were
covered under this scheme. The availability of these
grants, just when small, electricity-producing windmills
came onto the market, undoubtedly contributed to their
rapid diffusion. Windmills, like most other renewable
energy systems, entail rather high initial investment
costs. Riisager's 22 kW mill, the smallest available,
was costing in 1976 DKr. 70'000 (about $ 11'600).[9] Most
people would have to raise loans to finance the acquisition of such a mill. But interest rates of around 20 percent were a deterrent which the government grants helped
to overcome. Buyer response was correspondingly enthusiastic. The government felt compelled to reduce benefit
levels in January 1978 in order to bring the applications
in line with budgeted means.[10]

The electricity utilities also seem to have under-
estimated the demand for windmills. Riisager, when erecting his mill in 1975, was given the right to connect it
to the grid. He was paid the same price for his surplus
electricity that he had to pay for electricity bought
from the utility during wind-calm periods. Almost 50 percent of the first windmills were thus connected to the
grid. The utilities changed this generous policy once
they realized that the windmills were much more productive than they had assumed and that the applications for
connection to the grid were increasing much faster than
expected. Most utilities set the price for surplus electricity at 50 percent of the rate charged to customers.
They then failed however to increase it in step with increases in their selling rates when they began to pass
through higher fuel costs. The discrimination against
windmill producer was therefore increasing over time.

However, neither the government's nor the utilities'
change of terms seemed to be able to stop the spreading
of private windmills. The first two sales in 1976 were
followed by fifty in 1977 and more than 100 in 1978. Several hundreds were probably erected in 1979 and 1980
according to an estimate by Riisager. However, nobody
really knows how many windmills are sold every year. Estimates for sales in 1981 range from 500 to 1'000 windmills
with less than 90 kW capacity.[11] The latter figure is a
reasonable extrapolation from the 200 subsidy applications approved by the government in January and February
1981.[12]

A survey of the May 1981 list of windmill owners reporting monthly to OVE their windmill performance indicates that only eight of the 150 mills reported on were
erected before 1980.[13] If both figures reflect a correct
sample of the total windmill population at the beginning
of 1981, we would arrive at almost 3'000 mills already in
operation by that time. This seems to be exaggerated.[14]

This lack of precise knowledge about windmill sales and windmills in operation suggests that any forecast of future sales has to be accepted with great caution. The Ministry of Energy suggests that by 1995 100'000 windmills might be installed both for the production of heat and of electricity.[15] Together with other renewable energy resources, they would then contribute 4 percent of total energy consumption. A report published by OOA and OVE suggested in 1976 that renewable energy resources could cover up to 12 percent of energy consumption by that time.[16]

There were seventeen producers of small windmills in the summer of 1981 although here too some differences of opinion exist.[17] In addition, a number of small and large firms are producing important windmill elements such as generators and rotors. The government expects that the industry is exporting about seventy units during 1981.[18]

Small windmills with a capacity of between 11 kW and 90 kW are presently available. Most units sold have a capacity of up to 55 kW. Those windmills sold to a group of households or companies have a capacity of between 22 kW and 55 kW. The smallest windmill of 11 kW was costing in June 1981 DKr 110'000 ($ 15'500). The 55 kW mill had a price of DKr 325'000 ($ 45'600), in both cases including value added tax (VAT).[19]

Windmill development in two spheres. The revival of interest in wind energy focused primarily on the development of small windmills for individual household use. It was carried by three groups of actors with their own motivations and focus of action:

1. Riisager set out to develop a windmill for his private use. The thought about commercial production came only later when the machine proved successful, and when the oil crisis brought to the fore a latent demand. Riisager became the central commercial windmill producer in the second half of the 1970s.
2. Researchers in physics and the technical sciences became interested in the possibilities and past Danish achievements in the wind energy area. They supported with hard facts the argument about the economic and technical feasibility of the development of wind energy, arguments which other people often used more out of commitment than actual knowledge.
3. The environmental movement which created the OOA as the vehicle against the government's plan for nuclear power. The need to propose alternative solutions led it to consider and then propagate the use of wind energy. The spinning off of OVE was a consequence of this choice of an alternative energy development scenario.

These three actors proceeded initially quite inde-

pendent from each other. The oil crisis did not right a-
way change this situation. All that happened was that
additional individuals and groups began experimenting
with windmills. The Danish energy policy debate intensified leading to the consensus opinion that Danemark's dependence on vulnerable energy supplies should be diminished. This debate was widely reported in the mass media
and created a media interest in wind energy developments.
But governmental authorities remained in their passive
role towards wind energy.

The poor cooperation and coordination among the
three actor groups listed above can be explained by three
factors:

1. Small versus large windmills: The individuals experimenting with and developing windmills were exclusively interested in small windmills for the individual. The
academic researchers attracted to wind energy problems
were more interested in large windmills.

2. Diverse energy policy interests: OOA was primarily interested in stopping the development of nuclear power. Many researchers and windmill developers saw no con-
tradiction between wind and nuclear energy development.
They were for the development of both.

3. Different tactics: The researchers interested in
wind energy but also opposed to nuclear thought it nevertheless unwise to be seen associating with OOA. They felt
that it was safer to appear neutral with respect to the
nuclear question if they wanted to gain support for wind
energy research from a pro-nuclear government.

The above mentioned mass media reporting of the
energy debate and the decision to remove OOA from direct
involvement in the promotion of renewable energy use,
and to transfer this task to a new organisation, the OVE,
was decisive for overcoming this split between the forces
positively inclined to the development of wind energy:

1. The press in particular provided a discussion and
information forum in response to the publication of the
reports by ATV and their recommendation of a large windmill development program. The mass media reported on the
Tvind windmill experiment. It relayed the experiences
from a number of "energy summer camps" which built their
own windmills. And it presented the increasingly numerous
individual efforts to build windmills for the self-gene-
ration of electricity. The advantages and disadvantages
from a national energy supply perspective of both small
and large windmills were also discussed.

This activity contributed to the creation of a public opinion in favor of an increased exploitation of wind
energy -and this repeatedly forced the hand of the government and of the electric utilities. But it provided

all actors concerned with the development of wind energy
with information about each other. This facilitated the
establishment and strengthening of contacts among each
other despite all differences of interest and of opinions.

2. The formation of OVE, as a spin-off from OOA,
created an organisational focus on the development of
wind energy in particular, but all other renewable energy
resources more generally. OVE lacked any mandate to become formally involved in other policy matters. This made
it possible to gain support and cooperation from all individuals and groups working on or interested in wind
energy development irrespective of their specific interests and ideological orientations: individual windmill
builders and small producers of windmills, windmill owners, nuclear energy opponents without any practical experience with renewable energy systems, and engineers and
researchers involved in technical and economic analyses
of different windmill systems.

Some researchers remained sceptical of OVE because
of its identification with the small windmills developed
and built by non-professionals. Nevertheless even they
saw in OVE a positive force. OVE, in their eyes, was increasing the public interest in wind energy, and in this
way OVE was contributing to pressure on the state to provide financial support to wind energy development. This
money, however, was likely to be allocated to large windmill research, i.e., what they were interested in.

But there never really developed any close and sustained cooperation between the forces behind small and
large windmill developments respectively, although OVE
provided a meeting ground since 1975. Temporary cooperation took sometimes place within OVE but rarely was continued outside of it. If contact was sought, then it was
always the small windmill side which felt the need to
do so, never the actors interested in large windmill development. Small windmill development continued to take
place within the private sector and at the grass-roots
level. Large windmill development occurred in established
research institutes, supported by government funds.

The growing state involvement in windmill development since 1976 was never really designed to bridge this
gap. On the one hand, the state never really believed in
the future of the small windmills. It failed to provide
support for their development apart from subsidies which
were granted for other purposes --such as supporting
innovative activities or energy saving-- and which could
be used to support windmill construction. The test station for small windmills was the only concrete, though
indirect, support ever given.

On the other hand, the state naturally turned to
established institutions when it finally decided in 1976
to support a large windmill research program. In parti-

cular, it chose DEFU as the manager of the program. But DEFU was always looked upon with suspicion by the people behind the small windmill development.

Cooperation between supporters of small and large windmills is difficult because they are separated by the conflict over the division of state resources in their respective support. Small windmill supporters welcome the development of large windmills. They see them as a complement to the small ones. They accept therefore gladly state support for the large windmill development program. What they complain about is that the state is not also supporting the development of small windmills in a more active way.

Supporters of large windmill development are not necessarily against small windmills. But they do not see them as having a large supply potential. Scarce resources should therefore be concentrated on the most promising option, i.e., large windmills. The problem is that such a passive attitude has for example led the government and other established institutions to ignore the small windmill development, or to discriminate against it as in the case of most electric utilities. This has meant above all that nobody really has an overview over the real extent of small windmill development. And this seems to be a weak base on which to decide to exclusively bet on large windmill systems.

The actual situation of a dual government attitude and the concentration of the respective developments in two different spheres has led to two different institutional dynamics. Large windmill development relies largely on existing institutions and networks within the public sector. The only addition were some steering bodies for the government's wind energy program. But the representatives on these bodies do not represent new forces. Quite the opposite was the case in the small windmill sphere. Windmill producer and owner organisations were formed. Decentralized information and consulting networks were built up. Local energy offices help individuals and small producers to get started with windmill construction. And local social networks were activated to propagandize the case of the small windmill and to help others to gain access to one.

ACTORS AND THEIR ACTIONS

Institutions and structures, opportunities and constraints do not really change by themselves. Their transformation is sometimes the unconscious result of human action. But in general they change because human actors make them change. The previous section has shown how important individuals and groups have been in bringing about a new growth period in the utilisation of wind energy in Den-

mark. In this section we look at the most important actors and the roles they played in bringing about or hindering the development of wind energy utilisation in Denmark. These actors are the government, the electric utilities, the interest organisations supporting wind energy
use, the windmill buyers and producers, the political
parties, and the mass media.

The Energy Policy of the Government

The basic task of a government's energy policy is to
secure a sufficient and safe supply of energy given certain demand conditions. The import dependency for the
various energy resources is an important criterion for
evaluating a country's energy situation. A high import
dependency makes the country subject to international
events over which it has no control, certainly not a
small country such as Denmark. Supply stability for oil
--apart from the quickly forgotten lessons of the Middle
East wars in 1956 and 1967-- and falling real energy prices made superfluous an active governmental energy policy
prior to 1971. The market, i.e., electricity utilities
and oil companies, could be left alone in providing a
solution. This started to change with the first tremors
of the coming oil crisis in 1971. The government in Denmark became concerned and proposed an alternative nuclear
power scenario.

The nuclear option. The sharpening conflict between
the international oil companies and the major Third World
oil producing countries implied an increased uncertainty
about the future supply of oil. Oil covered by that time
about 90 percent of Denmark's primary energy needs. Energy policy concerns came into sharper focus in government
planning. The debate began on alternative strategies for
reducing energy supply uncertainty.
The Danish government wanted primarily to develop
nuclear power in order to reduce the dependency on oil
for the generation of electricity.[20] This supply side response, and the focusing on a centralized, capital and
skill intensive technological solution were not surprising. Traditional energy supplies were not available
domestically. Energy-saving as a strategy was unthinkable
at the time. The general optimism of the international
scientific, industrial and political milieus about the
potential of nuclear power provided an important "frame
of values" and a narrowly conceived choice of options for
governmental decision-makers, even for social-democratic
ones.[21]
Developing nuclear power would maintain import dependency. But the diversification of energy resources and
the shift to friendly export countries would still reduce
the risks inherent in this dependence situation.

The government was also looking for a strategy which would bring quick results and which was economically sound. Nuclear power seemed at that time still to fulfill these conditions. Wind energy was not considered a good alternative. Earlier experiences during times of international crises with wind-generated electricity had suggested that this electricity was uncompetitive. Eventual development of wind energy utilisation was dependent on the realisation of technological break-throughs. These were resource-demanding and time-consuming and their realisation was uncertain in the first place. In short, wind energy was at best a long-term solution, a view strongly shaped and supported by the electric utilities.

The new energy policy. The nuclear energy option had been basically developed by the government in cooperation with the utilities, industry and parliament. Other actors started only slowly to get organized and to make themselves heard. The oil crisis in 1973 and 1974 helped. But very important in generating public demands for the consideration of wind energy as an alternative were three developments. Public opinion had by that time become mobilized against nuclear power and in support of alternative energy utilisation. Technological improvements to small, electricity-generating windmills had brought closer the day of competitive wind energy. And scientific reports on wind energy took a positive attitude towards the further development of this technology, in part by pointing to important national gains which could be realized with wind energy.

The government's energy action program of 1976 was reflecting this new situation although it contained a rather partial action program. Three research areas for the development of wind energy were identified:

1. Evaluation, reparation and testing of the 200 kW Gedser mill (originally erected in 1956). This was to be done in cooperation with the U.S. Department of Energy and NASA.
2. Construction of two 600 kW windmills in Jutland for development and testing purposes. These mills were seen as precursors for the machines to be used in the construction of the large windmill system. Ancillary work on load management simulation was also to be carried out.
3. Establishment of a quality test station for small windmills open to all producers at their request and expense.

The research budget was set at DKr 35.5m ($ 5.9m), to be adjusted for inflation. All expenses were to be freed from VAT. These two clauses were quickly abandoned when inflation accelerated and the government deficits continued to grow. The real value of research funds available decreased therefore significantly during the plan period from 1977 to 1980.[22]

Support of small windmill development. The planned test station was the only production side support for the development of small windmills. No other direct support had been foreseen. However, the energy action program provided for grants in support of energy saving measures taken by households, farmers and industry. The purchase of a windmill was covered by this grant program. Coverage and accessability were initially lowered in response to budget problems, but then they were improved again when public pressure was applied.

Originally grants covered 25 percent (for households and farmers) and 40 percent (for industry) of investment costs. The response went beyond government expectations and rapidly exhausted available funds. The government changed the rules for the new budget year beginning in January 1978. Government support of energy saving was obviously a function of budgetary constraint. The government still did not consider that small windmills could provide a useful addition to national energy supply.

The new policy introduced maximum rates, set at 30 percent and 40 percent respectively. Payment of the maximal support was made dependent on low income levels. This rule was designed to lower the value of the average grant. In addition, applicants had to prove a pay-back on their investment of eight years. This was designed to eliminate a number of applications because windmills had a pay-back period, in the average, of ten years although their lifetime was estimated to be anywhere between fifteen and thirty years. This rule could only be fulfilled by buyers with a relatively high electricity consumption located in areas with good wind conditions given the rules applied by most electric utilities for connecting windmills to the grid. Large farms with a lot of mechanical equipment were likely to qualify, but they had also the greatest capacity to finance a windmill out of their own pocket. Households, if they wanted to qualify, had to maximize consumption of their own electricity. The government kept within its budget and windmill buyers realized financial optimality at the price of wasteful consumption of electricity.

The qualifying criteria were relaxed as of the beginning of 1980 in response to public pressure concerned with the consequences of the 1979 oil crisis. The income criteria were dropped. The pay-back clause was replaced with the requirement of a quality certificate for the planned windmill issued by the test station for small windmills. This change in particular had the important although unintended side effect that it made producers become concerned about product quality. It also assured potential buyers about the quality of the product they

were going to by. This lowered risks and information cost
and in this way may well have convinced many a sympathetic wind energy supporter to go out and acquire a mill.[23]
The terms were changed once more in January 1981.
Farmers and households could now get grants of only 20
percent (instead of 30 percent) of investment costs. However, VAT on the windmill became now reimbursable. This
change was obviously intended to cut apparent budget expenditures and replace them with less visible tax expenditures. The VAT rate is currently 22 percent, which
means that a buyer in 1981 can count on a 18 percent price reduction for windmills costing between DKr 110'000
($ 15'500) for a 11 kW mill and DKr 325'000 ($ 45'600)
for a 55 kW one.

However, budget allocations to cover the grants have
every year proved insufficient due to the high demand.
Grant applications were therefore held up every year towards the year end to approve them at the beginning of
the new budget year. This treatment had however negative
effects on the stability of the production and sales of
windmills. The windmill producers, all of them small, had
problems coping with this fluctuation and they have become less cooperative with each other through their conflicts over remaining customers. Buyers too might have
been discouraged thus slowing down the diffusion of mills.

The introduction of more generous grant conditions
is largely the result of the international oil developments in the wake of the Iranian revolution, and of
their domestic repurcussions within Denmark. Iran was
Denmark's main oil supplier. The crisis induced therefore many people to become less dependent on traditional
sources of electricity and by doing so, to regain some
control over the development of their energy costs. This
desire was channeled through the two interest associations, OOA and OVE, which made skillful use of the oil
supply developments and their economic consequences in
Denmark to apply public pressure on the government to induce it to grant increasing support for the private exploitation of renewable energy resources.

Of course, one can wonder if the frequent alteration
of grant terms did not in itself have a dissuasive effect
on potential windmill buyers. Luckily, OVE and the local
energy offices were ready to inform and educate these
buyers and make them aware of the exact benefit available to them.

Conclusion. The government's nuclear and large windmill plans are in suspension while the small windmill
sector is developing quite vigorously. The government
plans to install between 1'000 and 2'000 large windmills
for a production capacity of around 1 GW. Attempts to select sites for the first series of mills have run into
resistance on the part of local authorities.

The government seems still committed to the nuclear option. Resistance to nuclear power, channeled through OOA, has paralyzed the decision-making power of both political parties and parliament. The issue is now to be decided in a national referendum which will take place sometime during 1982 or 1983. The forces responsible for this development are of course the same which have forced the government to become "passively positive" about the development of wind energy, although more so for large-scale than small-scale wind energy technology. Yet, it is again this same environmentalist movement which created the conditions where local authorities feel compelled to reject large-scale wind energy power. It seems then that the government will slowly have to realize that it cannot for much longer try to have an energy policy which is mostly ignoring the public interest in the small windmill option.

Electric Utilities and Wind Energy

Electricity is produced and distributed by a mixture of private and municipal companies.[24] They are organized in three regional units which manage the distribution of electricity over the grid. DEF is the overarching national organisation. Both DEF and its research and planning arm DEFU have always been committed to the development of nuclear power. They have also argued against an exploitation of wind energy from the beginning of the debate on it in 1971. The individual utilities themselves developed a differentiated attitude towards wind energy. They simply accepted small windmills when they appeared and permitted connection to the grid. Wind energy was not seen as a real alternative. It was simply considered as being basically irrelevant to the interests and activities of the companies.

Most small windmills are hooked up with the grid. The technical improvements to the mills realized by Riisager made such a link feasible and even desirable. The utilities permitted this connection at fairly generous terms. Many of them paid the same price for electricity received as they charged for electricity supplied. The attitude began only to change when the surge in windmill sales became apparent. DEF then prepared in 1976 a set of suggested conditions which should govern the integration of small windmills into the grid. The technical requirements imposed where unexceptional. But three other issues proved more controversial: the price paid for electricity received by the utilities, the refusal to let collectively owned windmills be connected to the grid, and the distribution of the costs arising from connecting the mills with the grid.

Electricity pricing. The 1976 rules went back on the

initial praxis of paying for electricity what the utility
was charging. DEF's rate setting guidelines suggested now
that the price difference should be equal to the fuel
costs saved and transmission losses averted because the
utility does not have to produce the electricity supplied
by the windmill owner.This saving was set at 50 percent
of total production costs. DEF consequently proposed that
the buying price be set at 50 percent of the selling price. Most distribution companies did do that at the time,
although some offered to pay even less or nothing at all.
     However, the buying rates were defined in nominal
terms. Selling rates began soon afterwards to increase
as rising fuel costs were passed through.[25] The buying
rates were not adjusted accordingly and the gap between
the two prices widened rapidly to the disadvantage of the
windmill owner. Government pressure in response to public
opinion forced the utilities to increase buying rates by
about 30 percent in late 1979. This still did not reesta-
blish the initial condition of 1976 and the renewed increases of electricity prices after the Iranian revolution took quickly away the benefits of this adjustment.
It seems clear that the utilities do not intend to honor
the rate setting guideline of 1976. And we are obviously
far away from the U.S. policy of a positive discrimination in favor of the individual producer-consumer of
electricity.[26]

Collectively owned windmills. Larger windmills which
produce electricity for a group of households are about
20 percent more economical than single-household mills.
The DEF rules however prohibited the integration of these
mills into the grid. Obviously the utilities wanted from
the beginning prevent their development and adoption. The
government-enforced rule change in 1979 was ambiguous on
this issue. On the one hand, these windmills could now
be hooked up with the grid. On the other hand, permission
to do so depended on severe restrictions. Windmill owners
could not consume more than 60 percent of the mill's production, yet self-consumed electricity could not be more
than 55 percent of total electricity consumption. This
penalized such mills because the price bias against
electricity delivered by the mill owner would have
suggested a mill capacity as close as possible to total
electricity consumption.

Connection costs. Linking the windmill to the grid
entails establishing the link between the mill and the
existing grid   and often strenghtening the grid at
the connection point. The mill owner bears the hook-up
costs in any case. DEF rules leave it open who should be
paying for the costs of improving the grid at the connection point --often a necessity in the rural areas. Many
utilities finance all the work as it is often a necessity

for the satisfaction of future needs. Others charge the customer with a small contribution. A few utilities demand full cost coverage from the windmill owner. This adds up to DKr 50'000 ($ 9'000) to investment costs. People interested in buying a windmill have always argued that this is patently unfair. Grid improvement benefits the utility and all its other customers too. Conflicts about sharing these costs have sometimes led to delays in getting permission to link the mill to the grid. More usual is the negotiation of a compromise.

DEF has clearly attempted to reduce the profitability of small windmills used for the generation of electricity once it became clear that many households were going to adopt such mills. This strategy seems to have been inspired by three motives:

1. The fear of competition: Utilities are accustomed to their monopoly control over the local electricity system. The introduction of a new type of electricity producer --who was at the same time an electricity consumer-- introduced an unknown quantity into the system. Windmills are also small-scale technology, not exactly something which fits easily into the world as seen from the utility management's viewpoint. In addition, this development occurred at the initiative of the windmill owners and this threatened the utilities with a loss of absolute control over system development. These factors created the ideological and value base for looking for more rational reasons to reject small windmills.

2. The commitment to nuclear: The utilities were committed to introduce nuclear power. They had invested resources in planning for this event. Nuclear looked cheaper than oil and coal-based electricity according to DEF calculations. DEF knew that wind-generated electricity in the past had been more expensive than other forms of electricity. They felt that economic sense spoke for nuclear and against wind. Load management problems were likely to emphasize this cost difference. Finally, this new source, even if only of a marginal size, might just have been enough in combination with lower demand growth than anticipated to delay the construction of a nuclear power plant. Delay was, however, only going to strengthen the anti-nuclear movement.

3. The load management problem: DEF argued that wind energy was going to increase the gap between peak and base loads. The necessity to provide additional expensive peak load capacity would simply accelerate the rate of increase in electricity prices.[27]

It seems that none of these factors really justify the negative position on the development of the wind energy resource. DEF did in fact reduce its opposition to

to wind energy when the government prepared its first
energy action program in 1976. This was partly out of
loyalty to the government and the national interest in a
different energy policy. But, realism also suggested that
the government might well sanction the utilities if they
did not act in accordance with official goals and did not
help the government to appease public opinion. The government's timid support of wind energy development did
not undermine its commitment to the nuclear option preferred by the utilities. Moreover, the utilities also realized that the government's commitment to the development of large windmills meant that the their leading role
in developing and managing the electricity systems was
going to be preserved.

DEFU consequently became involved in the national
wind energy research program. And DEF will end up running
the program to build the system of large electricity-generating windmills which is foreshadowed in this research
program. DEFU contributed DKr 7m ($1.1m)of its own money
to the large windmill program. It is the manager of this
program, including the building and testing of the two
600 kW mills. And it has three of the five seats on the
board of directors of the program.

Some have questioned the comprehensive engagement of
DEFU in this wind energy program. They feared that DEFU
might utilize its position to introduce its bias against
wind energy into the interpretation of the test results
from running the two experimental mills. This could easily be done as the mills are designed to facilitate technical testing and not to produce electricity at least
cost.

These fears seem exaggerated. Interests hostile to
DEFU and supportive of wind energy are strong and sophisticated enough to prevent DEFU from getting away with
such a tactic of discreditation of wind energy. It was
also simply efficient to let DEFU run the program as it
still possessed the organisational memory from earlier
experiments with wind energy to run the present program
along efficient lines. Finally, DEFU seemed the appropriate choice for manager if DEF will later on run the
commercial windmill program.

Conclusion. DEFU and DEF are of course in a strong
position to control the wind energy program because the
government has delegated in the past all planning and
operational decisions with respect to the electricity
system. They have a monopoly on knowledge and expertise
in all things electrical. The government has therefore to
give them an important voice in formulating the government's energy policy. In the past they have used this position to hinder the adoption of a wind energy scenario.
To-morrow they might support it, although it will be a
scenario suited to their interests. Unfortunately consu-

mers have in general no way to directly influence utility
decision-making. They have to proceed indirectly, using
the political process to induce the government to intervene on their behalf. Luckily, OOA and OVE have the
strength and the capacity to mobilize public opinion in
favor of wind energy. It might therefore well be that
DEF can be brought to become more supportive of large as
well as small windmill development.

Interest Groups for Wind Energy

There is no doubt that the mobilisation of public
opinion has played an important positive role in the Danish wind energy development. Two organisations in particular have been crucial here, OOA and OVE. They have also
played an important information and educational role both
in the political and the socio-cultural spheres. They
identified opportunities for using renewable energy resources and then propagandized concrete solutions. The
OOA, founded in 1973, has played a more general and more
political role. The OVE, founded in 1975, acted more specifically to promote the use of renewable energy resources, wind energy among them.
OOA is an organisation devoted to the fight against
the introduction of nuclear power. Most of its efforts
have gone in this direction. It began to argue for the
development of domestic, alternative energy resources
because it needed a positive alternative to the development of nuclear power. OOA mobilized and expanded a
public which was the result of a long shift in the normative climate throughout the 1960s in most industrialised countries. This increased orientation towards environmental values such as an "untouched" nature and a pol-
lution-free environment was used to mobilize this public
against nuclear power. In so doing, it introduced this
public to the problems of energy policy in general.
The linking of an anti-nuclear position with one in
support of renewable energy resource use proved however
to be problematical. Many people, among them politicians
and windmill builders, for example Riisager, failed to
see an opposition between the use of nuclear and of renewable energy resources. They refused therefore to actively support OOA, thereby weakening the pursuit of their
own goal, i.e., the promotion of renewable energy use.
This unsatisfactory situation led some people within and
without OOA to form OVE in 1975. Another incentive for
going this way was that OOA simply did not have the resources to pursue both of its goals. The inability to mobilize all supporters of renewable energy resource use
was of course one reason for this inability.
The need for a separate organisation became urgent
when Riisager presented his new, small windmill. The decision to concentrate efforts to promote wind energy in a

separate organisation proved fully justified by subsequent developments. Engineers began joining OVE and this in turn enabled the organisation to start up consultant services for windmill builders and buyers. This was a powerful tool to help overcome the barriers to the diffusion of a small-scale, yet complex technology to generally non-technical individuals. In addition, OVE began organizing seminars for the windmill producers and builders in order to promote technological exchange and cooperation among them. This too was important because Riisager had achieved several crucial technical break-throughs. Most builders were also quite helpless in organizing the commercial production of windmill equipment.

OVE also launched general educational campaigns both at the national and the local levels. OVE representatives contacted national and local politicians in order to directly and indirectly generate pressure on the government so that it would increase its support for the development of small windmills, or so that it would at least create favorable contextual conditions with incentives for individual buyers to adopt wind energy technology.

OOA and OVE are both associations of local units. OVE had forty-four local groups and ten energy consulting service units associated with it in March 1979. These units have great independence of action as long as they observe the basic goals of the organisation. This freedom has provided the different units with the flexibility necessary to adopt branch activities to local conditions. Such an organizational set-up matches well with Danish tradition, organizational as well as political.

The existence of past, concrete experiences with the use of windmills has of course been a great support to the activities of both OOA and OVE. It was also helpful to be able to point to concrete developments in other countries. Pointing to earlier periods of extensive wind energy use in Denmark suggested that it could be easily done again. This way of arguing and appealing to personal memories was especially important before 1975, before the new generation of small windmills became available.

This historical experience had had also another, very useful consequence. The state of the art of Danish windmill design and construction principles had been incorporated in the 1950s in a engineering textbook. This book is compulsory reading for all mechanical engineering students. This ensured that basic technical knowledge about windmills was widely distributed in most technical milieus. This knowledge formed the base on which the innovators of the 1970s could build. It also facilitated in a later phase the rapid diffusion of information about the new windmill designs.

The quick establishment of OVE's credibility was not only supported by this collective memory of past windmill experiences and design principles. The early support gi-

ven to OVE and its ideas by Sørensen, a physicist from
the reputable Niels Bohr Institute in Copenhagen, was also very helpful. His review of the state of art of past
Danish windmill technology established windmills as more
than a crackpot answer to the current energy crisis.
The success of OOA and OVE is unquestionable. We
have already seen that these organisations managed to put
the government under pressure through public opinion mobilisation, bringing it to include wind energy in its
energy policy planning. OOA and OVE can also credit themselves with the responsibility for having induced the government to improve the support given to individuals wanting to acquire and use windmill equipment. Similar pressure induced the utilities to improve the conditions for
linking windmills to the grid. This was important because
this linkage provides a cheap way of resolving the energy
storage problem which so often decisively affects the
economics of renewable energy systems.

OVE has become a recognized expert on wind energy
questions thanks to its consulting service and its technical cooperation with windmill producers. As a consequence, two of its engineers were recruited into central
positions at the governmental small windmill testing center.

Another achievement is that OVE is running a windmill evaluation program on a voluntary basis. About 150
windmill owners send in monthly data on their windmill
performance and their energy consumption patterns. This
is the only large and systematic evaluation of small
windmill performance. It helps monitor the productivity
claims made by windmill producers. This will help keeping
them from making exaggerated promises whose non-fulfill-
ment often generates a climate of uncertainty and buyer
backlash. In addition, the program will provide detailed
information on wind patterns in different locations and
this should help in two ways. For one, it helps identify
good windmill locations. And secondly, it helps determine
the optimal combination of windmill type and location. [28]

The only failure of OVE seems to be its inability or
unwillingness to establish an information gathering system for the determination of windmill sales. Of course,
this should be the task of the government. But failing
this, OVE could also benefit greatly from itself trying
to know what exactly is the development of the wind energy branch.

In closing, it should be pointed out that both OOA
and OVE were helped in their tasks by excellent initial
conditions. The many people still remembering the extensive use made of wind energy in earlier periods were
apparently the first ones to take a positive stand on the
renewed development of wind energy. Many of them functio-
ned as informants and opinion leaders in their local,
educational and work environments. This activation of lo-

cal social networks is probably one important reason why Danes are such positive and enthusiastic believers in the prospects of wind energy.[29]

Windmill Buyers

Most windmill buyers are farmers or other inhabitants of rural areas. The larger windmills are bought by companies, larger farms, and groups of people also located in the rural areas. The number of small, electricity-generating windmills currently in operation is certainly more than 1'000 at the end of 1981. A majority of this windmills are connected with the electricity grid, using it as an otpimal supply equalisation system. Wind conditions are best along the western and southern coasts. But windmills are also in use in the flat inland areas.

Early buyers of windmills have generally been technical enthusiasts with a desire and an ability to themselves build a windmill. Or they were ecologically committed people also interested in alternative lifestyles and independence from large, centralized organisations. The economics of windmill use was not important and not necessarily a deterrent to the acquisition of a windmill although these people used their political clout through their interest organisation to pressure the government to help them improve the economics of their passion. These early adopters played an important role in convincing others to adopt windmills.[30]

The presence of a widely visible windmill in the backyard simply attracted attention and very often led to personal contacts between owners and interested passersby. We have seen that Riisager --the technical innovator-- got convinced in this way of the commercial potential of his windmill. This visibility has been responsible for the maintainance of a process of "keeping-up with the Jones's", something which does not work for heat pumps hidden away in the cellar.

But these early buyers were also actively helping to convince others to also buy a windmill. One way to do so was to participate in the information spreading process organized by OVE. Important here was the spreading of detailed measurements and accounts of windmill performance, showing under what conditions windmill electricity could be an economic way of covering private electricity needs. A journalist at a big Danish newspaper and one of the first windmill owners himself used his newspaper in this way.

Another tactic was to use local social networks to convince neighbors, friends and acquaintances to consider buying a windmill.

Windmill owners contributed to the spreading process when they managed to get the government and the utilities to improve the conditions under which one could acquire

and use a windmill. This activity, run through OVE as
well as outside of it, was quite important in improving
the economics of windmill use. And this improvement is
crucial for maintaing the diffusion process now that a
second generation of buyers, less committed morally or
ideologically to alternative energy use, begins to take
the relay from the first.

Windmill owners formed the Danske Vindkraftværker
(DVKV - the Danish Wind Energy Producers) in May 1978.
This organisation was used to strengthen contacts among
mill owners, to exchange information on their experience,
and to serve as the negotiation body in dealings with the
government and the electricity utilities.

The DVKV played a decisive role in bringing about
the recent bancruptcy of a windmill producer. This producer made great claims for the economic profitability of
his windmills. One buyer in particular, a company, found
that its mill did not reach the promised production level. Discussions about a partial reimbursement of the
purchase price broke down. DVKV began to spread the news
about this case and considered starting a court case a-
gainst the producer for making dishonest claims. The impact of this negative information was drastic enough
in terms of a collapse in windmill orders that the producer was forced to declare bancruptcy.

Windmill Producers

We have mentioned the important technological innovation in small windmill design made by Riisager and
other windmill builders. None of them received any public
assistance while experimenting with windmill designs.
The main motives behind the initial efforts have been a
desire to secure an independent supply of electricity
and to solve technological challenges. Their efforts
could have ended here. But their creation of a suitable
windmill technology coincided with a growing interest on
the part of others in having their own electricity. This
interest in turn was fanned by the ecological movement
and the oil crisis.

This situation created the opportunity to change
from an initial phase of individual tinkering to a phase
of commercially producing windmills. Most early windmill
builders had not considered such a possibility. But once
they decided to do so --helped by the activities of OVE--
they were in themselves an important factor in spreading
information about wind energy possibilities.

There existed seventeen producers of windmills in
July 1981.[31] In addition there are a number of large and
small companies providing windmill parts such as generators and rotors. Most producers were originally carpen-
ters, car mechanics, and blacksmiths. They started small-
scale production on their local premises. Most of them

have less than ten employees.

One recent development had the association of black-smiths present the plans for a new windmill type. the plans are to be cheaply sold to association members. The aim is to establish windmill production points all over the country among the more than 1'000 members of the as-sociation. Potential windmill buyers should thereby be encouraged to buy locally, thus contributing to the main-tenance of a decentralized production structure.

Initially, windmill builders were driven by an idea-listic interest in and commitment to windmill energy. They were therefore willing to exchange with each other their technological knowledge and operational experience. This enabled OVE to organize technical seminars where producers could learn from each other. The producers also agreed to provide their plans through OVE to any indivi-dual who was interested in building his own windmill. This attitude obviously helped speeding up the branch de-velopment process.

This phase has now ended. The widening of the market increased profit opportunities and the increasing number of producers heightened competitive pressures, so that producers have begun to think first about their economic interests before being concerned with the general well-being. The demand fluctuations induced by the government's handling of its subsidy program for windmill buyers have also contributed to this development. Technical coopera-tion is now insignificant. Riisager has by now lost his technical advantage so that this may not matter much. It is maybe also time that the logic of branch development changes away from technological development more towards an extension of production runs.

The windmill producers created the Foreningen for Danske Vindmøllefabrikanter (FDVF - the Association of Danish Windmill Producers) in the spring of 1979. It re-mained very inactive until its reorganisation in the spring of 1981.This might explain why this organisation does not have an overview over windmill sales develop-ment either. The goal of the reorganized organisation seems mainly to be the exploitation of export opportuni-ties. As already mentioned, the Danish government foresaw windmill exports of about seventy units during 1981.

Political Parties

The exploitation of renewable energy resources has never been a contentious issue within and between the parties. Each party has its supporters of renewable ener-gy development. The arguing has been about the degree of public support for the development of wind energy utili-sation for example. The fiscal crisis has made it easy to find a majority for limiting this support.

The socialist parties have many supporters for wind

energy exploitation. But only the Socialist People's Party is strongly for wind energy, and this because it is strongly against nuclear power. The communist party is for nuclear power and supports wind energy only weakly. The social democrats are more seriously split between supporters of nuclear energy and opponents, which, by necessity are strongly for wind energy. The bourgeois parties are generally for nuclear power. This is even true for the Venstre although most windmill owners, like many people living in rural areas, are voting for it. And many of the owners are also against nuclear.

The political parties have therefore adopted an equivocal stand on wind energy development. Most politicians do not really believe in the future of wind energy. Yet they have received many signals from local politicians that large parts of the population are in favor of a stronger public involvement in the development of renewable energy resources. They have therefore supported the government's two energy action programs where about 15 percent of the funds are allocated to the large windmill research and development program. But the chronic shortage of funds to satisfy all the grant applications from windmill buyers shows that this support is quite selective and limited.

The Mass Media

the media have played an important role in the spreading of knowledge and information about developments in the wind energy field. They have been very open to the debates around wind energy questions. They have presented extensive reviews of relevant research reports and discussion papers. Newspapers, and radio and television have prepared and presented their own reports on different wind energy projects, such as the Tvind mill. Interviews with producers and buyers of windmills about their experiences and plans have been frequently made and rapidly diffused. There is no doubt that the mass media have played a central role in public opinion formation and mobilisation on renewable energy questions.

PROBLEMS AND CONSTRAINTS

Denmark is flat and has long coast lines. It has therefore a lot of wind. The potential to use wind energy is significant. However, different groups of actors have divergent views about the extent to which it is technically, economically, and politically feasible to transform this wind energy potential into a concrete contribution to national electricity supply.

The uncertain economics of the wind-generation of electricity is of course one reason for this divergence

of views. The most pessimistic estimates about the future
share of wind energy in national energy supply are however based on considerations of environmental impact and
of load-management problems in the electricity system.

The Environmental Impact of Windmills

Even an extensive use of small windmills is unlikely
to make a significant contribution to national energy
supply. The development of wind energy implies therefore
the use of many large windmills, a situation underlying
the government's decision to support a large windmill development program.
Small windmills with up to 90 kW capacity can only
be installed on the 200'000 farms and homesteads, at
least as long as one assumes that the current resistance
to erecting windmills in urban areas will persist. If all
farmers would put up 22 kW mills with an average yearly
output of 40 MWh, one would get a total production of
wind-generated electricity of about 0.7 mtoe. This would
amount to 3.4 percent of national energy consumption
both actual in 1977 and expected in 1985, or to 37 percent and 27 percent respectively of actual and planned
electricity production in these same years.[32]
If only twenty percent of the farmers are willing to
buy a windmill, one would arrive at correspondingly lower
contribution rates. This, as we will see later, would
solve the load-management problem. The Ministry of Energy
expected the use of 100'000 windmills in 1995, not all of
which would be used to generate electricity. We would
then maybe get a 20 percent contribution to electricity
supply. This is appreciable but not extraordinary.
Extending this contribution would therefore require
the considerable use of large windmills with tower
heights above 40 meters, possibly even as high as 80
meters. The government plans are based on the installation of up to 2'000 of these windmills. Large windmills
have a significant visual impact, especially in Denmark
where they will be standing on large tracts of flat land.
The selection of building sites is presently governed by
three criteria:

- the land should not be used for intensive agricultural purposes,
- the land should be flat for 3 km around, and
- there should be an electric transmission line with
  sufficient capacity nearby.

Mapping the sites fulfilling these conditions puts them
almost all into popular recreation areas. Visual impact,
noise, and the need to close off security zones around
the mills would severely reduce the recreational value of
these areas. These areas are already in short supply. The
large windmill plan clearly contains the potential for

conflict even within the environmental movement itself.
The conflicts can already be spotted within the movement
and within the Ministry for Environmental Protection.
It would seem politically impossible to choose this
siting structure when realizing the large windmill plan.
In fact most local authorities have protested when recently faced with the possibility that one of the
first 200 mills might be located on their territory.
The logical solution would be to concentrate windmills in clusters. Windmills would have to be placed 200
meters apart. There are probably not many suitably large
and flat areas available to place all the planned mills,
and these areas might still lie within the recreational
zones. Sørensen has proposed to put the windmills out to
sea just far enough from shore so that they would become
invisible. This would maybe resolve the esthetical objec-
tion. But transmission cost are likely to be higher than
for a land-based solution.

The Load-Management Problem

There is little practical experience with load-management of a system with many very small production units
combined with a few very large power generation stations.
A study made by one of the leader's of the governmental
large windmill development program has concluded that up
to 10 percent of total electricity production could come
from wind energy without it creating a management problem. A solution would therefore have to be found only for
the long-term. The government's wind energy research program is studying load-management problems.
The management problem is particular to the electricity system prevalent in Denmark where practically all
electricity is produced in oil and coal-powered generating stations. DEF has always made this point in the debate about wind energy in Denmark. These power stations
cannot be turned on and off at a moment's notice. Minimi-
sation of production costs requires lead times of eight
hours and almost 24 hours for nuclear power stations.
Wind data from one location suggests that periods of high
or low winds are followed by similar periods in four out
of five cases.[33] Some power output equalisation might come from locally different wind conditions in a region.
But it seems obvious that any solution to the load-management problem will at least require an excellent meteo-
rological forecasting service.
There is another aspect to the load-management problem. In Denmark a lot of district heat is produced in cogeneration plants. The main wind season, winter, is also
the time when maximal heat output is needed. These stations can therefore not be used for management purposes.
But this might not be necessary because the high electricity demand in winter implies the use of pure electricity

generating stations and they should give sufficient flexibility to the load manager.
The combination of nuclear power with its large
blocks of inflexible base load might well worsen the management problem. The often assumed compatibility of nuclear and wind power should also be investigated from
this viewpoint.

Economic Aspects of Wind Energy

Different groups of actors have quite different information about the economics of wind-generated electricity. We would like to dicuss three factors here which
might explain part of these differences: windmill types
in combination with their location; financing conditions;
and energy price developments. The judgement will be of
course also affected by the choice of an individual or a
national perspective.

Windmill type and geographic location. The economic
result of the generation of electricity with windmills
is very much dependent on the correct match of windmill
type, essentially production capacity, with the locally
existing wind conditions. The larger the mill, the
stronger the winds which will be needed to start production of electricity with 220 V. A 15 kW mill can start
production at wind speeds above 2.5 m/second. A 22 kW
mill needs already speeds of more than 6 m/second. It
does obviously not pay to buy a mill which is so large
that it cannot be run very frequently. But it is also a
waste to have a mill that is too small to exploit frequent
strong winds. Unfortunately for many buyers, knowledge
about local wind conditions is not very good.[34]
The need to correctly match mill capacity with wind
conditions is emphasized by the rate structure applied
by most utilities to electricity sold to and bought from
them. We have seen that most utilities pay substantially
less than they charge. This situation implies that the
individual windmill owner does best if he chooses a windmill size which minimizes production of electricity beyond his own needs. This reason for a smaller mill is
however counterbalanced by the fact that investment costs
per installed kW of generating capacity are inversely related with mill capacity. A kW of capacity for the smallest mill of 11 kW cost in June 1981 DKr 10'000 ($
1'400). The corresponding price for a 55 kW mill came to
DKr 5'900 ($ 830). More or less fixed costs for the mill
foundation and the link with the grid are further empha-
sizing this economy of scale.
This investment rule suggests that individuals
should not try to maximally exploit the available wind
energy. A national perspective suggests of course just
the opposite as long as wind energy is a cheaper source

of electricity than other alternatives. Considerations of
balance-of-payment effects, reduced dependency, increased
employment and exports of windmills might further modify
this rule in favor of wind energy.

Financing costs. They are a crucial determinant of
the individual profitability of wind energy. Like any
other renewable energy source, wind energy trades high
investment costs for low operating costs. The present time with historically high interest rates, even in real
terms, is therefore a bad moment to make the switch from
conventional to renewable energy sources.[35] The time is
doubly difficult for such a transition because our societies have increasingly stressed the instant gratification
of material needs. The emergence of ecological values is
the beginning of a corrective movement and ecologically
minded people have therefore been ready to adopt wind
energy even if it was not strictly profitable.

However, most potential windmill buyers beyond the
fringe group of innovators will require some type of subsidy to enable them to make a loan-financed investment of
up to DKr 350'000, the price for the largest of the small
windmills.

The government grant program in support of the
buying of windmills is therefore important for supporting
the further diffusion of windmills. Government expenditures on these grants should be seen as the price paid by
the collectivity to gain the positive contribution made
by wind energy use to macro-economic, social and political goals.

Energy price developments. Assumed future energy
price developments affect the profit calculation of windmills in two ways. The low operating costs of windmills
remain basically unaffected by energy price developments.
But this is not true for other methods of generating
electricity. Underestimation of future oil price developments for example will make windmills look relatively
less profitable than they will actually be.

The price differential charged by the utilities for
electricity bought from the windmill owner and the electricity sold to him affects the owner's net electricity
costs. The smaller this gap the better he fares. But in
addition we have seen that a small gap makes it profitable to switch to a larger windmill which will permit the
sale of more surplus electricity to the utility at a lower cost to the owner.

It is therefore quite appropriate to doubt the wisdom of current government policy which lets the utilities
keep the price for electricity delievered to them at a
very low level, even below the level suggested by their
own rules.

CONCLUSION

Two aspects of the Danish wind energy branch development merit special emphasis. First, the renewed development of the wind energy technology was brought about
by complete outsiders to the established research and
production systems. "Alternative" people with their commitment to a more environmentally pleasing life style and
an artisianal ability to tinker with technology have
achieved signifiant technological break-throughs. These
individuals and small enterpreneurs have succeeded in
transforming their individual results into a vigorous
branch development process with a bright future even ad-
mitted to by the government. Yet they have done this
against the "traditionalist" attitude of the established
production system and with only minor and late support
from the political system.

It is true that two events outside their own control
helped them succeed. The rise of the environmental movement --of which they and their activity are themselves a
part-- has prepared a large part of the population to
expect much from wind energy. The oil crisis has helped
to transform what might have been a latent potentiality
into a concrete demand for electricity-generating windmills for individual households and small enterprises.
The oil crisis also liberated social energy and made
people become active in support of wind energy development.

Clever and successful organizational work and institution building represents the second characteristic aspect of this growth process. Of course, the original wind
energy enterpreneurs have benefited from this support but
they themselves have played a significant part in the
effort to make it happen. The formation of two strong organisations, OOA and OVE, in order to educate and inform
a basically sympathetic population and to mobilize it in
support of wind energy development made the break-through
possible or at least speeded it up tremendously.

OVE specifically has played a key role. Not only
did it create potential windmill buyers. It helped the
inventors to get ready for commercial production. And
last but not least it used its political clout to force
the political and the electricity production system to
become a little bit more forthcoming and provide better
conditions for the utilisation of individual windmill
technology.

We have stressed the importance of past windmill exploitation in Denmark. The still existent collective memory about those experiences provided a context within
which new arguments, technological changes, and early experiments could deploy all their power of persuasion.

Two decisions around the formation of OVE facilitated the tapping of this collective memory. First, the

disengagement of the wind energy question from the nuclear one was crucial. Their respective insitutionalisa-
tion in two different, though not antagonistic organisations allowed the tapping of social energies basically
supportive of wind energy development, but which had
hitherto been kept in limbo. Secondly, the concordance
between the decentralizing idea behind small windmill use
and the decentralized structure of the movement's interest organisations liberated a lot of localized social
energies, again in favor of promoting the adoption of
wind energy. One lesson from the Danish wind energy development is that the combined mobilisation of local and national social networks can be a powerful ingredient in
bringing about socio-technical change.

ABBREVIATIONS

AC	Alternating Current
ATV	Akademiet for de Tekniske Vitenskaper (Academy for the Technical Sciences)
DC	Direct Current
DEF	Danske Electricitetsværkers Forening (Danish Association of Electricity Utilities)
DEFU	Danske Elektricitetsværkers Forenings Utrednings-avdeling (Research and Planning Department of DEF)
DKr	Danish Crown
DVKV	Danske Vindkraftværker (Danish Wind Energy Producers)
FDVF	Foreningen for Danske Vindmøllefabrikanter (Association of Danish Windmill Producers)
OOA	Organisationen for Oplysning om Atomkraft (Organisation for Information on Nuclear Power)
OVE	Organisationen for Vedvarende Energi (Organisation for Renewable Energy)
VAT	Value Added Tax

NOTES

1. The plan is to substitute coal for oil, limiting
oil imports to 8.6 mtoe in 1985, a 41 percent share in
energy consumption (IEA, 1979:66).
2. DEF (1979:11).
3. The engineer who designed the mill refused to
sign the report by SEAS claiming high maintenance costs.
The operating costs of the restarted Gedser mill are today reputedly lower than those of the two new 600 kW
mills. This result might be simply due to a failure to
account for inflation over the last twenty-five years.
4. See Hvelplund and Linderoth (1976).
5. Riisager originally protected the technological

solution which enabled him to link his mill to the grid.

6. The Tvind mill was at that time the largest wind-mill in the world. Main parts were salvaged from ship-yards and factories (Tvind-skolene, 1977).

7. See ATV (1975). The Wind Energy Commission was established on the initiative of the owner of a construc-tion company who expected a windmill program to create a demand for concrete structures.

8. See ATV (1976).

9. This price compares to an approximate GNP per ca-pita of $ 7'500.

Throughout this paper we have converted DKr by using the average exchange rate for the relevant years. These were:

1975	1976	1977	1978	1979	1980	1981
5.75	6.05	6.50	5.51	5.26	5.65	7.12

(Source: IMF Financial Statistics)

10. Terms were again improved in 1980 as described in Section 3.

11. Flavin (1981:22)reports that up to 2'000 wind-mills were expected to be sold in the U.S. in 1981. Danish population is a little bit over 5 million.

12. As described in Section 3, the government always had to clear up a backlog of unsatisfied demands from the previous year because it had run out of funds. The January and February rates of approval might therefore be exceptionally high. A growing market on the other hand should produce rising numbers of applications throughout the year.

13. See Naturlig Energi (1981(11/12):15-18), the in-formation journal published by OVE. See also Farstad (1982:90).

14. Sales in 1979 and 1980 would have had to average around 1'400 units, and not several hundred units as suggested by Riisager. 1981 sales estimate would also look very small in comparison.

15. See Energiministeriet (1980).

16. See Bleega et al (1976:17).

17. See Farstad (1982:90) reporting the count made by the small windmill testing station. The Danish Natio-nal Report (1981) mentions "about" twenty producers, com-pared to 60 in Europe and 100 all over the world (accor-ding to Flavin, 1981:22). One company went recently banc-rupt and another one is preparing to enter the market with a 265 kW mill destined for exportation (Naturlig Energi, 1980(4):8).

18. Danish National Report (1981:9).

19. Naturlig Energi (1981(11/12):11).

20. The government made plans to substitute electri-city for oil by electrifying the railroads --so far ope-rating with diesel trains. First contracts have been let at the beginning of 1982.

21. Strong trade unions such as the construction workers and the metall workers are in most countries for nuclear power.

22. The new energy research program of 1981 established by the Ministry of Energy allocates DKr 200m ($ 21.8 m) to renewable energy research. This is about 36 percent of the total funds devoted to energy research. DKr 67m ($ 9.4m) will be spent on wind energy research if the distribution of funds among the different energy resources is the same as under the first research program.

23. See the contrasting cases of heat pump development in Germany (Chapter 6) and solar collector use in Israel (Chapter 3).

24. There were 120 companies in the period 1974-78. 11 of them are pure production companies, operating 18 power stations with an installed capacity of 6.3 GW. Some of these stations are co-generation units. The other 109 companies were basically distribution companies. Only 12 of them operated minor production capacity. 53 of the 120 companies are municipally owned (see DEF, 1979a).

25. Electricity rates charged to customers increased by 75 percent between 1973 and 1975 and doubled between 1973 and 1978 (Statistik Årbog, 1979:242-243).

26. See Chapter 8.

27. See the further discussion of the load-management problem in the next section.

28. This data is regularly reported in Naturlig Energi, OVE's house organ.

29. See for example the chapter on Nysted, a Danish rural municipality, and its energy savings efforts in Baumgartner and Burns (1982).

30. See again the chapter on Nysted in Baumgartner and Burns (1982).

31. See note 17.

32. Data is taken from IEA (1979).

33. The low-cost solution in the times when the forecast is wrong is to import electricity on short notice from neighboring countries. See Sørensen (1978) for the simulation results.

34. This illustrates the important nature of the OVE program of collecting monthly windmill performance data from 150 locations.

35. The comparison is of course biased against renewable energy resources. Many of the environmental costs of traditional energy forms are not capitalized as investment costs nor are they included in operating costs (for example health maintenance costs).

BIBLIOGRAPHY

ATV 1975 Vindkraft. Oversigtsrapport fra Vindenergiudval-
    get under ATV. Copenhagen.
ATV 1976 Vindkraft 2. Forslag til handlingsprogram. Vind-
    energiudvalget under ATV. Copenhagen.
Baumgartner, T. and T.R. Burns 1982 Facing the Energy
    Challenge. Lund: SIAR Research Report.
Bleega et al 1976 "Skitse til alternativ energiplan for
    Danmark." Copenhagen: OOA and OVE.
Danish National Report to the UN Conference on New and
    Renawble Sources of Energy. New York: UN A/Conf.100
    NR/34, 1981.
DEF 1979 "The Electricity Supply in Denmark." Copenhagen.
DEF 1979a "Dansk elforsyning 1978." Copen gen.
Energiministeriet 1980 "Vedvarende energi, elvarme m.v.
    i Varmeforsynings-planlægningen." 3. delbetenkning
    fra Energiministeriets Varmeplanutvalg. Copenhagen.
Farstad, H. 1982 Fornybare energi og grasrot-initiativ.
    Olso: Instituttet for Sosiologi, Universitetet i
    Olso, Hovedoppgave.
Flavin, Ch. 1981 Wind Power: A Turning Point. Washington,
    D.C.: Worldwatch Paper Nr. 45.
Hvelplund, F. and H. Linderoth 1976 "Kraftværksøkonomi på
    danske betingelser." Århus: Handelshøjskolen.
International Energy Agency 1979 Energy Policies and Pro-
    grammes of IEA Countries. Paris: OECD.
Sørensen, B. 1978 "The Regulation of an Electricity Sup-
    ply System including Wind Energy Generators." Paper
    presented at the Second International Conference on
    Wind Energy Systems.
Tvind-skolene 1977 "...lad 100 møller blomstre."Ulfborg:
    Skipper Klement.

6
Heat Pump Use in the Federal Republic of Germany

Hans Diefenbacher

No real market for heat pumps existed in the Federal Republic of Germany (FRG) until the middle and even the late 1970s. Electric utilities started to promote air-water heat pumps in 1979. Large gas and diesel heat pumps for swimming pools, sports centers and office buildings began to be installed as of the middle 1970s. Today they become more current in larger appartment buildings and housing developments. Small gas and diesel heat pumps are expected to reach the mass production stage by 1983 at the earliest.

Heat pump sales reached about 40'000 units in 1980 compared to a stock of about 25'000 housing units connected to heat pump and solar collector systems as of 1979. A further rapid sales expansion expected for 1981 failed to materialize. It is now thought that only 20'000 units were sold during 1981.

Expected technological breakthroughs and low construction activity may explain this sales stagnation. However, legal confusion, complex administrative regulations and subsidy programs, and an uncertain cost outlook seem to form important barriers to a more rapid adoption of heat pumps, especially by individual houseowners. The infrastructure for installing and servicing heat pumps is weakly developed. Disappointed buyers add therefore to the discouragement of potential buyers.

Almost 100 enterprises are engaged in the branch with research and development, production, and marketing and servicing activities. There is no clear branch leader. Only a few enterprises are exclusively engaged in the heat pump branch. Most enterprises are small or

Hans Diefenbacher has an economics degree from the University of Heidelberg and a doctorate in economics from the university in Kassel. He is now working at the Protestant Institute for Interdisciplinary Research (FEST) in Heidelberg where he is responsible for energy, development and industrial democracy problems.

128

medium-sized although the German subsidiaries of Japanese and American multinational corporations attempt to
rapidly expand their market share by exploiting their
low production costs due to home market mass production.[1]

INTERNATIONAL HISTORICAL DEVELOPMENTS

Heat pump systems compete with many other heating
systems. This differentiates their development process
from the one of their technical twin, refrigeration
systems. This difference largely explains the different
speeds with which heat pumps and refrigeration equipment
developed.
The principle of the heat pump is known since around
1850. First installations were realized around 1900.
Subsequent developments occurred mainly in Switzerland,
the UK, and the USA, albeit with significant ups and
downs.
However, only the recent changes in the energy
price and supply situation generated impulses for a broad
process of technical innovation and product development.
These changes also created for the first time a widespread demand for small, mass-produced heat pumps.
Luckily, today's development could draw on technical and
operational knowledge readily available in two places.
For one, producers here and there had built and installed over the years a number of large, custom-built heat
pump systems. Secondly, refrigeration techniques had
been continuously developed while heat pump development
was stagnating. This store of knowledge was a ready
source for a transfer of technology.
The early heat pump developments in Switzerland,
the UK, and the USA followed quite different paths.[2]
In Switzerland, the first heat pumps were installed
around the turn of the century. The shortage of coal
during World War I gave an additional impetus to their
further spreading. A number of enterprises used heat
pumps to satisfy their internal needs for heat. This
development was interrupted by the end of the war and
the return to normal fuel supply conditions. The rapid
electrification using cheap hydro-power resources contributed also to kill off further development of heat
pumps. Only a few pumps were installed during the 1920s
and 1930s.
Renewed fuel shortages during World War II however
revived demand for heat pumps. All major energy machinery producers -- Brown Boveri, Escher Wyss and Sulzer --
produced and installed such equipment, mostly using
water as the source of heat. Some of these systems are
still in operation today. But the earlier cycle repeated
itself once more with the end of the war and the succeed-

ing period of falling real energy prices. The three
firms continued to build a few large systems but a sustained commercial development had to wait until the
energy crisis of the 1970s.

In the UK, a prototype heat pump for house heating
purposes existed as early as 1928. But development failed to take off. Calculations suggested that such a heat
pump would probably be economic only in countries which
lacked indigenous coal resources. The UK, as a major
coal producer, was obviously not going to provide the
home market on which to build an export industry.

Growth in heat pump production and use has been
most sustained in the USA. The beginning however was
rather hesitant. The main orientation of heat pump development shifted several times. Heat pumps for the heating of office buildings appeared in the early 1930s.
Air heat pumps were installed in single family houses
with some success in the late 1930s But disinterest
of the electric utilities induced the producer to aban-
don production. A new development phase startet after
World War II linked to the spreading of air-conditioning
to single family homes. Product development focused here
on the creation of year-round room-conditioning equipment. A few hundred units had been sold during the years
up to 1950. At that time, eleven producers, nine electric utilities and fifteen universities were working on
heat pump development and production. They had so far
invested $ 10m and continued to invest about $ 1.5m
annually.

It is interesting to look at the subsequent developments as the state of heat pump development in 1950
in the USA has been reached in the FRG in the late
1970s. In fact, Cube and Steimle argue that many discussions, development programs and experiences in the
FRG today are simply duplicating the earlier US experiences and developments.[3]

The introductory phase of heat pump development in
the USA ended in 1954. Sales had reached almost 2'000
units. Heat pumps were listed in the industrial statistics as a separate item as of that year. More than half
of the 129 electric utilities had initiated special marketing programs, organized exhibitions and sometimes
even provided free hook-ups to the grid in order to further the use of electric heat pumps. Sales grew annually
by more than eighty percent. Sales growth became much
less vigorous in the early 1960s although there were now
fifty producers competing in the market. Sales peaked
in 1964 with 120'000 units sold, about half as many as
had been predicted in 1954. The initially rapid growth
had destroyed the existing demand potential.

The expansion of the servicing network of many producers failed to match the growth in sales and in maintenance requirements. Maintenance requirements were

higher than expected because demand pressures had led to
carelessly calculated pump capacities and shoddy pump installations. Frequent equipment failure was the consequence. Rapid demand growth had also incited some producers to sell untested and badly constructed heat pumps,
and, in so doing, using high pressure selling tactics.
Operating costs much higher than expected and advertised
were the inevitable result leading to a general loss of
confidence on the part of potential buyers.

Heat pump prices remained rather high although the
large number of producers prevented the emergence of an
oligopolistic market. But this fragmentation led to individually small production volumes, excluding thereby
the capturing of economies of scale. Falling energy prices were of course another cause for this sales stagnation.

This sales stagnation facilitated paradoxically a
consolidation of the market, preparing therefore the way
for the renewed expansion of today. The elaboration of
semi-official measurement, quality, and safety norms and
their incorporation into the construction norms applied
by a leading housing finance corporation were important
factors in this consolidation. The corporation denied
financing if the planned heat pump did not already have
a satisfactory operating record, if its capacity did not
match the heating needs, and if the producer could not
guarantee an adequate after-sale service. In fact, warranty periods run for five to ten years and are an important factor in reassuring non-specialist buyers.

BRANCH DEVELOPMENT IN THE FRG

As already pointed out, a heat pump branch and market did not really exist until the middle of the 1970s.
Test installations, theoretical investigations, and research projects were dominant activities until a few
years ago. Energy suppliers, above all the electric utilities, were showing only a minimal interest in heat
pumps. Only in 1979 did some of the utilities begin to
advertize the advantages of the electric heat pump, undoubtedly in an attempt to build up demand for their
emerging surplus generating capacity.

Heat pump installations became more frequent as of
1975. But these were all custom-built, large units for
public swimming pools, sports centers, and a few office
and administrative buildings. Four swimming pools were
equiped with gas heat pumps from 1977 to 1979. The gas
heat pump at the sports center in Paderborn, one of the
world's largest heat pump with a capacity of 3'700 kW,
became operational in September 1977. In the same year,
a gas heat pump was for the first time coupled to a solar
collector to produce all the heat and sanitary hot water

for a sports and school center. Some diesel heat pumps
were also installed during this period.

This preference for gas and diesel heat pumps is explained with their high energy efficiency of 160 percent
and more. The heat pump in Paderborn has so far produced
an energy output of 209 percent of the primary energy
input. Peaks of 228 percent have been reached.[4] The gas
heat pump at the natural gas storage complex in Frankenthal has so far achieved an energy ratio of 192 percent.[5]

Installations of larger gas and diesel heat pumps
in apartment buildings and housing developments are also
becoming more frequent. A building in Bochum with 36
apartments is fully heated and supplied with sanitary
hot water down to outside temperatures of $0^{\circ}C(32^{\circ}F)$.
Heat pumps in larger housing developments work like small
district heating 'islands'. And an old people's home with
46 living units built in 1978 combines for the first time
a heat pump with a solar absorption roof.

Gas heat pumps have also been installed with increasing frequency in small and large production enterprises, e.g. a greenhouse complex, the natural gas storage complex in Frankenthal, and a few slaughter-houses.
A favored heat pump application in industry is to re-
cuperate waste heat. The best known example in the FRG
is the glassworks Süssmuth in Hesse which is developing
its system in cooperation with an 'appropriate technology' program at the university in Kassel.

A pilot project in Waiblingen is a first insofar as
it combines the use of waste heat, district heat and
heat pumps in one integrated concept.[6] The cleaned water
from the municipal sewage treatment plant serves as the
heat source with a temperature between 9° and $20^{\circ}C$ $(48^{\circ}$
and $68^{\circ}F)$. The primary energy input for the heat pump is
the low-calory methane gas generated by the decomposi-
tion of the sludge from the sewage treatment process.
The surplus gas is burned in a boiler to boost the temperature of the water coming from the heat pump to $90^{\circ}C$
$(194^{\circ}F)$. The district heating system links a few public
buildings: an indoor swimming pool, the town hall, a
community center, and the building of the fire brigade.
These are up to 2.5km away from the heat pump complex.
The hot water flows first to buildings equiped with high-
temperature heating systems, then to buildings which have
low-temperature heating systems. Construction costs of
the system of DM 6 to 8m should be amortized in about
eight years according to calculations of the municipal
building engineer. Total energy cost savings should add
up to at least DM 50m over the estimated lifetime of the
heat pump of twenty-five years.[7]

Larger gas heat pump installations have been growing from the four pilot systems in 1977 to about fifty
operational systems in 1979. However, smaller gas and

diesel heat pumps, which are favored by ecologists over electric heat pumps, will not be in mass production until 1983 at the earliest. Electric heat pumps are still without competition in this market segment despite their relative low energy efficiency of between seventy-two percent and ninety-five percent (when calculated over the whole system including the electricity power station).

Data about sales and installations of heat pumps in general are very unreliable. Forecasts about sales during the 1980s diverge substantially and have already been proven wrong in different directions. Table 6.1 presents one such forecast. However, in October 1980, a

TABLE 6.1
Estimated and Forecasted Heat Pump
Installations in the Housing Sector

Year	Electric HP	Gas or Diesel HP
1980*	2'800	1'000
1985°	12'000	19'100
1990°	56'900	92'300

* Estimate;   ° Forecast

Note: Figures are for housing units connected, not for HP proper.
Source: BMFT, 1979:85.

high official of the Ministry of Research and Technology thought it possible to have one million heat pumps installed by 1990 (instead of the much lower number necessary to connect the approximately 650'000 housing units implied in Table 6.1). The electric utilities thought it even possible at one moment to have 4.2 million electric heat pumps alone in operation by 2000.

The electricity industry estimates that about 6'000 heat pumps were installed during the years up to 1978. Another 8'000 units were installed in 1979 according to this view, and around 45'000 units, about equally split between heating and sanitary hot water applications, in 1980.[8] However, three of the larger producers have privately indicated to us a production volume which for them alone would add up to 48'000 units for 1980.

Whatever the exact numbers, actual sales and installations in 1980 were clearly greater than those predicted by the government (see Table 6.1). We have seen in the case of the USA that such a rapid market expansion tends to produce negative feedback effects. It is quite likely that the disappointing sales in 1981 reflect such a development. Sales in 1981 are thought to have reached about 20'000 units, far less than the 50'000 units expected as recently as the end of 1980.

Forecasts about the split of future sales between different heat pump types are also quite controversial. Most experts agree that small gas and diesel heat pumps suitable for the typical four-family house will become available in the late 1983. The government forecast presented in Table 6.1 predicts that these pumps will quickly outsell electric heat pumps even in the market segment for small heat pumps. But sales of electric heat pumps would be growing at sizable rates nonetheless. And we have seen that the electric utilities themselves were much more optimistic than the government (at least until recently). In addition, the compressor heat pumps mentioned so far might experience quite soon serious competition from gas absorption heat pumps. These are reputed to be more cost-effective under German climatic conditions than the more energy-efficient compressor heat pumps. To the surprise of experts, such an absorption heat pump was exhibited jointly by three producers at the 1981 Fair for Sanitation, Heating and Climatization. The market introduction of this absorption heat pump is expected shortly.

The final split between the different heat pump types will depend on heat pump and energy price developments and both of them can be influenced to some extent by enery suppliers and producers. Electric utilities could obviously offer better rates and connecting conditions than they do now if they really wanted to push the electric heat pump. A continuation of the demand contraction of 1981 might induce all producers to become more aggressive in their pricing strategies. The market entrance of giants such as Volkswagen might also put pressure on prices. VW is expected to offer a diesel heat pump based on its car engines. It could obviously decide to compensate stagnant car sales with aggressively marketed heat pumps. And this could not but change the heat pump market.

The heat pump branch is currently made up of between sixty and ninety enterprises. Some of them are actually only distributors and installators. Others are still only engaged in research and development activities. Only a few of the producers are exclusively engaged in the heat pump branch. Most branch members are medium-sized or even small, almost artisanal enterprises, especially those that are presently producing gas and diesel heat pumps. There is no clear market leader.

However the situation is likely to change. The Ministry of Research and Technology tends to concentrate its subsidies on the large enterprises. The appearance on the market of such sophisticated and large enterprises as Volkswagen with their small diesel heat

pumps is likely to squeeze out competing small enterprises. Another likely source of market concentration is the
attempt by the local subsidiaries of large American and
especially Japanese multinational corporations to increase their market shares. These firms can exploit their
technical experience and economies of scale which they
gained in their much more highly developed home markets.
The German subsidiary of Mitsubishi aims for a market
share of eight percent in 1981. Mitsubishi has twenty
years of heat pump experience in Japan and is currently
operating there two production lines which have an hour-
ly capacity of twenty units each. Hitachi began to seriously compete in the German market in 1981. It concen-
trates for the moment on heat pumps for the production
of hot sanitary water, offering them at extremely low
prices.

The distribution of heat pumps is mostly in the
hands of installators which, however, do not specialize
in the installation of heat pumps. Only small producers
deliver generally their pumps directly to final users,
although Happel, one of the larger German producers, is
also selling some of its pumps directly to users. Established wholesellers and distributors of conventional
heating systems are surprisingly little involved in heat
pump distribution. The installators, which provide under
these conditions the link between users and producers,
are unfortunately and in general quite unfamiliar with
heat pump technology. Some producers are therefore very
much involved in technically supporting installators.
But it is already apparent that further sales expansion
in the 1980s is becoming constrained by the weaknesses
of the distribution, installation and servicing infrastructures, a development which is similar to what had
happened in the USA in the 1950s as described above. We
will return to this point in a later section.

PROBLEMS AND BARRIERS TO THE INTRODUCTION OF HEAT PUMPS

In this section we are discussing the more general
problems and regulations of heat pump use in the FRG
under the three headings of sources of heat, of energy
inputs, and of costs and prices. The following section
will then deal more specifically with the subsidy situation existing in the FRG for the installation of heat
pumps.

Sources of Heat

Heat pumps can draw on a number of sources of heat:
(1) water in rivers, lakes and underground reservoirs,
possibly also waste water and sewage systems;(2) air,
including the exhaust from ventilation and aircondi-

tioning systems; (3) the soil; and (4) solar energy and
the absorber liquid used in solar collectors. Technical
and legal problems exist for all of them, albeit to different degrees and in different forms.

Water. Lake and river water has been the commonest
heat source for the early heat pumps in Switzerland. There is no problem in withdrawing heat from large bodies
of water. Nor is there a problem if the water bodies used
lie downstream from large users of water for cooling purposes, such as power stations. Here the resultant cool-
ing-down is even acceptable from an ecological viewpoint,
at least if it is kept within limits.
The current legal situation in the FRG makes all
forms of water use subject to permission, even if the
water is returned after use. The right to withdraw heat
from water is however not explicitly regulated. Yet, the
Water Economy Offices (Wasserwirtschaftsämter) will in
most cases prescribe a minimal temperature of $2^{\circ}C$
($35.6^{\circ}F$) for water returned to rivers, lakes and underground reservoirs. In addition, the lay-out of the intake and rejection pipes have to conform to floodwater
rules. The offices sometimes will issue detailed rules
with respect to the maximum quantities of water that can
be used, varying them seasonally according to water level
and temperature.
The use of water is subject to several cost barriers. Polluted waters, above all with phospates, lead to
heavy growth of algae on the surfaces of the heat exchanger. This drastically reduces the efficiency of the
heat exchanger and requires frequent cleaning operations
for which there are no really good methods available.
Avoiding this problem and its cost consequences would
require the three stage treatment of sewage including
the elimination of phospates and the control of agricultural run-offs. Treatment costs in this case are socialized unless the heat pump operator himself builds a
water treatment plant at the intake, a possibility open
only to large industrial plants.
The costs of connecting the body of water serving
as a source of heat with the heat pump grow rapidly with
the distance between the two. But these costs are almost
independent of the volume of water put through the heat
exchanger. This source of heat is therefore only economical for large projects close to the body of water concerned. This is another potential source of conflict
between this 'soft' energy alternative and environmental
values. Such projects are therefore likely to remain restricted to already urbanized and heavily built-over
areas. In the FRG, only projects in the public domain
have so far managed to pass all the regulatory hurdles.

Underground water reservoirs. This is an attractive source of heat. Relatively constant water temperatures allow heat pumps to be optimally designed, thereby providing a high energy ratio. The main problem is that reservoirs often contain low quality water leading to corrosion of and deposits on heat exchanger surfaces. Operation costs may therefore turn out to be rather high. The use of underground water is heavily regulated. The Water Economy Offices have to approve the plans for the well. This plan has to provide construction details and a description of soil conditions. It has also to include a guarantee that the well corresponds to the industrial (DIN) norms and that the drilling of the well will proceed according to the relevant norms of the building industry.

Discharge of the water has also to be approved even if it is reinjected into the ground or the public sewer system. In the latter case, a fee of between DM .40 and DM .90 per m^3 (about $ 4 and $ 10 per 1000 cubic feet) has to be paid. Permission to discharge the water into rivers or lakes is usually refused if the salt content of the water is high, which is frequently the case.

These legal requirements and conditions influence greatly the economic profitability of heat pumps. Authorities have recently tightened even further the conditions under which groundwater can be exploited for heat pump purposes. Administrative delays have become longer and the degree of specificity of the conditions imposed has grown.

Air. Although ubiquitous, large temperature fluctuations, often moving against energy needs, and relatively low average temperatures in winter time make air a heat source of limited usefulness in the FRG. These temperature conditions either lead to the installation of an over-dimensioned, and therefore inefficient heat pump, or they require the installation of a bivalent system including a conventional furnace. Heat pump systems may require a defroster on the heat exchanger for temperatures below 7°C (45°F).

The optimal combination of a heat pump with a conventional furnace is difficult to calculate, as is also the temperature at which the mode of operation should be changed. However, in many cases it is the electricity company which, in the case of an electric heat pump, decides the point at which the system has to switch (see also p.147). The utility is setting this point according to peak load management needs. This does not necessarily coincide with the optimal point for the heat pump system, thus possibly making the system rather uneconomic from the viewpoint of the individual owner.

Another problem with air heat pumps is that the necessarily large air flows may create substantial

noise pollution. Decisive here are local noise regulations which determine the necessary amount of noise insulation.

Larger buildings and industrial plants may often
use exhaust air from their ventilation and air-conditioning systems as a source of heat. Heat recuperation
systems are especially suitable for buildings (often in
the public sphere) such as hospitals, old people's homes,
indoor swimming pools, which require relatively high
room temperatures.

Solar energy. This combination had been proposed
in the FRG as early as 1955. It has recently been taken
up again especially by supporters of decentralized, soft
energy systems. Large industrial firms planning to enter
the branch picked up this idea around the middle of the
1970s. They switched their designs relatively early from
the use of solar collectors to solar absorbers where the
absorber liquid of the heat pump is directly circulating
through the piping system in the roof of a house. These
energy-roof systems are still in the testing phase. They
benefit from massive financial support by the Ministry
of Research and Technology, channeled through its Frauen-
hofer Research Institute for Construction Physics. Alternative systems using different types of solar collectors are also proposed but have not yet gone beyond
the planning stage.

Problems and constraints seem to be minimal, at
least at this point in time. But mass production of this
system has not yet begun. It is therefore not yet economically profitable given present energy prices. Another
barrier could arise in the form of local building codes
which are limiting the use of solar collectors for esthe-
tic reason. But such a barrier seems to be surmountable.
It is therefore possible that one day this technology
could provide up to thirty percent of total energy consumption in the FRG, just about the share of household
energy use in total energy consumption. At least this
is the view of the chairman of the Federal Association
for Solar Energy, an industrial interest organisation.
This man is also occupying a high managerial position
in one of the largest electric utilities. He could
therefore contribute to making this forecast come true.

Soil. Practically nothing has happened in this
area since a patent for exploiting the accumulation of
heat in the soil has been patented in Switzerland in
1912. An economical exploitation of this source of heat
requires extensive knowledge of the local physical soil
characteristics and of heat exchange design best adapted
to them. The acquisition of this knowledge is expensive
the more as there do not yet exist official guidelines
or industrial (DIN) norms which would standardize the

138

investigation and design procedures. The resultant costs
and uncertainty are probably a substantial barrier to
the spread of this technology.

Soil is a good medium for heat storage. But low winter temperatures in Germany require that pipes are laid
rather deep (1 to 2m, i.e., 3 to 7 ft) and rather far
apart (80 cm to 1.5 m, i.e., 2 1/2 to 5 ft) in order to
prevent freezing of the soil around the pipes. Such a
heat exchange system requires rather larger surfaces
than are available in a typical housing plot in suburban
areas.[9] The installation of such a pipe grid would require extensive and costly earth movements. Repairs,
when required, are also likely to be expensive as it is
difficult to locate leakages in the piping system without digging up the whole area.

Costs of such a system are therefore high. The determination of the optimal heat pump capacity acquires
therefore great importance. A capacity large enough to
satisfy peak loads is almost out of the question. Not
only would this maximize the costs of the items mentioned above. It would also lead to very high depreciation charges as the pump would work at full capacity
only for a few hours every year. This technology requires therefore a bivalent system with the heat pump
satisfying base loads only. The pump could then work at
full capacity for almost three times longer than in the
case of a monovalent design.

Of course, here as well as in the case of other heat
pump or 'soft' energy systems, one should investigate
the possibilities for modifying energy consumption patterns so as to match them better with heat pump energy
production patterns. The discussions about optimal heat
pump systems always take for given the demand pattern
and adjust the production capacity accordingly. It may
well be more 'cost effective' to change behaviour patterns underlying the energy demand patterns. The resultant loss in 'comfort' might be less serious than the
increase in investment costs implied by all the 'soft'
energy systems, and which threaten ever more individual
access to housing property in our densely populated
areas of Western Europe.

Energy Inputs

Electric heat pumps dominate the market in the FRG.
They are the only pumps readily available below a power
of 10 kW. AWAK started to offer a short while ago a gas
heat pump with a power of 9.2 kW, sufficient for the
heating of a typical four-family house. A few producers
started to design gas heat pumps with a power rating of
two and three kW as early as 1977. But mass production
is not expected before 1983. Gas and diesel heat pumps
with a rating of 10 kW and up to 600 kW are offered by

FIGURE 6.1
Energy Flows in Different Heating Systems

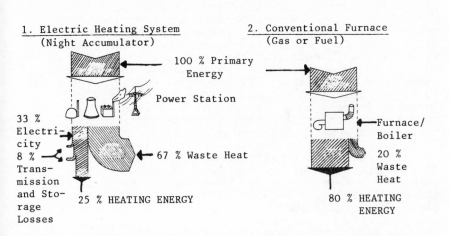

1. Electric Heating System
   (Night Accumulator)

2. Conventional Furnace
   (Gas or Fuel)

100 % Primary
Energy

Power Station

33 %
Electri-
city

8 %
Trans-
mission
and Sto-
rage
Losses

67 % Waste Heat

25 % HEATING ENERGY

Furnace/
Boiler

20 %
Waste
Heat

80 % HEATING
ENERGY

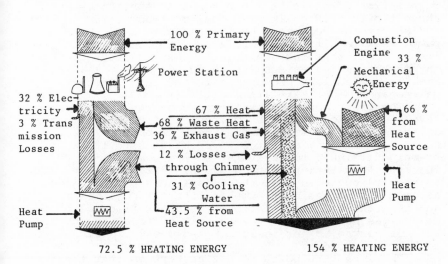

3. Electric Heat Pump

4. Gas and Diesel Heat Pump

100 % Primary
Energy

Power Station

Combustion
Engine 33 %
Mechanical
Energy

32 % Elec-
tricity
3 % Trans-
mission
Losses

67 % Heat
68 % Waste Heat
36 % Exhaust Gas

12 % Losses
through Chimney

31 % Cooling
Water

43.5 % from
Heat Source

66 %
from
Heat
Source

Heat
Pump

Heat
Pump

72.5 % HEATING ENERGY

154 % HEATING ENERGY

Source: Ruske and Teufel, 1980:53. Numbers for the HP
systems are slightly changed from the original
ones.

most producers. Larger units, while readily available,
have still to be custom-built.

Producers of electric heat pumps, and those electric
utilities which   favor heat pumps, sell them with the
argument of energy savings of up to 70 percent. This
holds of course only for the direct energy use of the
owner of the heat pump, and not for the total energy
system including electricity production and distribution.
Figure 6.1 indicates that the total system reaches an
energy ratio between final energy output and primary
energy input of between 72.5 percent and 90 percent, a
ratio which is also reached by the conventional oil
furnace. Calculations with recent data even suggest
that the monovalent electric air-water heat pump uses
more primary energy than the conventional oil-burning
furnace with the same heating capacity (see figure 6.2).

The much better performance of gas and diesel heat
pumps compared to electric ones is due to that the heat
pump in the former case has to raise the temperature of
the absorber liquid only to 40°C (104°F). The end temperature of 70°C (158°F) can be reached through the recuperation of the heat contained in the exhaust gases and
cooling water. This advantage is generally recognized.
The debate in the FRG turns around the exact magnitude
of the energy ratios. The results from the large gas
and diesel heat pumps in the FRG suggest that their average ratio of at least 190 percent is substantially
above the theoretically predicted minimum of 150 percent
to 185 percent suggested by the supporters of these heat
pump. Peak results go beyond 220 percent.It is of course
less certain that the small units destined for the housing market will also achieve these efficiency levels.
Small size and less professional (and less frequent)
maintenance might take its toll.

The other contentious issue concerns the pollution
levels of the overall systems, especially when comparing
a large number of small diesel heat pumps with electric
heat pumps relying on large power stations. It is extremely difficult to arrive at a good comparative evaluation of pollution outputs of the different systems.
Figure 6.3 suggests that the diesel heat pump is almost
as good as the gas heat pump in terms of CO_2-emissions,
and that the electric heat pump is about twice as bad
as the gas heat pump for every unit of final energy output. Of course, other pollution indices would also have
to be considered.[10]

The important point to notice here is that these
unsettled controversies lead on the one hand many ecologists to oppose electric heat pumps, especially because they are convinced that electric utilities are
pushing them to justify their nuclear power programs.
The supporters of the electric heat pump on the other
hand tend to predict worse outcomes for the diesel heat

FIGURE 6.2
Primary Energy Consumption for Different Heating Systems
and Same Room Temperature

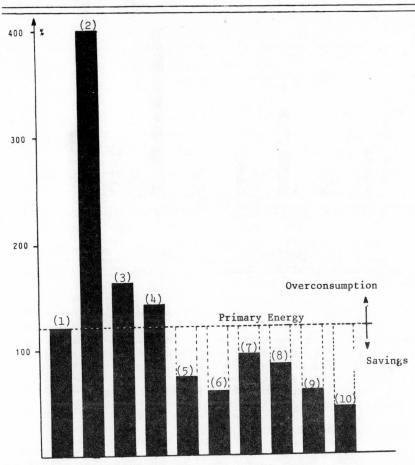

Legend:
(1) Fuel-burning Furnace; (2) Electric Water Heater, night accumulator; (3) Electric HP, monovalent, air-water; (4) Fuel-burning Furna-
ce/Electric HP, bivalent, air-water; (5) Gas Absorption HP, air-water; (6) Gas or Diesel Compression HP, air-water; (7) Fuel-burning
Furnace, additional insulation for 20% energy savings; (8) Fuel-burning Furnace, additional insulation for 30% energy savings; (9) Fuel-
burning Furnace, additional insulation for 50% energy savings;
(10) Gas Absorption HP, additional insulation for 40% energy savings.

Source: Borsche, 1981:11.

142

FIGURE 6.3
Relative CO_2-Emissions for Different
Heating Systems

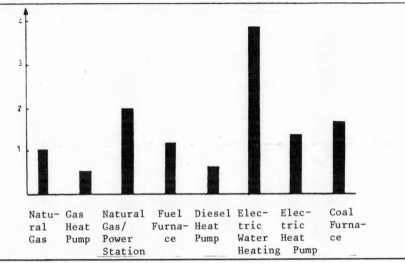

| Natu-
ral
Gas | Gas
Heat
Pump | Natural
Gas/
Power
Station | Fuel
Furna-
ce | Diesel
Heat
Pump | Elec-
tric
Water
Heating | Elec-
tric
Heat
Pump | Coal
Furna-
ce |

Note: Normalized for Natural Gas Furnace.
Source: Borsche, 1981:16.

pump than are likely to obtain. The overall effect is
however the production of a climate of uncertainty. Especially smaller houseowners with limited scientific insight are deterred from even investigating the usefulness
of installing a heat pump of any type. Governments (at
all levels) and responsible administrative bodies consider it prudent to hold back with the elaboration of
norms and recommendations, possibly even subsidy programs, until the debate has become less emotional or has
generated some consensus.

Such developments contribute to maintaining confusion and uncertainty on the part of final buyers. Demand
for heat pumps will certainly develop much more slowly
and unevenly than under non-controversial circumstances.
This scenario also entails a low amount of investment in
research and development because the market is not predictable. The learning curve is therefore much flatter.
The outcome is high equipment prices and therefore further delays in the creation of a mass market with all
their negative dynamic consequences.

Cost and Prices

Here we discuss first the problems involved in the
norms and guidelines which are used to calculate required

heating system capacities. We then point to the cost consequences these norms and guidelines can have. A third
section looks at maintenance and repair costs. And the
fourth section discusses the impact of energy price as-
sumption on comparative profitability of different
systems.

Capacity calculations. The comparison of heat pump
with conventional heating systems involves a number of
difficulties. Conventional systems are chosen and evaluated according to the VDI-guideline 2067 dealing with
heat supply systems. However, these norms are not fully
applicable to heat pump systems. But special norms have
not yet been established. For example, VDI-norms assume
an efficiency ratio for oil furnaces of between 74 percent and 82 percent. Many experts believe this to be too
high. Similarly, the norm assumes for the calculation of
heating needs an average outside air temperature which
is too high to be realistic. These calculations disadvantage the heat pump which has a comparatively much
smaller energy consumption.[11] This situation of course
opens up the way for debate and the spreading of contradictory claims which only serve to confuse the potential buyer.
A similar problem exists with the DIN norms
used to determine the heating needs of a building. The
way they are set up leads normally to a generously if
not overdimensioned furnace. This has no great consequences for a conventional system. Investment costs are
a little bit higher than necessary and efficiency will
be somewhat lower without this becoming noticeable.
However, the application of this norm to heat pumps,
especially electric ones, makes them absolutely uneconomic, at least under existing rate structures.
The selection of an optimally sized heat pump
system, and therefore the creation of comparability with
other heating systems requires:
1. The exact determination of the heating requirements of a building is required. This should include an
evaluation of the effects of improved housing insulation
(see Figure 6.4). It should again be stressed that 'cost-
less' behavioral changes might lead to substantially reduced peak loads and thus a reduction in required heating
capacity.
2. The system should be optimally designed by taking
into account the capacity of the pump, the source of
heat, and the energy input to the pump. An optimal design has in most cases also to evaluate bivalent systems.
3. Energy price developments should be correctly anticipated because different systems have different structures of investment and operating costs. This requires
also a careful evaluation of the different discounts

offered by the electric utilities.

Clearly the evaluation of alternatives requires some sophistication. Individuals interested in installing a heat pump cannot do this work on their own. Unfortunately the branch has not yet managed to train sufficient manpower to guarantee a high quality of evaluation. Errors, misjudgement and confusion are the consequence, leading to buyer dissatisfaction and ultimately resistance as we have seen in the case of the early developments in the USA.

Of course, such a comparative analysis will always remain somewhat ambiguous because of the uncertainties surrounding the forecasting of energy price developments. Heat pumps have lower direct operating costs than conventional furnaces, but higher investment costs in exchange. And the energy part in the operating costs are lower for heat pumps than furnaces. Underestimation of energy price developments, a common occurrence in the last few years, operates to the detriment of the profitability of the heat pump. This is especially the case when energy costs increase faster than the costs for maintenance and repair services.

The 1974 guidelines for the calculation of operating costs of heating systems issued for example by the Ministry of Finance of the Land of Baden-Württemberg have had a similar effect. They in fact require cost calculations over 25 years, assuming this as the equipment lifetime instead of the usual 10 to 20 years. It is of course impossible to make serious energy price forecasts for this length of time. Comparative cost calculations are therefore always subject to large margins of error, so large that in fact the ranking of the systems might become uncertain. The implication is that the government should therefore make decisions on grounds of larger energy policy requirements, which tend to favor the introduction of heat pumps on a larger scale.

Investment and installation costs. Annual depreciation charges depend of course on the assumptions made about equipment lifetime and interest rates. The above mentioned VDI-guidelines for heat supply systems assume an interest rate of 6.5 percent. This tends to favor the capital-intensive heat pump system, at least as long as interest rates remain much higher than that. But the real problem is that this norm creates a difference between calculated and actual costs, opening up another source of surprise, disappointment and confusion.

Experience wit heat pumps is not yet large enough to allow for good estimates of equipment life time, especially not for the smaller heat pump types. Lifetime assumptions for calculatory purposes vary therefore a lot, reflecting often partisan interests. Experiences with many of the early, larger heat pump installations are very good. Some of these pumps are still operating after satisfactory service over twenty-five to thirty years. It might be that the experimental character of these systems induced their owners to follow careful maintenance and repair schedules, thus prolonging equipment life. Today producers commit themselves to lifetimes of at least fifteen years, but expect in practice much higher average values. Volswagen and Fichtel und Sachs expect for their small diesel heat pumps about 20'000 to 40'000 operating hours. This is equivalent to ten to twenty heating periods. The Ministry of Research and Technology assumed for its sales forcasts made in 1979 (see Table 6.1) an average expected lifetime of only ten years, rising to twelve and fifteen years respectively for systems installed in 1985 and 1990. These conservative assumptions affect negatively the depreciation calculations of heat pumps. These negative results stick in the public's consciousness as they emanate from a trustworthy public body.

Expected equipment price developments are also subject to uncertainty. Both the Ministry of Research and Technology and the equipment producers assume falling real prices for the heat pump proper. However, the price fall will not duplicate the one realized with electronic calculators. The Ministry's study predicts an annual real price reduction of 1 percent for electric, and of 3 percent for gas and diesel heat pumps, in the latter case however only as of 1983. Capital costs for construction work and connection to the grid are likely to increase in real terms. But so will costs of conventional furnaces. Overall price developments may well provide heat pumps with a slight but increasing price advantage even if total real costs remain constant for heat pump systems.

Up to now, installation costs for heat pumps have been varying quite a lot between installers. A private survey of firms by us and a similar investigation by the electric utility in Hamburg suggests a variation by a factor of ten. Costs can be as low as DM 1'400 and can go as high as DM 12'600 for exactly the same heat pump unit. The producer price for such a heat pump large enough for the typical single family house is about DM 15'700.[12]

One gains the impression that installers follow completely different pricing strategies as we will discuss later on page 159. This cost diversity if not chaos is creating increasing confusion among potential buyers if it does not dissuade them right away. The already optimistic operating cost analyses proposed by the heat pump producers are completely destroyed through this situation in the installation market.

Maintenance and repair costs. Lack of operational

experience, especially with smaller heat pump types, is
making estimates of these costs a hazardous business.
Calculations often rely on the VDI-guidelines. The Ministry of Research and Technology assumes annual repair
costs in addition to normal maintenance costs equal to
three percent of systems purchace price. Experience with
existing systems has again been better than this. Cube
and Steimle report a total for maintenance and repair
costs which adds up to only 1.5 percent of purchase price
per annum and in the average for an operational life of
20 years. The size of these costs is likely to be very
sensitive to the choice of system parameters.[13] In addition one also has to assume that these values presuppose
the widespread availability of qualified installators.
We know however that this is far from the case.

Real prices for maintenance and repair services
will probably be increasing over the coming years. This
development is the more likely the slower the growth in
the service capacity of the branch. We have already suggested that such a lag is very probable and will have
negative consequences not only for prices but also for
the quality of services rendered.

Energy price developments. The direct operating
costs of heat pumps are essentially made up of energy
costs. Forecasts here are of course extremely uncertain.
Electricity and gas prices are likely to evolve at different speeds. Anyway, these prices are essentially monopoly prices and can therefore change according to the
energy suppliers' marketing strategies. The forecast of
the Ministry of Research and Technology in 1979 assumed
an annual real price increase for light fuel oil of 5
percent. But the price actually doubled within the span
of 14 months from October 1979 to December 1980.[14] It is
clear that this development has invalidated all cost
comparisons between conventional system and heat pumps
and between different types of heat pumps which have
served as the basis for forecasting demand for heat
pumps in the 1980s.

The problem with the energy cost calculations for
electric heat pumps is somewhat different. Electricity
rate structures vary from utility to utility. They also
contain a number of charges which can be avoided if the
heat pump operator accepts restrictions on when to run
his pump. Yet it is these variations which determine if
a heat pump can be economically run or not.

The situation in the city of Mannheim (in late 1980)
can stand as an example. The installation of electric
heat pumps with a rated power from 2 kW on is subject
to permission by the electric utility. The operation
of the heat pump without any limitations entails the
payment of:

1. A <u>connection fee</u> of DM 117 per year and per half kW of rated power above 2 kW.
2. An <u>electricity price</u> proper of DM 11.50 per 100 kWh during the day (6 am to 9 pm) and DM 7.90 at night between 9 pm and 6 am.
3. A <u>meter charge</u> of DM 78 in total for a dual rate system.

VAT and a special tax on electricity consumption are added to the bill.

Various discounts are given if the heat pump is kept operating only during the hours of low electricity demand. Disconnections cannot be more than two hours at a time, and not more than 6 hours per any 24 hour period. An interruption has to be followed by a period of at least equal length during which electricity is supplied. The monthly connection fee in this case is replaced by a one-time contribution in the amount of DM 20 per kW rated power. The night rate for electricity is also lowered by 25 percent.

The load-dependent mode of operation is only possible if the company can centrally control the heat pumps. Other, less flexible solutions entail an automatic cut-off as soon as the outside temperature falls below a certain level, or the meter starts to charge such a high rate that the operation of the pump becomes uneconomic (and the operator presumably turns it off himself). Another version limits operation to pre-determined periods with weak network loads. The connection fee is then dropped.

The gas utilities have not yet developed special rate structures for heat pump operators. But as in the case of fuel, lower gas consumption, for example as a consequence of installing a heat pump, leads to a higher per-unit-charge. All large gas-driven heat pumps in operation today benefit from special supply contracts.

<u>Conclusion.</u> The determination of the economics of heat pumps and of different heat pump types is a rather complex business full of many uncertainties. Nonetheless, several authors have recently argued that some electric heat pump types cannot be amortized. Borsche for example has calculated the total cost figures for a number of heating systems over an operational period of fifteen years (see Figure 6.4).[15] The energy price assumptions made favor the <u>electric</u> heat pump. Heat pump prices and average installation costs reflect the situation in the spring of 1981. Yet, the electric heat pump in both its mono- and bivalent mode are only better than the electric space heating system with night-time accumulator. Kemmer arrives at a similar result, calculating an annual loss of DM 1'344 for an electric heat pump of the size suitable for the average single family house. He concludes sarcastically that "that person acts rationally which

FIGURE 6.4
Cost Comparison of Alternative Heating Systems

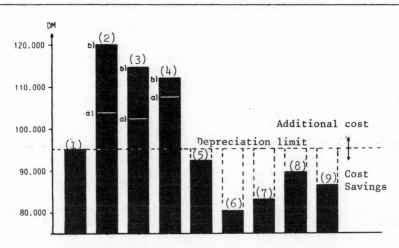

Assumptions:
(1) Annual price increase of 10% for oil and of 5% (a) and 7.5% respectively for electricity.
(2) Only operating costs are shown for fuel-burning furnace. Capital costs for burner, boiler and tank come to about DM 5'800.

Legend:
(1) Fuel-burning Furnace; (2) Electric Water Heater, night accumulator; (3) Electric HP, monovalent, air-water; (4) Fuel-burning Furnace/Electric HP, bivalent, air-water; (5) Gas or Diesel Compressor HP, air-water; (6) Fuel-burning Furnace, additional insulation for 20% energy saving; (7) Fuel-burning Furnace, additional insulation for 30% energy saving; (8) Fuel-burning Furnace, additional insulation for 50% energy saving; (9) Gas Absorption HP, additional insulation for 40% energy saving.

Source: Borsche, 1981:23.

convinces the neighbors to install an electric heat pump in order to lower the price of fuel that he himself is continuing to burn in his good old furnace."[16]
    Figure 6.4 also suggests that it is already cost-effective to switch away from the conventional furnace and replace it with a gas or diesel heat pump. Falling prices as a consequence of mass production should further accentuate this advantage.[17] The gas absorption heat pump for a typical four-family-house (larger than the house assumed in Figure 6.4) is also supposed to be profitable in combination with an increased house insulation.

But such cost-benefit calculations are highly complex and even dependent on the exact geographic location
within the FRG where regional and even local energy suppliers charge different prices. It does therefore not
come as a surprise that it was mostly industrial enterprises, corporate property owners and public administrations which went ahead and installed the first heat
pumps. Only these actors have the competence to make
complex evaluations and decisions. In addition, their
heat pumps have the necessary large scale to generate
the savings which can pay for the high information and
decision-making costs. The typical household cannot
follow here and has to look for help from professional
advisors. This costs money and might still not provide
independent advice. Hence the need for public guidance
and help. Yet, the following section will show that this
has not been forthcoming. To the contrary, government
regulation and incentive programs are so complicated
that a potential heat pump buyer is likely to require
professional help to find his way through this maze.

GOVERNMENT REGULATION AND INCENTIVE PROGRAMS

The regulatory situation and the structure of incentives faced by potential buyers of heat pumps in the
FRG is complex if not chaotic. Regulations are issued
and financial incentives provided by all three levels
of government, the federal, the Länder, and the municipal. Sometimes they complement each other, at other
times they are contradictory. Some incentives are cumu-
lative, others exclude each other. The administrative
rules and guidelines developed by the Länder to apply
federal law are far from uniform. The rules and guidelines to all kind of laws are in many cases revised and
modified quite frequently. Many subsidies and incentives
can but do not have to be granted. To complicate matters
even further, the energy suppliers, often organized on
the municipal level, have also tended to observe different attitudes towards heat pumps.

It is therefore impossible to provide a generally
applicable description of the regulatory environment and
incentives available. For illustrative purposes we chose
to provide a description of the situation a heat pump
buyer in the city of Mannheim in the Land of Baden-
Württemberg would have encountered at the end of 1980.
Improvements have occurred since then. But Mannheim is
also a municipality with support programs which are far
better than the average in the FRG.

The Federal Law on Housing Modernization and Energy Savings

This is the basic instrument with which the federal government is supporting the introduction of heat pumps. This law is important because its revised version of 1978 together with its administrative rules and guidelines has shaped all other support measures taken at the lower political levels. Energy savings is obviously only part of the goals of the law. And heat pumps were originally included in the supportable measures almost as an afterthought. The revised version of the handbook issued by the Ministry of Land Use, Construction and Urban Planning in 1979 deals more explicitly with heat pumps as a means to save energy. But the main argument is that ground water is the ideal source of heat, and that heat pumps make economic sense only in connection with improved housing insulation. These are both questionable views.

However, this law indicates that the federal government considered heat pumps to be an acceptable and applicable technology as of July 1978. The budget allocation under the law reserved for supporting the purchase and installation of heat pumps is rather modest. But the importance of this law for the development of the heat branch is not lying here. Rather, the inclusion of heat pumps on the list of supportable measures gave heat pumps an official certificate of acceptability. This counts in the FRG, especially as rulemakers at the lower level often simply copied the list of supportable measures when preparing their own support programs for energy saving activities.

Heat Pump Subsidies Available in Mannheim at the End of 1980

A heat pump buyer in Mannheim can consider seven different sources of financial support. All sources are ultimately administered on the local level although they do not always add up to a coordinated package.

Federal energy savings subsidies. Relevant here are the guidelines issued by the Land of Baden-Württemberg to the federal law on housing modernization and energy savings. There is no right to a subsidy. Application for the subsidy is made to the municipality. Construction can begin only after approval has been given. The subsidy however is paid only when the project is completed.

Heat pump subsidies are given both for retrofits and for new buildings. Total project costs however are limited to DM 12'000. Costs per apartment have to reach

at least DM 4'000. The affected apartments have to have
a usable life of another thirty years. Rental increases
are limited. The income of the owner of the affected
apartment cannot reach above a certain level.

The subsidy consists either of a loan with a low
interest rate of 3.5 percent, a principal pay-out of 98
percent, and an annual repayment of 6 percent (i.e. repayment takes a little bit more than thirteen years), or
a lump-sum payment equal to twenty-five percent of sub-
sidisable costs. It should be noted that this program
supports only the introduction of heat pumps into the
housing sector.

Federal subsidies for urban renewal. This law de-
signates a number of urban renewal areas. Forty percent
of allowable renovation costs, including the costs for
a heat pump, can be paid for by the government.

Income tax law. The costs of a heat pump can be
deducted from income in ten yearly even installments.
There is no upper limit but this benefit cannot be cumulated with a subsidy under the federal energy savings
law. The deduction has to be claimed every year, but the
deduction is a right and has to be accepted by the tax
authorities. This subsidy is obviously of special interest to high-income earners. They are likely to be unable to fulfill the income and rent conditions set out
in the federal energy savings law. It seems that the
laws favor high-income buyers of heat pumps.

Subsidies under the wealth formation programs.
Three federal laws support the accumulation of savings
which in part can be used to buy housing property. Heat
pumps are an acceptable element for a house purchased
with these funds.

Urban renewal program of the Land of Baden-Württemberg. The purpose of the program is to maintain
housing stocks near the city centers. The areas where
housing renovation can be supported are delineated by
law. The rules and conditions of the federal law on energy savings apply. But the subsidy element is somewhat
greater.

Protection of monuments. In the case of Mannheim,
up to 75 percent of renovation costs, including the installation of a heat pump, can be paid for by the Land
and the city for a building with a historical or cultural value.

<u>The Mannheim program for supporting the moderniza-tion of apartments</u>. Rules and constraints are similar to those of the federal law for housing modernization and energy savings. This subsidy cannot be cumulated with the federal one or the subsidy given under the programs of the Land.

Conclusions

The installation of a heat pump in the housing area can be supported under a number of governmental programs. Some of these programs have a very restricted applicability. Support for urban areas is much better than for villages and rural areas. Failure to get support under the federal energy savings law can be compensated with support from similar Länder or city programs in the case of some city locations. No alternative supports seem to be available for the more rural cases. The only support available in these cases comes from the various programs subsidizing saving for wealth formation and property acquisition. But they are also available and can be cumulated with the other supports for city locations.

Many of the structurally similar programs contain different cut-off limits and subsidy elements. This needlessly complicates the choice between the different programs. It also creates delays in realizing energy savings measures as one cannot begin to build or apply to other programs unless the first decision has been forthcoming.

Finally, it is not yet clear to what extent these various cost minima and maxima exclude certain projects from benefiting from the various programs. Nor is it clear to what extent the discretionary power in granting the subsidies under some of the described programs has really limited the spreading of heat pump installations. However we know that people have not necessarily executed those measures which would have been most cost efficient. We also know that low-cost measures predominate and that only about three percent of all house owners have engaged in more expensive energy savings measures, among them the installation of a heat pump. Finally, it seems that a large number of people have used the subsidy programs to install double-glazed windows without taking additional, complementary energy savings measures. And we know that most of these people would have done so even if no subsidies had been available.

ACTORS, PROBLEMS AND PERSPECTIVES

There is nothing natural in the process of introducing a new technology into an existing social system.
Heat pumps have to fit into an already existing, struc-
tured system of interests, institutions, rules and be-
haviors. Problems can but do not have to be resolved.
Opportunities might exist, but they may not be realised
because blockages and resistances arise. In the following sections we look in turn at governments, energy
suppliers, producers, installers, consumers, and ecologists and their views of the situation, their problems,
and plans. This approach will help us to increase the
understanding of the constraints and opportunities which
have shaped in the past and which are likely to shape
in the future the heat pump diffusion process in the
FRG.

The Role of Governmental Institutions

We have seen that governmental institution-building
is still open to improvement in a number of areas.
Technical standards and norms are still quite underdeveloped or, where existing, often inappropriate. Legal and
administrative rules for granting permits and subsidies
for the installation of heat pumps could benefit from
greater harmonisation, increased stability, and yet
further development.
Technical norms, safety regulations and warranty
conditions for heat pumps have in many instances not yet
been fully elaborated. If they exist, they have in most
cases not yet acquired the semi-legal or legal status
which alone can make them effective. Many engineering
and construction norms have not yet been adapted to the
specific requirements of heat pump installations. Those
concerning insulation of buildings and the determination
of heating capacity and need are just now in the process
of being inserted into the relevant statutes.
The procedures for approving the installation of
heat pumps fall within the competence of the Länder administrations. These have made uneven progress in elabo-
rating them. The existing rules and procedures differ
from Land to Land, often quite substantially. Some Länder
do not yet have regulations governing access to surface
or underground water bodies which could serve as a source
of heat. Yet, the federal law on energy savings favors
exactly this type of heat pump system. Bavaria and Lower
Saxony stipulate special safety requirements to prevent
leakages of absorber fluid. This introduces special design requirements, thereby increasing system costs.
Baden-Württemberg is reserving underground reservoirs
for large projects. And so on. The time involved in
getting the necessary permits to exploit water bodies

and to construct heat pump systems differs substantially among the Länder.

The confusion and uncertainty is especially great in the area of subsidies for heat pump installations. The frequent modification of the administrative regulations for the federal energy savings law are partly responsible for this situation. Partly it is the result of the fact that the regulations differ between the Länder and that the federal subsidy program is complemented by a great variety of widely differing regional and municipal subsidy programs. Partly, it is the consequence of the failure of these regulations to explicitly define the concept of 'allowable costs'. The cost of the heat pump itself is 'allowable' for subsidy purposes. But it is not clear if the different subsystems required, such as the heat exchanger with the source of heat and the heat distribution system within the house, are also included in this concept. Nor is it certain that one can include the auxiliary furnace in 'allowable costs' despite the fact that only a bivalent heat pump system will work efficiently and economically under most German climatic conditions.

It is not only the Länder governments which are to blame. The federal administration had not yet written in October 1980 the administrative guidelines to the paragraph of the income tax law which made heat pump costs deductible from income when the tax offices had to send out the tax bills for 1979. It is not surprising that in these circumstances tax rulings on the deductibility of heat pump costs have been far from uniform among the regions.

This administrative chaos creates a substantial disincentive effect on the buyer's side. This is especially true for the small individual house and apartment owner who can hardly be expected to find his way unaided.[19] It could therefore well be that the forecasted sales expansion in the 1980s, based on the coming availability of small gas and diesel heat pumps, will fail to materialize unless this situation is quickly corrected. A failure to do so could have serious repercussions on the producers' side. A failure to realize planned sales and amortize investments made in new heat pump products and production capacities could quickly lead to disenchantment, increased conservatism and hence a much less vigorous market dynamic.

It is essentially the federal government alone which intervenes on the producers' side. The Ministry of Research and Technology uses funds from its research support program to finance heat pump research and development. A little bit more than 1 percent of these funds went to non-nuclear research in 1972. This had risen to 37 percent in 1979. But only a small part of these funds is going to 'soft' energy technologies. Federal support

for heat pump development is therefore quite minimal.
Much of it goes to the development of the 'energy roof'.
The remaining funds are just sufficient to support a few
development and demonstration projects.

Yet, even this minimal support can have structural
consequences. Small and medium-sized enterprises in the
branch have great difficulties to get financial support
for their research and development projects. A support
strategy biased towards larger enterprises is quite common in industrialised countries as it minimises administrative effort, costs, and risk. Larger enterprises may
be better able to realise economies-of-scale and hence
push prices down. They may also possess superior marketing and this too could push up sales. But heat pumps
will be only one among their many product lines. They
may therefore fail to push heat pumps as much as smaller
enterprises more dependent on them would do. Smaller
enterprises also tend to be more innovative. The consequence of this governmental support strategy could therefore be the generation of substantial initial technical
and product breakthroughs relatively early on in the
branch development process. The subsequent development
however might then turn out to be more sedate than if
the strategy would have been to support small and medium-
sized enterprises.

Energy Suppliers

Electricity and gas distribution companies play a
decisive role in the further shaping and spreading of
heat pump use. Rate structure and levels, connections
and sales efforts and supports are important factors
in the determination of economic efficiency and buyer
interest. So far the electric utilities had the field
to themselves. This will change once the small gas and
diesel heat pumps will appear on the market after 1983.

The electric utilities are quite independent organisations. Federal and Länder governments do not exercise any direct control over them. Municipally-owned
utilities could be open to local political influence.
But they lack real economic independence from the utilities supplying them with electricity. Anyway, political
influence over rate setting seems to be minimal. Utilities in the electric and the gas sector do not compete
as they all possess geographic monopolies. Local gas and
electric utilities have so far not competed in the heat
pump market because each one was in the possession of a
non-substitutable product. Large heat pumps were best
run with gas or diesel fuel, small heat pumps with electricity. This will change in 1983 and it is quite unclear what will happen then.

The local monopoly situations enable the utilities
to set rates and sales conditions according to their

business strategy. National energy policy goals do not really influence these decisions. RWE, the largest utility agreed only at the end of 1977 to treat industrial enterprises who were co-generating part of their own electricity like any other pure electricity consumer. This change of mind required the intervention of the federal cartel office. Yet, the Minister of Research and Technology felt compelled in 1979 to threaten the electricity industry with nationalisation if it did not finally proceed to buy electricity produced by such enterprises at a reasonable price.

It is therefore no surprise that the attitude of the electric utilities towards heat pumps is generally ambivalent, often confusing, if not outright obfuscating. The German electricity industry is extremely growth oriented. Realisation of this growth requires an increase of the industry's share of the energy market. This in turn implies that electricity has to break into the market for house heating. Only in this way can the industry justify --in retrospect-- its nuclear power program, and avoid losses on it.

Heat pumps fit only partly into such a growth concept. Electric heat pumps are a new source of demand. They present one opportunity to enter the market for household heat. But heat pumps are also a relatively energy-saving method for producing heat and hot water. As such they are a threat to the profitability of the electricity industry.[20]

Utilities which consider heat pumps to be a means to enter the market for household heat push them with the argument of a 70 percent reduction in fuel consumption, surpressing the fact that the social benefits are far less substantial. However, even these utilities often set policies which discourage the adoption of heat pumps. Utilities fear that the massive introduction of electric heat pumps will further increase their peak loads just at a time when the nuclear power program is making it imperative to increase the base load. Hence they propose rate structures, cut-off periods, and interruptability to eliminate peak load demand coming from heat pumps. Other companies make sure that heat pump clients provide a guaranteed minimal contribution to company profits. RWE, for example, guarantees to the first 1'000 heat pump clients a fixed rate which is almost as low as the night rate. However, this rate is charged for a minimum of 10'000 kWh even if annual consumption falls below this amount, for example because the house is well insulated.[21]

Utilities which consider heat pumps to be an undesirable alternative to all types of electric space heating refuse to offer special rates to heat pump users. Or they demand high connection fees thus making uneconomical the operation of a heat pump.

This differentiated attitude towards heat pumps on the part of electric utilities has the consequence that "geographic location of the heat pump user determines in the end the profitability of the heat pump" and not any intrinsic quality of the pump.[22]

Gas utilities assume positions similar to the electric utilities. Several instances are known where unfavorable rates were offered to make potential heat pump users change their minds.[23] It seems clear that the general behavior of the energy suppliers does not exactly favor the adoption of heat pumps although it neither does prevent it outright.

Heat Pump Producers

We have already pointed out in the historical overview that the branch is made up of mostly small and medium-sized producers. There does not exist a clear market leader. Large companies, among them especially the European subsidiaries of Japanese multinational corporations, are presently pushing into German heat pump markets. Only a few producers are exclusively engaged in the heat pump branch.

The steep sales growth until the summer of 1980 has in the mean time turned into a drop in sales, disproving all forecasts and disappointing many expectations. We have suggested in the preceding sections some of the causes for this development, not all of which are really under the control of the producers. Some of them are clearly a consequence of the branch structure, i.e., the lack of an industry leader and of a strong branch organisation. Only these could muster the political strength and the interest to force the administrations to resolve the regulatory and subsidy problems. It probably would require a strong branch organisation to resolve the collective action problem of ensuring high quality services for installing, maintaining and repairing heat pumps.[24]

Interestingly enough, the producers behaved until recently as if they were part of a strongly cartellized branch. They apparently were increasing their prices in the beginning years in parallell to the increase in subsidies which became available to heat pump buyers.

It would of course be extremely difficult to manage the technological development process whatever the organisation of the branch. Presently most potential buyers seem to hold back in anticipation of the announced cost-effective small gas and diesel heat pumps expected to appear on the market sometime during 1983. Even IBM has difficulties after all to smoothly manage the market introduction of technologically new products.

Producers are divided in their views about the future development. Some profess to already see signs

of a lessening of the skeptical attitudes towards heat
pumps held by distributors and buyers alike. Happel, one
of the more important German producers is among them.
But then Happel had prepared for the expected sales boom
in 1981 by continuing to acquire production capacities
until late in 1980. Its optimism could therefore be part
of its sales strategy. Other producers, among them
Küppersbusch, expect a longer period of stagnating sales.
Their only hope is more expensive oil. Heat pumps in the
cellar are unfortunately less prestigious acquisitions
than the visible solar collectors on the roof. The market
potential of buyers committed to the heat pump path to a
soft energy system irrespective of negative economic returns has obviously been exhausted by now. Appeals to
macro-economic and social reasoning will therefore fail
to work as long as the individual profit calculations do
not show a positive result.

The end of the sales expansion has already led to
increased price competition. This development is reinforced by the already mentioned aggressive entrance of
foreign producers into the German market. But the effect
of falling equipment prices on demand should not be over-
evaluated as long as installation costs can make up 50
percent of total system costs. In any case, the 110 heat
pump exhibitors at the 1981 international fair for sanitation, heating and climatisation were predominantly
skeptical about future technical developments and sales
possibilities.

Installers and Other Service Sectors

Producers of heat pumps in Germany only rarely install their own equipment. Installation work is typically the task of specialised enterprises, very often of
small, artisanal ones. Producers do not plan to change
this division of labor despite the great and dangerous
problems persisting in this area. Happel's sales manager
for example explained Happel's reluctance to create an
enterprise-internal installation and maintenance service with the need to protect the cooperation between
Happel and installers in other product areas. Choosing a
different arrangement for heat pumps would undermine and
weaken the relationship Happel is using to sell its other
products.

The installers themselves have a differentiated attitude towards heat pumps. This explains the great variation in installation charges and the frequent problems
encountered by heat pump buyers:

1. Most craftsmen and installation enterprises lack
experience with and training in installing heat pumps.
Only a few of the larger and better known heat pump producers maintain enterprise-run training centers or employ

specially trained advisors visiting installers.

2. A large number of installers refuse therefore categorically to even install heat pumps.

3. Some installers seem to take a very generous approach to the calculation of installation costs. They charge high prices because they enter unknown territory. Some must have experienced losses with their first attempts and now want to eliminate further risks. Others consider those wanting to install a heat pump as being slightly silly, but obviously rich clients. They increase their profit margins accordingly.[25]

4. A minority of installers has actively tried to prepare itself for the new tasks and problems. Most successful in this were those installers which limited themselves to the products of one producer, especially if this producer has his own training program.
The installers themselves are unhappy with their cooperation with the producers. The director of the national organisation of craftsmen is quite critical of the business practices of many producers. He feels that too many had promised unachievable energy savings. Others are apparently for months late with their deliveries of spare parts. Producers sometimes started to deliver a new pump type months before they were really ready for production. The price formation of many producers is extremely chaotic. The great variety in heat pump types and designs is also contributing to the deterrence of potential buyers. In short it is not the fault of the installers if "the people do not know anymore what they should buy" as the director of the heat technology division of Krupp was summing up the situation.[26]

Heat Pump Users

Originally heat pump buyers were motivated by goals of a rational use of energy even at the price of higher costs and administrative problems. This positive orientation however was never as strong as in the case of buyers of solar collector equipment. The desire to be independent of imported energy resources may also have played a role. This buyer type is probably becoming less frequent, leaving his place to a much more cost conscious one. Potential users are in general favorably inclined towards the electric heat pump, apparently being unaware of the difference between private and social costs and benefits. The information being spread about the forthcoming small gas and diesel heat pumps may by now have changed even this attitude. Most potential users today seem however to hold back from actually buying and installing a pump because:

1. The price of fuel stopped to rise during the winter of 1980/81. Consumers apparently consider the supply situation for oil as being safe again. Appeals to fear do not produce sales today.

2. The costs of a heat pump installation cannot be amortised over a reasonable period of time. We have referred to authors who maintain that the electric heat pump fails to show a positive return at all.

3. News reports about the advantages of the forthcoming small gas and diesel heat pumps obviously incite buyers to sit out the next couple of years without buying a heat pump which is likely to be outdated when installed. The consumer does not know what to buy at the present moment.

4. The failures of installation and servicing infrastructures make the acquisition of a heat pump a risky and possibly very costly business. Information acquisition is the task of the potential buyer and this implies substantial non-monetary costs. Information offices of utilities and administrations are not yet really oriented towards promoting the use of heat pumps.

5. The legal situation is complex and confused. The outcome of administrative decision processes are difficult to foresee. New legal and technical norms might be forthcoming shortly thereby reducing the risks on the part of buyers and getting them a product of higher quality. Increased subsidies in the future might also increase the profitability of heat pump systems bought at a later point in time.

In short, there are many reasons which explain the hesitation of potential buyers of heat pumps. Energy saving has not yet become an urgent task in the mind of the average consumer. Occupation with the heat pump has still the character of a luxury good. The heat pump remains "a way for the middle class to trim its central heating bill."[27]

The Ecological Movement

Ecological research institutes have studied very intensively the heat pump question.[28] They all agree that the purchase of an electric heat pump is to be discouraged. At a minimum, this heat pump type fails to save energy at the national level. Instead the installation of such heat pumps provides the nuclear power industry with arguments, actually wrong ones, for a further expansion of electricity production.

Ecologists frequently advise to first introduce a substantive insulation program which would not only make

economic sense, but which would also realise an optimum
on energy saving. People interested in heat pumps are
mostly advised to wait until the small gas and diesel
heat pumps are introduced in the market. Ecologists prefer the gas absorption heat pump especially when combined with greatly improved insulation. Some authors
therefore request an end to state subsidies for electric
heat pumps.[29] State subsidies should be increased in support of heat pumps which run on primary energy forms.
For this purpose they propose: (1) Research subsidies to
small and medium-sized enterprises; (2) subsidies to consumers who intend to buy such heat pumps; and (3) the
use of the powers given to the state under the Federal
Energy Rate Regulation to intervene and regulate the
rates charged for users of gas heat pumps.

CONCLUSIONS

     The arguments presented here about the development
and diffusion of heat pumps in the FRG allow one to make
the following conclusions on a number of levels:
     1. The explanation of the past diffusion of heat
pumps and the making of prognoses about future developments has to fall back on a differentiated analysis of
different heat pump types, different with respect to heat
pump principles, sources of heat, and energy inputs.
     2. Only a few heat pump technologies are developed
far enough to consider them ready for market introduction. This is true of the electric heat pump and the
larger gas and diesel heat pumps. Small gas and diesel
heat pumps will not be ready before 1983 at the earliest
although absorption pumps may appear before compressor
pumps. This market situation contributes to the sluggish
sale of the already available heat pump types.
     3. Other reasons for the present sales stagnation
are complex. But they all reflect the initial problems
of a not yet established new technology. Important considerations here are:

   o   a product range which lacks standardisation, a
       problem compounded by sometimes almost fraudulent
       offers. These developments are favored by the
       small-size branch structure.
   o   an equally chaotic price structure where some-
       times prices charged are simply too high, espe-
       cially in the case of installation enterprises.
   o   installers are insufficiently trained, in part
       difficulties with the delivery of spare parts.
       Repairs can therefore become difficult.
   o   legal uncertainty and great geographic variations
       in legal interpretation. Administrative proce-
       dures are sometimes very cumbersome and involve

long delays.

4. Recent price developments for heating fuel have
led to renewed doubts about the private profitability of
heat pumps, especially the electric one. However in making such comparisons one should consider that the normed
calculations underlying such judgements tend to disfavor
the heat pump compared to conventional heating systems.

5. Only heat pumps running on gas and diesel fuel
are clearly advantageous from a national perspective.
Electric heat pumps generally increase total energy consumption. Electric utilities frequently favor the adoption of electric heat pumps as the means to increase
their share of the energy market. Rates and regulations
are used to favor the diffusion of electric heat pumps
in order to use this development to justify an expansion in the base load electricity generation capacity,
actually an argument to justify more nuclear power.

One can conclude that the recent change from a
boom in sales of heat pumps to a sales stagnation reflects a surprisingly rational behavior on the part of
consumers and heat buyers. This sales stagnation is
likely to be overcome only when:

o   the promised technological innovations really
    begin to appear on the market.
o   the legal norms become less complex and more
    uniform, and when they can be consistently ap-
    plied by administrators.
o   state subsidies and tax expenditures provide
    new financial incentives.
o   the cooperation between producers and installers
    has dramatically improved thereby increasing
    market transparency.

Heat pumps can be fruitfully used already today in
larger, often public buildings such as swimming pools,
schools, administrative buildings, housing developments,
etc. This is especially the case if they are combined
with other recent technological developments such as
small district heating networks, decentralized neighbor-
hood cogeneration units, recuperation of waste heat,
etc. This use of heat pumps can benefit from a creative
application of technological possibilities, a process
which unfortunately is too often blocked by bureaucratic
heavy-handedness.

NOTES

1. I am thankful to Dieter Gersemann (Oeko-Institut Freiburg), Lorenz Borsche (IFEU Heidelberg) and Thomas Baumgartner for their many suggestions and contributions to an earlier version of this report.

2. This section draws heavily on Cube and Steimle (1978) and on the Edison Electric Institute (1953) for the developments before 1951.

3. Cube and Steimle (1978:179).

4. Urbanek (1980).

5. Riemann (1980).

6. Kutzbach (1981).

7. Costs and prices are all given in DM. Its $ value fluctuated between $ .56 (Summer 1980) and $ .45 (December 1981).

8. Dehli (1981:15).

9. The surface covered by the coils in the soil is about three times the surface to be heated. This excludes the energy required to produce hot water.

10. See Gersemann (1981) and Borsche (1981).

11. Cube and Steimle (1978:87).

12. Compare also Kemmer (1981).

13. Cube and Steimle (1978:202).

14. Prices per 100 liters varied in late 1980 with the quantity of fuel bought between DM 57.70 for more than 14'000 liters ($ .91 for more than 3'700 gallons) and DM 72.50 for less than 750 liters ($ .1.14 for less than 200 gallons).

15. Borsche (1981:20).

16. Kemmer (1981).

17. Increased insulation in combination with the traditional oil-fired furnace is definitely the most profitable option. The large gains on an additional 20 percent insulation reflect the low costs of the required material or, respectively, the relatively high costs of the more sophisticated material needed to achieve larger insulation gains. However, a more rapid increase in energy prices quickly reverses the order of profitability. An annual oil price increase of 12 percent (instead of the assumed 10 percent) makes the 30 percent insulation option the most profitable one.

18. Gersemann (1981) provides a review of existing legal norms.

19. It is not surprising then that most early applicants for subsidies under the federal law on energy savings were in one way or another personnally connected with municipal administrators.

20. The Minister for the Economy of the Land of Hesse warned in parliament in 1979 that further electricity savings measures would reduce an already insufficient demand and would threaten the utilities' profitability (Brandt, 1979:32).

164

21. Cube and Steimle (1978a:90).
22. BMFT (1979:139).
23. Cube and Steimle (1978a:91).
24. The response of some producers to design integrated heat pump units, while positive, fails to resolve
the problems in the important retrofit market.
25. See Kemmer (1981).
26. Müller (1981).
27. Harper and Boyle (1977).
28. Kinchen and Witzel (1979); Ruske and Teufel
(1980); Borsche (1981).
29. See for example Borsche (1981).

BIBLIOGRAPHY

BMFT (Bundesministerium für Forschung und Technik (ed.)
1979 Wärmepumpen für Heizung, Kühlung und Energie-
rückgewinnung. Köln.
Borsche, Lorenz 1981 Heizen mit Wärmepumpen, Oel, Gas und
Strom. Heidelberg: IFEU-Institut für Energie- und
Umweltforschung.
Brandt, G. 1979 "Dezentrale Wärme-Kraft-Kopplung (WKK)
statt Kernkraftwerke." Prisma, Nr. 19.
Cube, H.L. and F. Steimle 1978 Wärmepumpen. Düsseldorf.
Cube, H.L. and F. Steimle (eds.) 1978a Wärmepumpen in
staatlichen und kommunalen Bauten. Karlsruhe.
Dehli, M. 1981 Energie von der Sonne. Bonn: Informations-
zentrale der Elektrizitätswirtschaft.
Edison Electrical Institute 1953 Bibliography of the Heat
Pump through 1951. New York.
Gersemann, Dieter 1981 Abschätzung der Umweltverträglich-
keit energierelevanter Rechtsnormen. Rechtsnormen-
dokumentation Wärmepumpen.
Harper, P. and G. Boyle (eds.) 1977 Radical Technology
(2nd ed.). London.
Kemmer, Heinz-Günter 1981 "Geschäft mit den Dummen - Der
Kauf von Wärmepumpen lohnt noch nicht." Die Zeit,
May 29.
Kinchen, D. and W. Witzel 1979 Wärmepumpen. Unterrichts-
material aus dem Oeko-Institut Freiburg.
Kutzbach, Carl-Josef 1981 "Heizen mit dem Klärwerk." Die
Zeit, October 16.
Müller, Mario 1981 "Die Leute wissen nicht mehr was sie
kaufen sollen." Frankfurter Rundschau, March 20.
Riemann, R. 1980 "Die Gas-WP des Erdgasspeichers Franken-
thal." Sonnenenergie und Wärmepumpe, Nr. 2.
Ruske, B. and D. Teufel 1980 Das sanfte Energiehandbuch.
Heidelberg: Reinbek
Urbanek, Axel 1980 "Gas-WP in zwei Jahren amortisiert."
Sonnenenergie und Wärmepumpe, Nr. 2.

Part III

Producer-Oriented Technologies

7
Geothermal Electricity in California

James Ward

During the 1979 Senate hearings on the Geothermal Energy Development and Commercialization Act, Senator James McClure stated, "I suppose most people in this country still don't know what geothermal resources are."[1] This statement, nineteen years after the first commercial geothermal power plant came on stream, illustrates a fundamental problem the geothermal industry has faced - lack of recognition and public awareness.

The industry's unique evolution may be responsible for geothermal's relative lack of public recognition. Geothermal's low profile among new energy sources has in turn impeded industry development by placing the industry on a weak footing in competing for government R&D funds and in lobbying for legislation to remove institutional and economic barriers to geothermal commercialization.

To an extent, the geothermal industry is an anomaly among new energy industries, having initially developed without the backing of major institutions such as federal and state governments, public interest groups, universities and large corporations. Yet, the industry is substantial compared to other emerging energy industries. Revenues of geothermal energy producers probably exceeded $100 million in 1981. The market value of their assets is in the $2 billion range. Geothermal is making a significant contribution to local energy supplies, meeting the needs of over one million California residents.[2] Geothermals relative obscurity is therefore a distinctive feature which sets the industry apart from other emerging energy technologies of recognized potential. Even today, geothermal holds a weak position relative to other energy technologies in terms of major institutional support.

James Ward has an MA in economics and has completed work towards a Ph.D. at Stanford University. He has also worked in the Norwegian oil industry.

THE ENTREPRENEURIAL ERA, 1920-1963

The first forty years of the geothermal industry were a period of entrepreneurs. The industry parallelled in many ways the petroleum industry. The most significant development, the Geysers project, was conducted by individuals and small private corporations on privately held land. Due to the nature of the geothermal resource, many early industry participants such as geologists, drilling engineers, lawyers and financeers came with petroleum industry experience.

Methods brought from the oil industry were gradually modified and adapted as the geothermal industry developed. In addition to adapting drilling methods, leasehold agreements and geological techniques, a direct technology. transfer occured as representatives of U.S. geothermal interests were sent to Larderello, Italy to learn of the Italian experiences with geothermal electric generation.

Marketing was the area in which the petroleum industry model was inappropriate and this became the industry bottleneck. Oil was barrelled and sold on competitive markets while geothermal required strong promotion to find a market.

The Pioneer

The first attempt to generate electricity with geothermal steam was initiated by a Healdsburg, California, merchant in the 1920s.[3] John Grant, who lived near the Geysers Hot Springs, purchased land in the Geysers region in 1919 with the ultimate goal of constructing a power plant for the town of Healdsburg, located about sixty miles north of San Franscisco on Route 101.

The Geysers Hot Springs had been a well-known resort since the 1860 but no attempt had been made to utilize the region's hot springs for anything except bathing. Upon purchasing land surrounding the Geysers Hot Springs Hotel, Grant approached the town of Healdsburg with a proposal for a small power plant. The town would install the turbine and transmission lines of about fifteen miles to Healdsburg and Grant would supply steam to drive the plant.

To profile and develop his resource, Grant formed the Geyser Development Company (GDC) and raised about $400'000 through a highly promoted stock offering. The funds were to be used to buy additional land in the Geysers and to begin drilling development wells. The Healdsburg newspapers encouraged this opportunity for local control and participation in Healdsburg's energy supply. However, none of the original company directors was at the time from Healdsburg. Instead the board consisted of three San Francisco businessmen including E.O. McCormick, then Vice President of the Southern Pacific

Railway, and one Santa Rosa merchant.

GDC was clouded in controversy from its inception. The company was rife with overpromotion and questionable practices. For example at the July 16, 1923 stockholders' meeting "President Smith stated that he was in receipt of an offer of ten million dollars for the power rights, but when pressed for more particulars it proved to be nebulous...". There were also public debates on two classes of stock, common and preferred. Inside stockholders generally held common stock, which carried no limit on dividends, while the public bought preferred carrying a fixed dividend rate.

Similar financing arrangements were typical for this period, especially in the speculative petroleum industry. Financing often followed a pyramid strategy where directors overpromoted the company to increase the value of a company's stock. If the promotion was successful and the stock price rose, more stock was sold at the higher price.

GDC shareholder meetings during 1923 were rancorous and within a year the company's non-local directors were removed. By August 1923, GDC's board had expanded to eight with six members from the Healdsburg - Santa Rosa area, and in 1924 the board was composed entirely of local residents with John Grant as president.

The feasibility of generating electricity from geothermal steam had been demonstrated by the geothermal plant at Larderello, Italy, which came on stream in 1904. In late 1923, a GDC stockholder, who was also a neighbor of Grant, visited the Italian plant at Larderello. By 1923 the Italian plant had considerable capacity and nineteen years of operating experience. His report back to GDC evaluated the Geysers as having more potential than Larderello with twice the steam pressure and fewer corrosive chemicals.

A small 250 kW unit was installed at one of the first GDC wells in 1923. The company had no contract to sell the steam nor any transmission lines out of the Geysers, so the unit was used to provide electricity for the Geysers Hot Springs Hotel. By 1925, a total of eight wells had been drilled. All were reported to be commercially viable but seven of them blew uncapped and remained unutilized.

With no revenues and considerable drilling and land acquisition expenditures, GDC began seeking additional funding to continue operations. A San Francisco investment banking house, E.H.Rollins was offered a 50 percent interest in GDC for $2.5 million. L.C.Decius, a Stanford educated geologist, was hired by Rollins to make a geological evaluation of the properties and submit a recommendation on purchasing the half interest. Decius' report was the first professional geological study of the Geysers and concluded that the source of the steam's heat was the molten mass of the earth's magma. The water from which the steam was produced was both magmatic and meteoric. Magmatic water was thrown off when the earths' magma solidified, while meteoric water referred to sur- face or rain water which found its way down to the heat source.[4] Decius felt that both the heat and water sources were of long duration. He recommended that "the exploita- tion of electric power be developed by drilling wells to secure steam in the fumarole area is fully warranted.."[5]

Nonetheless, Rollins, the investment bank, declined GDC's offer on the properties apparently due to uncer- tainties in finding a market for the power. While Decius' report may have allayed a common concern at the time that the steam would suddenly cease, it was a geological study, not a marketing plan. GDC still needed a buyer with the financial resources to construct a power plant at the Geysers and transmission lines to end users.

The sales options for GDC were governed by federal laws regulating public utilities. The power could be sold to Northern California's public utility, Pacific Gas and Electric (PG&E) or to a municipal utility. At the time, Healdsburg was the only city in the area operating its own municipal utility. The town purchased power from PG&E which was in turn distributed through the Healdsburg municipal system.

While deals with the Healdsburg system were often proposed, the town was probably too small to finance and construct the plant and fifteen miles of transmission lines. With a population under 5,000 and no other munici- pal systems in the area for a possible joint venture, PG&E was the only realistic buyer for power generated at the Geysers.

PG&E was largely a hydro based utility during the 1920s. In 1925 they had a peak demand on their system of 380 MW and a hydroelectric generating capacity of 399 MW. In addition, PG&E had four steam-electric plants with an installed capacity of 142 MW for load balancing and peak load demand.

New hydro projects were under construction and PG&E's steam plants were fired with fossil fuels the real price of which was falling due to new oil discoveries in Cali- fornia. Consequently, PG&E had no real interest in deve- loping geothermal power.

By the late 1920s GDC had exhausted its capital raised in stock offerings and was unable to find a joint venture partner. With the coming of the depression in 1930 any hope of additional capital for GDC disappeared. The Geysers project lay dormant through the 1930s and 1940s. A few attempts at further development occurred but none progressed beyond the proposal stage.

The Post-War Period

The modern development of the Geysers began around 1950. A Los Angeles lumber merchant, B.C. McCabe heard about the Geysers and began acquiring leases from GDC. By the early 1950 McCabe had leased 3620 acres with a 10 percent royalty to GDC. McCabe established the Magma Power Company and drilled his first well, Magma No. 1 in 1955. The earlier GDC wells ranged from 47 to 94 meters; Magma No. 1 was 249 meters deep producing 150,000 lbs/hr of dry steam.

Magma used standard drilling tools which were usually applied to low pressure areas. Magma lost the well as it blew out and had continuing problems controlling the well. Magma was also undercapitalized and joined forces with a newly formed company, Thermal Power. Magma gave Thermal a 50 percent interest in their leases in exchange for $230'000 to be used for further drilling. Thermal raised $200'000 of this through a public stock offering in 1957.[6]

Magma and Thermal contacted L.C. Decius, the geologist who had evaluated the Geysers in 1924, for drilling advice. Decius recommended using rotary tools and pumping mud into the well for control and to prevent the possibility of a blowout. Decius brought in a drilling superintendent from Associated Oil (a Southern Pacific Railroad subsidiary) to supervise the well which came in successfully. The previous wells had all blown using standard tools, but from 1957 on only rotary drilling was attempted at the Geysers. Six wells were successfully completed by Magma and Thermal by yearend 1957 with depths ranging from 161 to 431 meters.

Although McCabe and Dan McMillan (the president of Thermal) were convinced that the Geysers project was commercially viable, no market for the steam had been found. In 1957, McCabe sought assistance from Alf Hansen, a General Electric engineer. Hansen had visited the Geysers in the late 1940s and was familiar with the region's potential for power generation. Hansen was also impressed by the small power plant providing electricity for the hotel which was still operating after more than twenty years. On McCabe's urging, Hansen visited the Geysers and ran tests estimating the quantities of power that could be generated from the completed wells. In exchange for the engineering report, McCabe sold Hansen a small interest in the project.

The Entrance of the Utility

Armed with Hansen's report, McCabe approached the engineering department of PG&E. Hansen was well known and respected by the PG&E people. Based on his estimate that Magma No. 1 alone could produce 5 MW, PG&E assigned an engineer to the project. Previously PG&E had shown little or no interest in geothermal generation. Even at this point PG&E's involvement may have been largely defensive. If Hansen's estimates were correct, the Geysers had enormous electric potential. Were PG&E not to develop the resource, there was a strong possibility that the local communities surrounding the Geysers would eventually use them to supply a municipal utility right in the middle of PG&E's system.

In an attempt to further develop the project, Magma and Thermal sent Hansen to Larderello. The Italian installation had by now a production capacity of about 300 MW. Hansen spent time with Italian engineers discussing their experiences and problems, especially their experience with various metals and sealants.

On October 30, 1958, Magma and Thermal signed a contract to supply steam to PG&E for operation of a 12.5 MW power plant. PG&E was still cautious and initiated a search for a used generator. Although the pressure on the wells drilled in the 1920s had not diminished, PG&E was still concerned about the longevity of the steam. A used turbine was located in a Sacramento junkyard and reconditioned by General Electric using Hansen's notes from his Larderello visit. In early 1960, the plant known as PG&E No. 1 came on stream, with plans for a similar plant (PG&E No. 2) to commence operations in 1963.

As mentioned previously, PG&E's move may have been partially motivated by the desire to keep a large municipal utility system out of its service area. When PG&E No. 1 was contracted for, PG&E received the option on the use of all future Magma and Thermal steam production, thereby precluding the possibility for municipal development of the Geysers.

However once PG&E was motivated to seriously evaluate geothermal electric generation, it found it to be its lowest cost electric source. In 1957 PG&E had a 60-40 steam-hydro mix and new hydro sources were becoming both more difficult to find and more expensive to develop. With the rapid growth in PG&E's market area hydro's relative share was likely to continue to drop as expensive fossil fuel steam plants came into operation.

PG&E was also planning at that time to build a 180 MW nuclear power station at Dresden through the Nuclear Power Group, Inc., of which it was a member. The plant was estimated to cost $45 million or $250 per kW capacity. [7] In contrast, PG&E 1 and 2 at the Geysers had a combined capacity of 26 MW and a cost of $3.8 million or $146 per kW gross generating capacity. The Geysers also proved to be cheaper than PG&E's new fossil fuel plants. The 1959 fuel costs for producing steam were about 4 mills per kWh of electricity produced. Under the contract with Magma and Thermal, PG&E agreed to pay 2.5 mills per kWh generated from the steam of PG&E units 1 and 2.[8]

PG&E had the option to purchase future steam developed by Magma and Thermal, but they were not obligated to do so. While PG&E was continuing to design additional nuclear, hydro and fossil fuel projects, both Magma and Thermal felt PG&E should put a stronger emphasis on accelerating geothermal development. By 1963 Magma had proven a minimum power potential for the Geysers of 600 MW and with further drilling over the next year this minimum potential was increased to 1,000 MW. At this time Magma and Thermal had developed a total of 3,200,000 lbs/hr of steam, capable of producing 160 MW, but PG&E's plans through 1970 called for construction of only an additional 54 MW to the 26 MW already exploited with the first two units.

The problem was tactfully stated in Magma's 1965 shareholders'report:[9]

> We are endeavoring to have the Pacific Gas & Electric Co. accelerate the consumptive use of the present steam supply now available. We are confident that given such assurance of acceleration by Pacific Gas & Electric Co. we can continue to develop a minimum of 50,000 kW of power annually for many years from the area that can now be classified as proven geothermal steam land. This appraisal of increased steam supply could be accelerated beyond this volume if an additional drilling rig is used. The location of The Big Geysers property is only 80 miles from San Francisco, and there are no important problems of transmission of electricity into areas where the power demand is rapidly increasing. We believe that a constructive program can be developed with Pacific Gas & Electric Co. based upon their system requirements, of an accelerated utilization of the energy supply of The Big Geysers area.

Both Magma and Thermal were highly endebted and could not afford to develop capacity that would lie unutilized for at least six years. The cost of drilling wells ranged from $10'000 to $300'000 depending on depth and drilling formation and both companies had already borrowed extensively against future revenues. While Magma had already arranged borrowing against unit No. 1, no lender would provide funds against a cash flow that would not begin for at least six years.

If PG&E had made a firm commitment on accelerating production from the Geysers, Magma and Thermal felt they could have stepped up drilling and developed at least 150 MW annually. PG&E's moderately paced development of the Geysers was apparently based on continuing doubts about the longevity of the steam resources at the Geysers.

THE EMERGENCE OF A MODERN INDUSTRY

Until 1963 geothermal activity was largely confined
to the Geysers. Around that time Magma and Thermal started to broaden their geographical horizon. A number of
additional companies also began to enter the industry.[10]
Oil companies had already a foot in the industry because for over fifty years they had been finding hot
water while drilling for oil and gas. In many cases they
were still holding leases on these properties although
they had so far never planned exploiting the geothermal
energy. Standard Oil of California (Chevron) was the
first major oil company to actively enter the industry
although this was a rather accidental step. While drilling a 4,000 meter oil exploration well near Brawley,
California, Chevron encountered a sodium-chlorine brine
with a temperature of about 500°F (about 260°C). This
was a very unusual find among the oil company finds of
geothermal resources because of the exceptionally high
temperature involved.
Around the same time, Earth Energy, a division of
the Pure Oil Company, completed what they claimed was the
first well by a major U.S. oil company producing superheated steam.[11] Earth Energy planned to produce electricity with the steam and extract the chemicals found in
the associated brine for sale. Over the next two years
Pure's subsidiary became a major competitor of Magma and
Thermal, obtaining leases and drilling in the Imperial
Valley and Clear Lake regions of California and in Brady,
Nevada. In addition Pure began acquiring leases in the
Geysers region adjoining the Magma and Thermal properties.
The success of the Geysers established the potential
of geothermal resources, but as the industry broadened,
two major barriers to further development became simul-
taneously apparent. One was federal leasing policy; the
other was the need for further technological development.

Federal Leasing

64 percent of the acreage containing the most promising geothermal prospects outside the Geysers within the
Rocky Mountain and Pacific Coast areas are situated whol-
ly or partially on U.S. government owned land.[12] The federal government had no established policy for geothermal
leases in the mid 1960s. Companies therefore began taking
federal leases under the Mineral Leasing Act of 1920
hoping to convert these to geothermal leases if and when
a federal geothermal policy was established. This strategy was based on the logic that water, having a definite
chemical composition, was a mineral and that steam was a
mineral gas.

In 1964, Senator Alan Bible of Nevada introduced a
bill to address the issue of federal geothermal policy.
A modified version passed the Senate as S.1674 in 1965.
The bill was patterned after the Mineral Leasing Act of
1920 and allocated leases within 'Known Geothermal Resource Areas' (KGRA) by competitive bidding. The bill
called for a minimum 10 percent royalty to be paid to
the U.S. government based on the value of steam produced.
It limited each lease to 2,500 acres with a 51,000 acre
total limitation per company or individual within each
state. The bill also allowed the government to readjust
royalties at five year intervals. Although the bill passed both houses of Congress it was vetoed by President
Johnson in 1966.

The points of contention focused on the disposition
of claims filed prior to the bill, the 10 percent royalty minimum with a readjustment clause, and the acreage
limitations. The last point especially became increasingly important over the years.

Established geothermal companies, especially Magma
Power, felt they should have first right on leases in
areas where prior claims had been filed under existing
statutes. In both Brady, Nevada and Mammoth, California,
Magma had leased private land and had begun resource development on it with expenditures at Mammoth alone ap-
proaching $300'000. In both Brady and Mammoth the re-
source was largely situated on public lands and Magma had
established claims on these public lands adjoining their
private leases. Magma took the position that the value
of the leases on public lands was enhanced by Magma's
expenditures and development on adjoining private land
and that Magma should have priority in leases of adjacent
government properties.

In its 1965 recommendation on S.1674 the Interior
Department took exception to this view and presented the
administration viewpoint:[13]

> The Senate-passed bill, S.1674, also provides a pre-
> ference right or "grandfather clause" to those who,
> on January 1, 1965, were holders of valid mineral
> leases or permits or who filed valid mining claims.
> Such persons would have the right to convert such
> leases, permits, or claims to geothermal leases
> covering the same lands. In addition persons who
> were applicants on this date for mineral leases or
> permits may convert their applications for geother-
> mal leases and maintain the same filing date.

> We are convinced that it is good Federal policy to
> require that leases of the geothermal resources
> within Federal lands be issued only on the basis
> of competitive bidding. This requirement insures an
> objective consideration by which the fair market

value of the right to explore for and utilize this
resource may be obtained. There are undoubtedly numerous Federal areas where the potentialities of
geothermal steam development are known. In those
circumstances, we believe that it would not be in
the best interest of the United States to award a
lease to a particular individual based solely on the
fortuitous circumstance of his having filed the
first application therefore. Competitive leasing also would tend to promote actual development, with
concomitant economic gains to the West, in contra-
distinction to the acquisition and holding of leases
for possible appreciation of the value of the rights
derived from such a lease.

We believe that the preference right approach in S.
1674 will create substantial inequities. During
Senate hearings on this legislation, some people
testified that they had filed mining claims and applied for issuance of geothermal leases or the location of geothermal mining claims. We believe that
such mineral leases, mining claims, and mineral
lease applications should not be allowed to mature
into geothermal leases through this indirect, but
ingenious approach. We believe that a mineral lessee
and mining claimant now receives full fair value for
his lease and claims. He should not be awarded more.
The fortuitous or fortunate should not be rewarded
to the detriment of the less fortuitous or fortunate.

Established geothermal companies felt the administration's policy was running counter to its stated objective. With competitive leasing, companies with more
substantial resources could outbid undercapitalized geothermal firms for properties which had already been partially developed.
The royalty provision was also disputed, especially
the five-year adjustment provision. Companies felt they
needed a fixed royalty over at least 25 years to finance
exploration and field development.
The interface with federal policy therefore became
an increasingly difficult problem for the industry. Geothermal was not a high U.S. government priority. The
policy that was proposed treated geothermal as a hybrid
between an energy and a mineral resource and attempted
to fit the industry into existing institutions. The
acreage limitations, for example, were appropriate for
some minerals but inappropriate for a land-intensive
industry like geothermal. As shown in Table 7.1, the
2,500 acre limitation would have precluded even initial
development of a number of promising 'Known Geothermal

Resource Areas' (KGRA). In the Mono-Long Valley region
for example, an estimated 11,500 acres were required for
a 50 MW plant while in a number of other regions the
acreage requirements were even higher.

TABLE 7.1
'Known Geothermal Resource Areas' in the late 1970s.

Area	Acreage	Estimated capacity(MW)	Acres per 50 MW
Brawley	28,000	1,700-2,000	700
Coso Hot Springs	52,000	2,000	1,250
East Mesa	38,000	487	3,800
Herber	58,000	983	3,000
Lassen	79,000	133	30,000
Geysers	376,000	3,000	6,250
Mono-Long Valley	455,000	2,000	11,350
Salton Sea	96,000	2,800	1,680
Surprise Valley	72,000	150-200	18,000
Alvord	176,000	300	28,750
Raft River	30,000	100	15,000
Vale Hot Springs	23,000	500	2,300
Beowawe	33,000	500-1,000	1,650
Brady Hot Springs	98,000	1,000	5,000
Cove Fort-Sulfurdale	24,000	500-1,500	1,200
Roosevelt Hot Springs	30,000	500-1,000	1,500
Steamboat Springs	9,000	200	2,200
Thermo	26,000	50	26,000
Valles Caldera	168,000	1,500	5,500

Source: U.S. Senate (1979).

It seems that throughout the discussions on these
three points participants failed to ever come to an understanding that geothermal was a unique resource distinct
from oil, gas, and minerals and which therefore required
new solutions. Of course the geothermal industry did not
consistently argue for solving contentious issues in new
ways. In the area of taxation the industry argued hard
for being allowed to benefit from the same favorable tax
treatment enjoyed by the oil, gas and uranium industries.
The geothermal industry wanted to have the right to deduct intangible drilling costs and to reduce tax liabili-
ty with a percentage depletion allowance. The Internal
Revenue Service (IRS) denied these rights but was chal-
lenged by Magma and Thermal. The U.S. Court of Appeals
ruled in 1969 in favor of the companies, defining geothermal steam as a gas. The IRS disputed this ruling and
the issue remained a point of contention and uncertainty
until 1978 when the companies' viewpoint finally won. Of
course the uncertainty had a negative effect on the

companies'willingness to invest in geothermal power development.

Technological Barriers

The Imperial Valley discoveries by Chevron and Pure generated interest in the valley as an important geothermal region. However unlike the Geysers, the Imperial Valley discoveries were hot water resources, not steam, and contained high concentrations of dissolved corrosive solids.

The Geysers' technology was relatively simple due to its dry (or superheated) steam resource. Among the diverse geothermal resources known in the U.S., dry steam is the simplest to exploit for electricity production. Steam is directly piped through collector lines into the turbine. The spent steam is then evaporated from the plants cooling towers or reinjected into the reservoir.[14]

With a liquid-dominated system as found in the Imperial Valley a flash steam or binary cycle plant was required. In a flash steam plant geothermal fluids are brought to the surface under pressure. The pressure is reduced above ground to allow a portion of the fluid to flash to steam which drives the turbine.

In a binary cycle plant, the brine is pumped through a heat exchanger to heat a secondary fluid which in turn powers the turbine. The major advantage of the binary cycle is that the working fluids in the turbine are noncorrosive. The brine is confined under pressure and reinjected after passing through the heat exchanger.

Neither the flash steam nor the binary cycle systems were complex concepts. But neither had been demonstrated as a commercially viable technology. Demonstration required the construction of a small pilot plant, which, if successful, would be the forerunner of a commercial scale generating facility. In the mid 1960s there was not sufficient interest to arrange outside equity financing nor were government funds available for the development of liquid-dominated resources.

The Aborted Industry Development of the 1960s

The presidential veto of the geothermal leasing act and the technological barriers preventing development of water-dominated resources brought the flurry of activity of the early 1960s to an end. Development of the most promising KGRAs required a federal leasing policy and companies were reluctant to prove and develop a resource without assurance of continuing full control over the use of the resource.

In 1965, Pure Oil and its geothermal subsidiary Earth Energy, were acquired by Union Oil of California. Union was primarily interested in Pure's oil operations,

but they maintained Pure's commitment to geothermal with
continued drilling and leasing programs.

Pure had obtained extensive leases in the Geysers
and in 1967 Union agreed to merge its Geysers holdings
with the Magma and Thermal joint venture. Union took over
existing operations and future steam development. Union
was obliged to spend $1.75 million on development with
costs split 50-50 between Union and the joint venture of
Magma and Thermal thereafter. The agreement also specified that the first 200 MW of capacity belonged to Magma
and Thermal, the second 200 MW would be shared equally,
and the third 200 MW belonged to Union. Beyond this all
capacity would be shared equally.[15]

Although Magma and Thermal relinquished a valuable
asset, the deal freed especially Magma to pursue the development of new ventures. They would continue to receive
all revenues from existing power plants, but would be
freed from a major part of the expenditures for developing new capacity in the Geysers field. To further improve its cash position, Magma Power formed a new company in the late 1960s assigning a number of leases to
the new entity. Magma maintained control and sold a minority interest to the public to raise capital. While the
new firm, Magma Energy, paralleled many of the activities
of its parent company, its major new thrust was the development and demonstration of the binary cycle technology.

By this time it seemed unlikely that another vapor
dominated resource like the Geysers would be discovered
and industry entrepreneurs felt geothermal's future depended on the development of non-vapor resources and of
the technologies to exploit them. Magma's initial investment in the Geysers had been a high risk-high return
situation and the company continued with its entrepreneural philosophy by exchanging interest in a proven
operation for the riskier opportunity to develop new resources and the required technologies.

Federal Policies of the 1970s

The federal leasing issue was finally resolved in
1970 with the passage of the Geothermal Steam Act. The
Department of the Interior was given the authority to
issue leases for the development and utilization of geothermal resources on federal lands. In designing a leasing program, the Interior Department was given the conflicting goals of insuring orderly and timely resource
development, protecting the environment, and receiving
a fair market value for disposing of the government's
resources.

As enacted, the Act proved to be a compromise on the
issues debated during the 1960s. Leases were limited to
2.560 acres and were issued for an initial ten years

with a forty year renewal if geothermal steam production
had begun. The emerging leasing program closely paralleled federal oil and gas leasing policies. The Bureau of
Land Management (BLM) was responsible for approving and
issuing leases and for environmental assessment--respon-
sibilities the BLM also held for federal oil and gas
leasing. The competitive bidding for KGRA leases was
similar to the competitive bidding for oil and gas leases
that lie near known productive fields.

Although the 1970 Act became law in 1970, the first
competitive leases were not offered until 1974. No federal agency or office was given the responsibility to promote geothermal development and implementing the Act required years of coordination between the various federal
agencies. In May 1979, nine years after passage of the
Geothermal Steam Act, only 20 percent of the land in
federal KGRAs had been leased. Bureaucratic delays were
even longer in the case of non-competitive lease allocations. Only 19 of the 1,181 applications filed with
the BLM and the forest service of California had been
approved by the middle of 1979.

Another problem with the 1970 Act was the acreage
limitation. In an exceptional area a 50 MW plant might
require only 500 acres, but a more typical resource
would require 5,000 to 25,000 acres as had been shown in
Table 7.1. The 2,560 acre limitation precluded companies
from drilling a $400,000 exploratory well (a typical
4,000 ft. well) because they would be unlikely to have
adequate acreage to develop a commercial-sized plant.

The state limitation of 20,480 acres for any individual, association, or corporation was also a point of
contention. The industry felt this was too restrictive
in promising states such as Nevada and California. In
addition the 1970 Act allowed a family of four to lease
four times more acreage than a corporation. This led to
a situation where in 1979 members of one Texas family
held almost 100,000 acres of federal leases in Nevada
while corporations such as Chevron and Magma operated
under the 20,480 acre limitation.[16]

The Geothermal Loan Guaranty Program (GLGP) established in 1974 was the first federal program in support
of the geothermal industry. Given the risks involved in
geothermal projects, companies in the industry were rarely able to arrange debt financing for their projects.
GLGP provided a federal guarantee for loans on geothermal
projects up to $25 million. The loans were provided by
private commercial banks, but the federal government
guaranteed repayment to the banks if a project proved unsuccessful.

The GLGP was an innovative program in that it provided funds to the industry without direct outlay of federal funds. Banks received market interest rates on their
loans which were essentially risk-free due to the guaran-

tee. The federal government evaluated loan applications and could screen out projects of questionable economic viability, reducing the probability of loan defaults.

As with other federal programs, the program took time to implement, but by yearend 1978 $24 million in loans had been approved. Six months later this figure had increased to $43 million with four applications for another $65 million under review.

The federal government had failed to provide R&D funding for geothermal energy developments until the mid 1970s. Indirect funding of some extent came through projects supported by the National Science Foundation and the U.S. Geological Survey. A number of universities also sponsored projects by their geology or engineering departments which relied directly or indirectly on federal funds. These projects, however, were allocated less than half a percent of the Energy Research and Development Administration's (ERDA) 1975 budget.

In 1976, geothermal fared somewhat better capturing 1 percent of ERDA's budget. This compared with an allocation of 2.6 percent for solar and 55 percent for nuclear. The Carter administration continued to increase geothermal appropriations but they were far outdistanced by the increases in solar R&D. From near equal footing in 1975, ERDA's solar budget grew to $258 million in 1977 while 1977 geothermal outlays totalled only $53 million.[17]

The Development of a Two-tier Industry, 1970-1979

With the passage of the 1970 Act and the first Arab oil embargo in the early 1970s, a number of new companies entered the geothermal industry. Major oil companies such as Phillips, Getty, Occidental and Aminoil joined Chevron and Union by establishing geothermal divisions. In addition numerous small geothermal companies were established during the late 1960s to early 1970s.[18]

The rise in energy prices during the mid 1970s increased the potential rewards for geothermal energy production. A number of companies, particularly oil companies, allocated resources toward demonstration plants for resource discoveries outside the Geysers. Smaller independent firms began designing direct use projects such as geothermal residential space heating, food dehydration and geothermal greenhouses.

Magma Power had been working on a binary technology since the late 1960s. With internally generated funds, they began construction of an 11 MW dual binary plant in Southern California's Imperial Valley. In total, construction on six plants ranging from 10 to 50 MW was initiated using both the flash and binary technologies. Magma and Union each developed two plants while Chevron and Republic Geothermal developed the others. In addition flash plants outside California were startet by Union and

Phillips.
        The commitment to demonstrating geothermal technolo-
gies was largely attributable to the rapid increase in
the utilities marginal fuel costs. At the Geysers the
price of steam was linked to PG&E's prior year oil and
nuclear costs. As shown in Table 7.2 the Geysers' steam
price escalated rapidly after 1974. Although steam prices

TABLE 7.2
Price of Steam in The Geysers, 1969-1981, in mills per kWh

Year	Price	Year	Price	Year	Price
1969	2.65	1974	3.73	1979	17.08
1970	2.64	1975	7.39	1980	18.63
1971	2.74	1976	11.35	1981	27.76
1972	2.90	1977	14.10		
1973	3.15	1978	16.05		

Source: DiPippo (1980), Natomas Annual Report (1980).

are negotiated for each site, they are generally based
on principles similar to the Geysers contract.
        Under Union's management, the installed capacity at
the Geysers jumped from 78 MW in 1970 to 396 MW by yearend 1973.[19] This confirmation of geothermal's potential
coincided with the first Arab oil embargo and led to a
strong increase in drilling activity and renewed determination to develop non-vapor geothermal sites.
        In 1974, Natomas, an international oil company,
purchased Thermal Power from public stockholders for
$33 million. Thermal's main asset was a 25 percent in-
terest in the Geysers, giving Union and Natomas a combined 75 percent share, with Magma holding the remaining
25 percent.[20]
        The increased engagement of oil companies and the
entrance of new, small enterprises into the industry have
shaped a two-tiered industry structure. Oil and gas companies make up the first tier of the industry. They had
exploration and drilling expertise and the financial resources to support these activities. Oil companies tended
to conduct their leasing and exploration activities with
the aim of identifying a resource capable of sustaining
an electric power plant of at least 50 MW.
        The second tier of the industry is characterized by
independent entrepreneurs. With limited capital resources, these small companies have generally been unable to
compete in bidding auctions for sites with electric
potential. Over the period from early 1974 to the middle
of 1975, federal leases showing promise for electric
generation received an average high bid of $1,104 per
acre. With a typical lease in excess of 1,000 acres,

these properties are beyond the reach of small entrepreneural firms. Instead second tier companies have either
acquired unproven acreage where wildcat drilling is required or took leases on land in KGRA's with an estimated
temperature of less than 300°F (150°C). Leases in the
latter areas are dramatically less expensive, costing as
little as $11 per acre if no discovery well exists.[21]
 The segmentation of the industry into two tiers became almost complete in 1981 when Natomas purchased
Magma's 25 percent interest in the Geysers for $400 mil-
lion. This transaction gave major oil companies almost
95 percent of existing U.S. geothermal generating capacity.

CONCLUSION

 California's geothermal generating capacity today
is over 1,3000 MW. It is expected to reach 2,700 MW by
1987. Ninety percent of this capacity is and will be situated at the Geysers, where PG&E is the exclusive user
of geothermal steam. The Geysers are presently supplying
about 10 percent of PG&E's system requirements for North
and Central California.
 The successful establishment of the industry was
largely attributable to the determination and tenacity
of entrepreneurs. Early investors in Magma Power were
willing to provide equity capital on the basis of
McCabe's strong belief in geothermal's potential and his
determination to develop the Geysers. The geothermal industry, like any new private venture, required an entrepreneur with the ability to convince investors of the
industry's potential and with the marketing capabilities
to establish a market niche.
 The industry also benefited from the location of the
Geysers on private land and from equity markets during
the late 1950s which were favorable for new ventures.
Magma Power was thus able to establish geothermal's credibility without awaiting the determination of a federal
geothermal leasing policy and the provision of financial
support by the federal government.
 Geothermal development was hampered by PG&E's initially neutral view of geothermal's potential. Engineering studies always seemed to conclude that geothermal
was a competitive source of energy. But the utility was
concerned about the risks involved in utilizing a new
and unproven technology. They were particularly worried
about the longevity of the steam supply. Unfortunately
PG&E did not have the in-house staff to assess this
concern. Magma's marketing strategy was to minimize this
risk and to stress geothermal's cost effectiveness. The
hint that other utilities could become involved in the
utilization of the geothermal potential at the Geysers

184

should PG&E continue to decline its use was also helpful
in bringing about the decision to go ahead with the first
power plant.

However, Magma failed to convince PG&E to fully exploit its option and to expand electricity production at
a rate which was commensurate with the expansion of capacity and proven geothermal reserves. This reluctance an-
noyed Magma because the resource was PG&E's least-cost
source of energy and because this behavior saddled Magma
with substantial investments which failed to produce a
return. PG&E simply did not have confidence in Magma. The
utility changed its behavior once Union Oil took over
from Magma and began to manage the whole Geysers development including existing operations. PG&E apparently felt
comfortable working together with Union Oil. It considered it an experienced, competent, and professionally run
company, something PG&E never felt about the entrepreneurial newcomer which Magma was. In addition, Union's involvement gave credibility to the geothermal concept.

One of the most significant barriers to the expansion of the geothermal industry has been the inability
of the federal government to institute a strong, unified
geothermal policy. Definite federal leases to geothermal
areas were handed out for the first time in 1974. Most
industry participants believe that the present leasing
terms are too restrictive and that applications under the
new regime have been subject to excessive processing delays.

Both the Geothermal Loan Guarantee Program and Federal R&D funding during the late 1970s have been favorably
received by the industry. A number of programs which
could not have obtained private sector financing were
funded under these programs. This is particularly important since geothermal has had neither strong corporate
nor public interest group backing, placing the industry
on weak footing for the competition with nuclear, solar
and other energy technologies for federal R&D funding.

Yet even by the late 1980s, geothermal's contribution to total energy supply is unlikely to be significant
outside of PG&E's service area. Industry growth outside
the Geysers area will depend on the development and demonstration of cost-effective technologies for the exploitation of the corrosive hot water deposits.

ABBREVIATIONS

BLM   Bureau of Land Management
ERDA   Energy Research and Development Administration
GDC   Geothermal Development Company
GLGP   Geothermal Loan Guaranty Program
IRS   Internal Revenue Service
KGRA   Known Geothermal Resource Area

PG&E   Pacific Gas and Electric
R&D   Research and Development

NOTES

1. U.S. Senate (1979).
2. Geothermal energy contributed 0.5 percent to
California's primary energy supply in 1975.
3. This section is based on reports which have appeared in the newspaper published in Healdsburg called
the Healdsburg Enterprise during the period December 3,
1920 to April 2, 1925.
4. DiPippo (1980) gives a detailed description of
the geology of geothermal steam.
5. Decius (1924).
6. Thermal Power was a company especially formed to
provide new capital for further geothermal development
and to hold a 50 percent share in the Geysers leases.
Thermal Power's stock was controlled by the company's
president. Magma remained operator of the leases. But
Magma and Thermal acted for all practical purposes as a
joint venture with respect to the Geysers, as well as
other leases acquired elsewhere subsequently.
7. Moody's Utility Manual, 1958.
8. A mill is one hundreth of a cent.
9. The information here on Magma is drawn from
Magma Power Company's annual reports for the years 1964
to 1967. The passage is taken from the 1965 report.
10. The information on recent industry development
is coming from a number of interviews with involved persons in industry and government.
11. Pure Oil News (1965, Winter Supplement).
12. U.S. Senate (1979).
13. U.S. Senate (1965).
14. DiPippo (1980).
15. The $1.75 million which Union Oil agreed to in-
vest were largely sufficient to finance the development
of the agreed upon 600 MW of steam capacity. Magma-Ther-
mal therefore avoided to have to pay its 50 percent share
of the development costs for some time to come.
16. These issues were once again addressed in 1979
in two Senate bills which were combined in the Omnibus
Geothermal Energy Development and Commercialization Act.
The bill died however as the industry, the administration
and the Senate were unable to come to agreement. A critical issue was once again the tendency to classify geothermal with oil and gas on leasing and royalty policies,
and its grouping with solar and wind energy in terms of
'alternative energy' tax credits and R&D funding.
   The dominant political view during the Carter administration was supportive of renewable energy technologies. The oil industry in contrast was hit by the new

Windfall Profits Tax. Geothermal escaped this tax, but the political climate would not allow an easing of lease and royalty terms for an extractive energy industry.

17. Tax credits for geothermal were included in the Energy Security Act of 1979. In addition, geothermal's R&D allocation from ERDA continued to increase through 1979.

18. Information from the annual reports of Natomas Corporation, 1974 to 1980, and of Union Oil of California for 1976 to 1980 has been used here in addition to information gained through interviews.

19. PG&E continued to exercise its options for all the steam produced. The utility has remained up to today the exclusive user of Geysers steam.

20. The sale of Thermal was linked to the death of its main shareholder.

21. Leases without discovery wells but temperatures above 300°F (150°C) were going for $30 in the average. The data is given in McNamara (1979) and is based on 613 lease sales.

BIBLIOGRAPHY

Bruce, Albert 1961 "Experience Generating Geothermal Power at the Geysers..." Paper for the U.N. Conference on New Sources of Energy, August 21-23, Rome, Italy.
Decius, L. C. 1924 "Geological Reconnaissance of the Area in the Vicinity of the Geysers, Sulphur Creek, Sonoma County, California." (mimeo)
DiPippo, Ronald 1980 Geothermal Energy as a Source of Electricity. Washington, D. C.: Government Printing Office.
McNamara, Jack 1979 "A Preliminary Analysis of the High Bids at Geothermal Lease Sales..." (Reprinted in U.S. Senate, 1979).
Petroleum Information Corporation, 1979 The Geothermal Resource. Denver.
U.S. Senate 1965 "Hearing before the Subcommittee on Minerals, Materials, and Fuels...on S. 1674." Washington, D. C.: Government Printing Office.
U.S. Senate 1970 "Hearings before the Subcommittee on Minerals, Materials, and Fuels...on S. 368." Washington, D. C.: Government Printing Office.
U.S. Senate 1979 "Hearings before the Subcommittee on Energy Resources and Materials Production...on S. 1388." Washington, D. C.: Government Printing Office.

8
Wood for Industrial Energy in Northern New England

Mark Diffenderfer

Wood is a readily available, albeit finite, resource throughout northern New England. It also has a long history of use specifically as an energy resource. For the earliest settlers of the area, wood was probably the sole source of fuel. Along with wind and water, wood provided a solid foundation for the early stages of the industrial revolution. It provided charcoal for foundries,[1] steam for engines, and heat for homes and buildings.

However, by 1870 wood was surpassed by coal as the primary fuel for industrial use. While it continued as an important source of home heating well into the. 20th century, it was rapidly displaced by the introduction of inexpensive, labor-free oil heat. By the time of the 1973-1974 oil crisis, wood was burned in only about 1 percent of the homes in Vermont, one of the most rural and forested states in the United States.[2]

Today, however, we are witnessing a phenomenal re-emergence of the use of wood as an energy resource. Most people are aware of the extensive growth in residential consumption. By the winter of 1978-1979, 46 percent of all housholds in Maine and 43 percent of all households in New Hampshire and Vermont were heating with wood. Approximately 20 percent of the households in these northern states were obtaining more than half of their heat from wood. Even more significantly, there is an increasing tendency to burn this wood in efficient, air tight stoves rather than open fireplaces. Between the winter of 1976-1977 and 1978-1979, the amount of

---

Mark Diffenderfer is a Ph.D. candidate in the Department of Sociology and Anthropology at the University of New Hampshire.

wood burned in air tight stoves increased by an average
of 24 percent in these three states, while the volume
burned in fireplaces declined by an average of almost 48
percent. By the winter of 1978-1979, the wood burned by
households in northern New England provided about 8.9
million BTU's of heat energy, displacing almost 163
million gallons of oil. Furthermore, in New Hampshire
and Vermont 11 percent of all household heat was obtained from wood, while in Maine the figure is 9 percent.[3]

Certainly wood has begun once again to provide a
significant contribution to residential energy consumption of the region. Many people, however, do not realize that there has been a corresponding increase in industrial use of wood for energy purposes. While this
growth has not been nearly as extensive, it is becoming
significant. Today there are 150 wood burning enterprises in northern New England. Many of these enterprises are in industries that have traditionally burned
their wood waste -- the paper related industries, for
example. But many other industries have also begun to
change to wood use. And even among the traditional
users, new techniques are being employed to make a more
efficient use of our forest resources.

There are many factors, both positive and negative,
which are affecting this rejuvenation of wood burning in
the industrial sector of the economy. As opposed to the
residential sphere, where considerations of family security, independence, and environmental well-being interact with economic feasibility, the primary motivation
for adoption in the industrial sphere is economic. But
many additional variables impact on economic feasibility.
These include environmental and geographical conditions
which affect wood availability and transportation, technological developments, economic incentives provided
through tax programs, political legislation, the availability of information, and the behavior of other actors
in the system (bankers, ecologists, suppliers, etc.).

This paper is divided into two parts. First, there
will be a general discussion of those factors which tend
to enhance as well as deter the adoption of wood energy
systems. This is designed as a broad overview with the
intent to provide background information. Secondly, a
series of brief case studies will address more specific
issues concerning feasibility, the effect of various
programs on the adoption of wood, and the techniques
used by several industries to overcome difficulties.

While this paper will not be able to address the economic practicality of adopting wood for energy in specific industries, it should at least make potential adopters aware of what factors need to be considered. In
addition, by showing what has been done and needs to be
done in northern New England, it should provide insights
for decision makers in other areas who wish to develop a

coherent policy to facilitate wood use.

GENERAL INSTITUTIONAL CONSTRAINTS

Many problems are posed by the adoption of wood-burning technologies in industry. The primary difficulties faced by large users are the availability of supplies, storage and handling, financing, and meeting government regulations. For some small industries, the systems being developed still face technical problems.

On the other hand, there are many incentives for the adoption of woodfired energy systems. Its economic advantages are enhanced by tax policies and other programs designed to make use more appealing.

Environmental and Geographic Considerations

Availability. While there are many environmental and geographic conditions affecting the use of wood, the primary concern must be its mere availability. For some industrial users, there is a sufficient quantity of wood waste available on site to meet all of their energy needs. The small sawmills and furniture factories as well as the large paper and lumber companies currently make extensive use of bark, wood, and wood-derived black liquor (from the pulping process) to generate steam and, in some cases, electricity. But when we begin to consider the massive, centralized, electrical generating facilities currently being developed, wood availability is a more serious problem. We must concern ourselves with whether or not sufficient wood exists as well as with the impacts which its harvesting will have on the environment.

In general, New England, especially northern New England, is ideally suited for the wood energy alternative. For example, fully 90 percent of the state of Maine is forested. However, a number of industries -- notably the lumber, paper, and now energy-related industries -- are utilizing the forest resources although they do not necessarily compete for the same parts of the forest. In fact, the wood used for energy purposes tends to be low grade trees and residues which are not used by other industries or are left behind by their harvesters. Studies of potential sites of large facilities have usually found that there is sufficient wood available to fire plants for decades.[4]

However, long term availability is not the only problem. There are periods during the year -- after strong storms or during the spring thaw -- when the woods are inaccessible. Some method of storing large quantities of wood or otherwise assuring supplies for those periods (which, during the spring may last for four to six weeks) must be developed.

Environmental Concerns. While wood is a renewable resource, to assure supplies over generations we must take
into consideration the environmental impacts of current
policies. Many people have expressed concern over the
effect which practices such as whole tree harvesting,
clear cutting, or removal of forest residue will have on
soil nutrients. These are important considerations which
need to be addressed.

To the extent that harvesting is limited to the removal of low grade trees from the woods, the impact will
probably be negligible. As long as trees still stand in
the area, nutrients will be returned to the soil from
the leaves and needles. In fact, with proper forest management, this practice can actually enhance the growth
of the rest of the stand in much the same way that weed-
ing a garden enhances its yield.

The impact of whole tree harvesting and clear cutting
is more questionable. The leaves and twigs of trees contain a disproportionately high concentration of nutrients.
In addition, decaying wood provides locations for nitrogen fixation. Whole tree harvesting alone will have some
negligible impact, but if other trees are left in the
area, the annual fall of leaves will replace many of the
lost nutrients. When whole tree harvesting is combined
with clear cutting, the potential impacts are more serious. Most likely the effects will not show up until
the third or fourth generation. Some people argue that
when nutrition becomes a problem, we can begin to ferti-
lize. However, we should proceed with caution in this
area. Economic considerations alone may make fertiliza-
tion much less practical in a few decades. Careful
forest management practices are probably a more desirable alternative.

There are also other environmental concerns. Increased clear cutting could result in more non-point
sources of water pollution,[5] leading in particular to
erosion and water eutrophication. If clear cutting is to
be employed, it should be limited to relatively small
parcels. (Burlington Electric, for example, restricts
its suppliers by contract to clear cuts of no greater
than 12 acres, although in practice the clause has not
been used at all.)

Another problem involves the disposal of ash residue.
A 50 MW plant produces roughly 80 tons of wood ash per
day. Because of the concentration of heavy metals, care
must be taken in locating disposal sites. Improper disposal could result in contamination of water supplies.
An alternative to landfills is the use of the ash as a
fertilizer.

Finally, we must be concerned that the forests remain
suitable for wildlife and recreation. Once again,

extensive clear cutting could have negative consequences. However, selective thinning and removal of waste wood can actually enhance the forests.

Technology

In most instances, there are few if any technological problems associated with wood burning. For the most part, it is an established field and a great deal of experience has been gained. Even a technology such as co-generation, which many people regard as a recent innovation, has been in use since the 1880s.

However, there are two situations where technology plays a key role. The first is in those relatively new technologies such as fluidized bed burners or gasifiers. These are relatively recent innovations. As such, they have not yet been adopted by very many companies and their net contribution is negligible. Since they have not been widely used, they still have a few technical problems which must be solved. These do not appear to be insurmountable and more experience with the systems should tend to alleviate them. These considerations will be discussed in more detail in later sections.

The second way in which technology is important is through its ability to overcome environmental and geographic constraints. This may include the way in which technology facilitates the harvesting and the subsequent transportation of wood products. The ability to harvest large amounts of wood has been increased by the development of chip harvesters (which make it possible to use more of the tree) and feller bunchers.

There is also need for a good road net. Chips are transported in trucks having a gross weight of 40 tons. These necessitate sturdy roads which hold up during the thaw and bridges strong enough to support the trucks. In addition, the vans must be able to come to within a half mile of the cutting site. The road network at the delivery site must also be able to handle the increased truck traffic. A 50 MW plant will require approximately 105 truck loads per day. This averages out to fifteen oneway trips per hour or one every four minutes. This amount of traffic could have a significant impact on many areas.

Again, we must remember that these latter factors pertain only to the large, centralized facilities. These potentially negative factors should be considered because they play a very important role in site location. Otherwise they could easily turn into a deterrent to the further expansion of wood use.

Economic Considerations

Wood Prices and Operating Cost. Given the availability of wood, the strongest factor operating in favor of the adoption of wood energy systems is their economic advantage. While prices vary, wood chips can be harvested and delivered up to fifty miles away at a cost of $15 to $20 per ton.⁶ At $15, wood chips yield a cost of $2.71 per million BTU. Number 6 fuel oil, on the other hand, at $.65 per gallon, yields a cost of $5.42 per million BTU.

Such a cost comparison, however, is oversimplified. Significant increases in wood use for energy purposes are likely to drive up prices in the face of a relatively unelastic supply unless care is taken to spatially separate potentially significant users of wood chips. In addition, the operation and maintenance costs for a wood-fired system are twice as high as for oil or coal systems. This is due to the increased handling, the need for more equipment such as induced draft fans, and more labor. Costs may be decreased through greater automation or by retrofitting existing boilers. In addition, a variety of taxes and economic incentives act to reduce costs and facilitate adoption.

Federal Taxes. The Energy Tax Act of 1978 provides incentives for conversion by allowing industries an investment tax credit for converting from oil or gas to wood boilers. Tax credits are a greater incentive than a deduction since the amount of the credit is deducted directly from the taxes which a company owes. In this case, the credit includes both the normal 10 percent investment tax credit as well as an additional 10 percent credit for investment in a technology which displaces oil. Wood fuel handling equipment and air pollution controls are also entitled to this credit as "alternative energy property". The act allows for an accelerated depreciation allowance on oil or coal burners which are retired early by the transition.

State Taxes. Vermont is the only state to allow a property tax exemption for "alternative energy systems" but this is limited to electrical generating equipment. Maine offers a personal property tax exemption for forest products (logs, pulpwood, wood chips, and lumber). In addition, all three states exempt air pollution control equipment from property taxes by not including it in the assessed value of the property.

New Hampshire has no sales tax, and both Maine and Vermont exempt fuelwood sold for residential heating from these taxes. The sale of the equipment to burn the wood, however, is not exempted. In addition, Maine grants a tax-exempt status to the sale of air pollution

equipment and both Maine and Vermont give tax exemptions
for the sale of electricity (but only up to 750 kWh of
residential electricity in Maine). Finally, Vermont offers an income tax credit of 25 percent or $3000 (which-
ever is less) on the installation of renewable energy
systems.

Public Utilities Regulatory Policy Act. Prior to the
enactment of the Public Utilities Regulatory Policy
Act (PURPA) in 1978, a number of obstacles deterred the
adoption of cogeneration or other small scale electrical
power technologies.[7] These obstacles were: (1) utilities
were not required to purchase the electricity at reasonable rates; (2) some utilities charged excessive rates
for back-up services; and (3) there was the possibility
that cogenerators or other small power producers could
be considered electrical utilities, thus becoming subject to state and federal regulations. The PURPA legislation requires the utilities to purchase electricity
at rates which are reasonable, in the public interest,
and which do not discriminate against small scale producers. In addition, utilities must provide back-up
service at reasonable rates, and cogenerators or other
small producers are exempted from state and federal regulations concerning financing and rates.

Rates are to be set by the state Public Utility Com-
missions. They are designed to reflect the incremental
costs to the utility, defined as the cost of the electricity which would otherwise be generated by the utility or purchased from other sources.[8] In New Hampshire,
the rate which has been set for the sale of electricity
to the utility is .082 per kWh. When compared to the
rate of .065 per kWh which a consumer pays for electricity, the extent to which this is an incentive becomes
patently obvious. While ra es are not nearly as high in
Maine and Vermont ($.05 and $.078 respectively), they
still offer a substantial economic incentive to cogeneration.

Why would an individual be paid more for electricity
by the utility than it would have to pay in return? The
reason is that by encouraging cogeneration and small
scale electrical production, the utilities avoid the
costs of building new plants (which would yield more
expensive electricity) and also avoid using expensive
foreign oil (particularly in New England). Thus the
rate reflects the ability to avoid these otherwise
higher than normal costs.

Financing. In a survey of 100 potential industrial
users of wood-fired systems,[9] lack of financing was
listed as a major obstacle to conversion. There are
two factors contributing to this problem. The first is
the high cost of money. Current interest rates prohibit

many investments, not just energy-related investments.
In addition, bankers are hesitant to make loans to wood-
fired facilities. They are skeptical that wood supplies
can be maintained. Furthermore, they do not believe that
wood-fired systems compare favorably on a capital cost
basis with oil systems.

This problem could potentially limit the wood energy
industry. A number of steps should be taken to ease the
problem. First, there should be increased attempts at
demonstrating the sustainability of biomass by refining
techniques used to inventory these supplies. Secondly,
regional solar centers should employ financial consultants to aid industries in cost analysis.[10] Finally,
low-cost government loans or loan guarantees might be
used to facilitate adoption.

Insurance. Wood-fired boilers are subject to the
same insurance requirements as other boilers. However,
since rates are determined by the degree of risk perceived by inspectors, wood boiler owners should be aware
that rates may be higher since fuel and handling equipment pose different problems.

Governmental Legislation

Many of the preceding considerations are in essence
political decisions. The federal government continually
intervenes in the market through the use of international
trade policies, purchases, and, in the above instances,
through the implementation of tax policies designed to
assist certain industries. The government also intervenes in the market by attempting to control externalities -- those factors not subject to traditional market
forces such as pollution regulations. Such attempts are
normally regarded as deterrents to adoption but may,
nevertheless, be imperative. While these regulations
are extensive, a brief overview will be presented.

Federal Air Pollution Legislation. The burning of
wood produces a variety of emissions including sulfur
dioxide, nitrogen oxides, carbon monoxide, hydrocarbons,
and particulate matter. The sulfer emissions from wood
tend to be very low in comparison to coal and most oil.
Particulate emissions, however, are high in comparison
to oil. In practice, it is particulate emissions which
pose a problem.[11]

The Clean Air Act establishes national ambient air
quality standards as well as emission standards for hazardous pollutants. Air quality designations are based
on individual pollutants. States must report to regional offices whether areas within their region are in
attainment or non-attainment of federal standards.

Depending upon the designation as an attainment or

non-attainment area, different regulations are applied.
In an attainment area, industries are subject to Prevention of Significant Deterioration (PSD) regulations.
These attainment areas are further divided into three
classes. Class I regions are subject to strict regulation. Class III regions may have significant increases
in emissions. The majority of regions in New England
are Class III which allows for moderate emission increases.

In an attainment area, if a plant has the potential
to emit less than 250 tons per year of any pollutant, it
is not subject to federal regulation. It then needs to
meet only state requirements in order to obtain a permit.
Plants emitting more than 250 tons per year are subject
to PSD review. If the plant will emit no more than 50
tons with controls, it is subject to a one-stage review
involving a public notice. If a plant will emit more
than 50 tons per year with controls (or will affect a
Class I area), it is subject to a two-stage review and
it must employ the best available control technology
(BACT). It may also be subject to continuous monitoring.

In non-attainment areas, if a facility will emit no
more than 100 tons per year, it is subject only to state
regulations. If it will emit more than this amount, but
less than 50 tons with controls, it may obtain a permit.
If it will emit more than 50 tons per year with controls,
it must meet lowest achievable emission rate (LAER)
guidelines.

In New England, these guidelines have not proven to be
a significant deterrent. With current technology, 50
MW plants can keep emissions below 40 tons per year even
when fired only by bark.

State Air Pollution Regulations. In Vermont, the only New England state with its own standards for wood
burning, any facility with a capacity of greater than
90 horsepower is required to apply for a license. Any
plant which will not emit more than 100 tons of sulfur
dioxide, particulates, or hydrocarbons or more than
1000 tons of carbon monoxide shall be notified within
thirty days of its status. Otherwise, it must go through
a more intricate review procedure.

In Maine, any fuel-burning equipment with an output
of ten million BTU per hour must apply for a license. If
it will emit more than 100 tons, it must go through a
review procedure.

In New Hampshire, any wood boiler system must acquire
a permit. If it will emit more than 150 tons per year
of any pollutant, it is subject to review. Otherwise,
it must only establish that it meets emission limits.

National Forests Management Act.[12]   The National
Forests Management Act is the result of a suit which was
brought against the United States Forest Service for a
decision which allowed clear cutting. As a result of the
act, the Forest Service is required to conduct periodic
assessments of forest resources, analyzing the projected
supply of and demand for renewable resources. This analysis is required to take into consideration both tangible and intangible benefits.

Safety Regulations. The Occupational Safety and
Health Administration (OSHA) has established safety procedures for all steam boilers. For any boiler that operates at a pressure of greater than fifteen pounds per
square inch, an engineer must be on site. There must be
provisions for back-up systems in the event of a malfunction in any automatic equipment. In practice, most
systems converting to wood boilers already have oil or
coal boilers so there is no need for additional personnel.
In the following section, we will examine how these
factors have affected wood use in the four applications
for electricity and steam generation, cogeneration, and
gasification. We also discuss a few problems linked to
the use of wood in fluidized bed burners and in pellet
manufacturing. Not all of the above considerations will
apply to every case. We shall focus on relevant issues
and show the innovations which some industries have employed.

INDUSTRIAL APPLICATIONS

Electrical Generation by Utilities

Burlington Electric is the only utility to operate
a wood-fired boiler for electrical generation. Of their
three 10 MW oil boilers (which were converted from coal)
two have now been converted to wood. In addition, work
has begun on an $84 million, 50 MW boiler which should
be on line by the end of 1984. The plants currently in
operation provide approximately .2 percent of Vermont's
electricity, contributing about 115 trillion BTU.

Environmental and Geographic Factors. As mentioned
previously, one of the foremost questions is whether or
not there is sufficient wood available within an area
small enough to make transportation feasible. For practical purposes, this area is restricted to about a fifty
mile radius (possibly extending to seventy-five miles)
and should be within one state to avoid difficulties in
transportation regulations.

In the five Vermont counties surrounding Burlington, there is currently an unused, unmarketed supply of low-grade wood sufficient to fuel the plant for the next fifty years. Even at current rates of consumption, the annual growth is four times the amount removed from the forest.

The availability of wood has made Burlington a much more desirable site for a large wood-fired plant than many other places in northern New England. Maine and New Hampshire have much more extensive lumber and paper industries. Vermont, especially the northwestern part of the state, has very little industry which could make use of this wood. In fact, in the state as a whole, 80 percent of the saw quality logs are cut but only 20 percent of the low quality wood is being used. In northwestern Vermont there is a total lack of usage. Thus there is a greater and greater accumulation of this wood.

There are few harvesting constraints imposed by state regulation. Harvesters are required to keep the streams clean and prevent forest fires. In their contractual agreements, suppliers are required to abide by state guidelines. Clear cutting is permitted in only two situations: (1) land use conversions; (2) sylvicultural areas of 25 acres or less. Land use conversions are generally expansions of agricultural land. This implies that the land is already fairly flat and erosion is less of a problem. The 25 acre limit is self-imposed, but in practice this much acreage has never been cleared.

To assure against supply interruptions, supplies of chips are stored on site. The inventory will vary but it usually contains a two week supply, increased to six weeks for the spring. Storage is inexpensive since the chips are simply left outside. They are stacked as highly and steeply as possible and compacted. This technique makes the pile as impervious to water as possible. Percolation is limited to about the first ten to twelve inches. Compacting also increases the amount of tonnage which can be stored and prevents spontaneous combustion. The heat build-up in the piles can be great. It will dry the chips by as much as 10 percent. However, compacting the chips excludes air and prevents fire.

Techniques for waste disposal other than reliance on landfills are still being developed. The utility is currently employing a team of engineers to investigate the agricultural potential of wood ash. They are attempting to develop a process which would bind the ash into pellet form for marketing. It may prove to be at least a break-even situation in terms of costs.

Technology. As mentioned, there are no technical problems with the burning of wood. However, technological considerations influenced the choice of the site at Burlington. The first of these is the fact that it is a transportation hub of the state. This is a major consideration. Wood chips take up six times the volume of coal for equivalent BTU capacity. Thus, there will be much more shipping involved. The second is the increased efficiency of the transmission of electricity resulting from its nearness to the power lines. Other technological considerations regarding fuel mixtures will be discussed in terms of their impact on economic feasibility since they are not really technical difficulties but reflect economic choices.

Economic Considerations. The major incentive for the switch to wood-fired boilers has, of course, been economic (although the desire for a more secure fuel was also a major consideration). But the question of how to maximize the BTU output at the least cost is not necessarily a straight-forward one.

Green wood, due to its higher moisture content, generates much less heat than dry chips. But operating a boiler with dry chips becomes risky. Not only is it more expensive to build a drying facility, but also doing so makes you dependent upon its proper operation.

For these reasons, Burlington Electric, as with many other industrial boilers, burns green chips but mixes them with some other fuel. In addition to wood, the boilers are capable of burning number two oil and natural gas (and with modifications, coal). The most economically feasible mix is with the most wood possible. Currently, the mixture that is burned is 25 percent oil and 75 percent wood chips.

It is also more economical to sell the waste heat from the plant as hot water or steam to neighboring industries. While this is not the current practice, the possibility is at least being considered.

As a public utility, the construction of the new 50 MW facility can be financed by tax-free bonds because Burlington Electric is eliminating the use of oil. This financing is facilitated by the adoption of a wood-boiler. There is much less public opposition to such a plant than to construction of nuclear facilities.

In addition, construction of this facility will most likely not incur the cost overruns found in many other new plants. Without the delays caused by public opposition, which lead to higher construction costs, the final costs of the plant will most likely be very close to the $80 million estimate. In fact, costs for design and site preparation are below budget by a few million dollars.

Legislation. There have been no real obstacles posed by any current legislation. As mentioned, it is possible to control emissions with current technology. In fact, this proved to be an incentive to wood use since the pollution controls for the new plant will cost six to eight million dollars less than for a coal or oil facility.

In fact, as opposed to other states, the laws in Vermont are designed to facilitate the use of wood. The laws here are goal-oriented. They set standards and it is up to the company to meet those standards in any way it chooses. The specificity of the laws in Maine may act at times as a deterrent. There the laws are behavior-oriented, forcing industries to adhere to certain rules. Maine has been referred to in interviews as overly regulated.

In general, then, almost all of the difficulties associated with electrical generation are alleviated by siting the plant in Burlington. The availability of supplies and disposal sites, transport networks, and the legislative situation make probably for less problems than for simple steam generation in other states.

Steam Generation[13]

By 1979 there were over 150 wood-fired boilers in operation with a rated capacity of over 5000 pounds of steam per hour in the five New England states outside of Rhode Island. These boilers save the equivalent of about 34 million gallons of oil. More significantly, fully 120 of these industrial boilers were located in the three northern New England states, and over half of these (sixty-three) are situated in Maine.

The feasibility of wood-fired boilers for steam production varies. For industries with an available supply of wood either from waste or harvesting residue, adoption is almost imperative. For industries which must purchase their fuel from outside suppliers, the economic considerations are not as well defined.

This section will include a general discussion of feasibility. Special reference, however, will be made to the way in which one company -- Concord Steam, another public utility -- deals with difficulties faced by industries with no available biomass.

Environmental Considerations. The vast majority of wood-burning industries use their own waste wood as a fuel source. This accounts for the fact that 86 percent of the respondents to the Resource Policy Center (RPC) study are confident that supplies will be available in the future.

There is a greater uncertainty of supplies for those companies who do not generate their own wood residue or

who must supplement their supplies. However, a variety
of sources exist throughout New England. There are over
2400 companies producing mill wood residue throughout
New England and about 400,000 dry tons go unused annually. Loggers also produce another 2.3 million dry tons
of unused logging residues per year. Finally, many
logging operations are beginning to market wood chips
specifically for energy purposes. As time passes, however, the demand for these supplies is steadily increasing. Potential users should attempt to secure long-term
contracts to assure continued supplies.[14]

Concord Steam does not burn nearly as much wood as
Burlington Electric. When it originally switched to
wood use in 1978, it was burning about 20,000 tons per
year. Almost all of its needs were met by local sawmills. Today they burn almost 100,000 tons per year.
To meet these requirements they have diversified their
suppliers. While they still rely heavily on local mills,
they also obtain wood from construction and building residue, from railroad ties replaced by the railroads, and
from forest residue. They have tried to avoid the latter due to greater costs, but they have begun to find it
a necessity.

To the extent that wood is obtained on site or from
sources other than forest residue, supplies of wood are
not as susceptible to weather disruption. In addition,
reliance on waste other than forest residue will reduce
any impact which wood burning might have on wilderness
areas.

Technology. The boilers for wood burning range in
size from the factory-assembled boiler with a capacity
of 2000 to 20,000 pounds of steam per hour to the huge,
field-assembled boilers capable of producing up to
500,000 pounds of steam per hour. According to the RPC
study mentioned previously, the vast majority of operations (91 percent) have had no problems with the operation of their boilers. However, there is a greater tendency for retrofitted boilers to encounter difficulties
meeting start-up emission standards. This is important,
given the increasing tendency to retrofit boilers rather
than installing boilers designed for wood. However, as
greater experience is gained in retrofitting, these difficulties should be alleviated.

Most respondents to this survey (84 percent) also
report few or no difficulties with feeding mechanisms.
The most common problem encountered was due to the freezing of residues. This prevents their weight from
forcing them onto the screws or drag chains, thus preventing fuel from traveling along the conveyor to the
boiler. There is a greater tendency for such freezing
and bridging to occur when the storage bins lack adequate cover.

Unlike Burlington Electric, there is a greater tendency on the part of private industries to burn dry chips. On the average, residues have a moisture content of 25 percent. And, in fact, 38 percent of respondents to the RPC study burn residue with a moisture content of less than 10 percent. This varies greatly, though, from state to state. 67 percent of the companies in Vermont, as opposed to 10 percent of the companies in Maine burn residues with less than 10 percent moisture content. This is probably due primarily to the nature of the available supply, but it poses some technical problems since BTU output in the boilers must be maintained (which is difficult with wet chips). It also has an economic impact, as we shall see in the next section.

Economic Considerations. Of the respondents who provided information on fuel savings, the average amount saved by conversion to wood was $83,750. Approximately one third of these actually claimed savings in excess of $100,000 per year. It is savings of this nature -- although not necessarily of this size -- which have led so many enterprises to convert.

For example, Concord Steam was originally established as a coal-burning facility. It was built in order to diminish the effects of decentralized coal burning in the downtown area. By generating all of the heat necessary for the state office buildings and commercial stores from a central plant, the amount of pollution downtown was reduced.

When it became cost effective to switch to oil by the late 1940s, the change was made. And again, when it became obvious that wood energy provided a cheaper source of fuel than oil (or coal), the plant was converted once again (in 1978) to the use of biomass. As a public utility, there is always the possibility of recouping the price increases of fuels. But by reducing the cost of fuel, Concord Steam hopes to expand their customer base. They currently have about 130 customers, but 90 percent of these are government institutions. By obtaining cheaper fuel they hope to gain more residential and commercial customers.

But the savings for wood customers vary greatly depending upon the size of the boiler (and amount of wood used), the moisture content of the wood, investment characteristics, and so on. Some averages have been estimated, however, and are presented here as a rough guideline.[15]

Table 8.1 provides information regarding the annual costs of boilers varying in rated capacity. Note that the capital cost per 1000 pounds per hour decreases significantly as the boiler size increases. However, precise costs will depend upon specific characteristics. Total and unit operating costs for the same boilers

TABLE 8.1
Annual Capital and Operating Costs for Wood Boiler Installations (in thousands of $)

Costs	Boiler Size (1,000 lbs of steam/hour)				
	10	20	30	40	50
Installation Costs	310.0	437.0	612.0	708.0	813.0
Annual Capital Costs	21.1	29.8	40.5	48.4	55.5
Annual Operating Costs	46.5	65.6	91.8	106.2	122.0
Annual Unit Capital Costs ($/1,000 lbs/hr)	2.1	1.5	1.4	1.2	1.1
Annual Unit Operating Costs ($/1,000 lbs/hr)	5.7	3.3	3.1	2.7	2.4

Source: Berger and Lohnes (1979:7 and 10).

Cost calculations assume: 48% federal tax rate; 17% investment tax credit; 30-year plant life; depreciation of plant over 20 years for tax purposes; 8% annual inflation; 12% discount rate; 18 months of construction time; 97% capacity utilization; operating costs of 15 percent of installation costs.

will actually vary depending on whether or not an operator is present. But a general guideline is that operating costs will be approximately 15 percent of the purchase and installation price.

The price of the wood is also a major consideration. It will vary with market conditions, transportation costs, source, and moisture content. For those companies who can obtain fuel from mill wood residues, the cost will range from zero to twenty dollars per ton. Fuel from logging residues should range from five to twenty dollars per ton. If the wood is harvested specifically for the energy market, the price per ton should vary from $10 to $18.[15] Table 8.2 shows the total annual costs for wood boilers of different capacities using fuel ranging in price from $5 to $20 with a moisture content of 25 and 50 percent respectively.

When we begin to compare these costs with the costs of oil burners, we find that in spite of higher equipment, installation, and operating costs, the savings in fuel costs make wood very advantageous. In fact, the total annual unit costs of wood-fired systems are below the costs for an oil system operating on number six fuel oil except where the wood costs $15 to $20 per ton and has a moisture content of 50 percent.

For those plants which have wood waste produced on site with a moisture content of 25 percent, the instal-

TABLE 8.2A
Total Annual Costs of Wood Boiler, Fuel Moisture Content of 25%

Boiler Size*	Costs	Fuel Prices			
		$5/ton	$10/ton	$15/ton	$20/ton
10,000	Total**	113,300	159,100	205,100	250,900
	Unit***	11,330	15,910	20,510	25,090
20,000	Total	186,800	278,600	370,100	461,900
	Unit	9,340	13,930	18,500	23,100
30,000	Total	269,800	407,100	544,600	682,100
	Unit	8,990	13,570	18,150	22,740
40,000	Total	337,600	521,100	704,400	887,600
	Unit	8,440	13,030	17,610	22,190
50,000	Total	406,500	635,500	864,500	1,093,500
	Unit	8,130	12,710	17,290	21,870

TABLE 8.2B
Total Annual Costs of Wood Boiler, Fuel Moisture Content of 50%

Boiler Size*	Costs	Fuel Prices			
		$5/ton	$10/ton	$15/ton	$20/ton
10,000	Total**	152,100	236,900	260,500	405,900
	Unit***	15,210	23,690	26,050	40,590
20,000	Total	264,600	433,600	602,800	771,900
	Unit	13,230	21,680	30,150	38,600
30,000	Total	386,100	639,800	893,600	1,147,300
	Unit	12,870	21,330	29,790	38,240
40,000	Total	492,900	831,100	1,169,600	1,507,900
	Unit	12,230	20,780	29,240	37,700
50,000	Total	600,500	1,023,200	1,446,000	1,869,000
	Unit	12,010	20,460	28,920	37,380

Source for Tables A and B: Berger and Lohnes (1979:14 and 15)

*   lbs. of steam/hour
**   Sum of capital, operating and fuel costs
*** $/1,000 lbs. of steam per hour

lation and operation of a boiler with a 30,000 pound per
hour capacity costs $4,410 annually per 1,000 pounds of
steam. A similar oil boiler at today's prices would cost
$25,800 per 1,000 pounds of steam. The annual operating
costs would also be 47 percent less for the wood-fired
system.[16]

These figures are intended only as indicators of the
relative cost effectiveness of wood systems. The actual
savings for any company will vary with the local circumstances and existing systems. The decision regarding
adoption of wood should always be made in consultation
with specialists, some of whom may be available through
state energy offices.

Potential adopters should also remember the difficulties in financing new boilers. Bankers are still sceptical about supplies and about annual costs of wood systems. This is an important consideration.

Legislation. Many people feel that pollution legislation poses a major obstacle to continued development.
The fact that the companies previously mentioned had
trouble meeting start-up emission standards could well be
seen as an example of this. However, none of these companies had installed any scrubber or cyclone devices. The
same is true of other companies who have said that their
expansion was prevented by air quality standards.

Certainly at times the standards seem extreme. The
potential emissions are based on operations at 100 percent of capacity, 100 percent of the time. Not everyone
will meet these upper limits. About 50 percent of the
costs of new boilers involves air pollution equipment.
For Concord Steam, a new boiler and electrical generating
equipment which they are planning to install will cost
about one million dollars.

But the requirements are certainly not too extreme.
Many boilers currently operate with no pollution controls. And the costs of the equipment is not usually considered prohibitive. In fact, the rate at which change-
overs are occurring is increasing. Between 1920 and 1970,
there were about ten new wood boilers built per decade.
During the 1970s, eighteen new wood boilers were built,
with more being installed all the time. Thus, while there
certainly are some difficulties involved in wood use,
they are not unsurmountable by any means. The same is
true of wood use for cogeneration.

Cogeneration

Cogeneration, in its broadest sense, implies putting

waste energy to work. Frequently large energy producers
use large amounts of fuel to generate steam for manufacturing processes, hot water for space heating, or electricity. Much usable energy disappears, though, simply because
methods for using 'excess' power potential of the primary
energy are not employed. Cogeneration provides a means
using this excess energy.

The specific cogeneration system will depend upon the
primary energy needs of the industry. For the paper industry for example, steam must be generated for the manufacturing process. In this case, the leftover steam can be
used to drive a turbine to produce secondary electricity.
Thus cogeneration actually becomes a way of reducing the
cost of steam. For an electricity producer, however, the
role is reversed. When heat and electricity are produced
in excess of the company's requirements, the extra energy
is available to others.

This technology has been available for a century. In
fact, in the 1920s about 22 percent of all electricity
produced in the U.S. was cogenerated by industry. But
with the decline in demand for steam by industry and the
steadily increasing availability of less and less expensive commercial electricity, the contribution of cogeneration has declined to about 5 percent today.

Over the past few years, though, cogeneration has
again become increasingly attractive. In a 1979 survey of
wood users,[17] there were fifteen cogeneration facilities
in Northern New England alone (all but three of which
were in Maine) generating about 102 MWh of power. More
have come on line since the survey and by the end of February 1982 a new 40 MW cogeneration facility will be on
line at S.D. Warren in Westbrook, Maine.

In spite of this, a vast potential remains. It is
estimated that in Maine alone there is the potential to
generate at least an additional 150 MW, and perhaps as
much as 250 MW of electricity just in the forest products
industry. This is indeed a significant contribution to
the region's energy needs, especially since industry uses
about 40 percent of the electricity used in Maine. Here
we shall examine a few factors affecting enterprises which
already cogenerate.

Environmental considerations. The problems with wood
availability are the same with cogeneration as for any
other wood-fired boiler. If there is a sufficient supply
of wood, then cogeneration may become a consideration for
any plant which also can make use of steam. The wood does
not necessarily have to be produced on site. It can be
transported to a plant which has no tie to forest products

but wishes to convert to wood and also reduce the price of its steam. Such is the case with the Tillotsen Rubber Co. for example.

For a very large facility such as the one at S.D. Warren in Westbrook, Maine, the difficulties are essentially the same as for Burlington Electric. There must be assurance of large supplies, storage, and disposal. S.D. Warren has developed a number of innovative methods of alleviating these problems, especially those dealing with procurement.

The Westbrook boiler is designed to burn about 2,000 tons of chips per day, but it will probably burn about 1,500 tons in practice. Since about half of its radius is ocean, S.D. Warren would seem to face some difficulties in obtaining supplies. But the company has the largest tree farm in the country. 800 individual land owners with 180,000 acres of forest land are under contract to the company. It helps the families with land management in return for the assured supply. While not all of the wood actually goes to Warren, they at least have a captive supply. Today, within the economically feasible radius of fifty miles, the growth rate of low-grade wood is eleven times what is needed to fire the new boiler.

But Warren, due to its location, has very little storage area. While they have built one large, A-shaped building, it is capable of holding only about a ten-day supply. While some wood can be stored outdoors and a little within the mill complex, there is not sufficient storage to assure supplies during the spring thaw. To deal with this problem, the company has come up with two solutions. The first is the identification of 'mud lots' on the suppliers' farms. These are well drained lots, close to the road, which are accessible sooner than most lots. But this provides only a partial solution.

The most innovative technique is the diversification of supplies. Warren has some suppliers located far to the south in Massachusetts, others in far northern Maine. The seasonal differentiation between these areas is about four to six weeks. Thus, if the woods are inaccessible in the south, Warren's suppliers slightly to the north can still work. Cutting can then be proceeding northwards ahead of the thaw. When the northernmost woods are reached, they can once again harvest in the south. As an extra precaution, Warren can also obtain residue from local sawmills that stockpile for the spring.

Disposal of waste poses a problem in Maine. The surface geology of the land makes it possible that water supplies could become contaminated. However, some landfill sites are available and their later agricultural potential is being investigated.

Technology. In general, there are no serious technological difficulties associated with cogeneration. It is necessary to keep a steady BTU output which necessitates careful consideration of the fuel mixture. On the one hand, very dry chips (less than 50 percent moisture content) burn too quickly. But burning only green chips fails to produce enough heat.

To deal with this problem, it is necessary to find a correct fuel misture for each facility. At S.D. warren they will burn coal and wood in much the same manner as at Burlington Electric. Eventually they also may burn rubber. Portland is New England's largest tire recapping center, and a use for old tires is constantly being sought. A similar process is already being used at Tillitson Rubber in Dixville Notch, New Hampshire. In addition, if their wood is too low in moisture, they try to mix it with something that has more bulk and burns more slowly.

This all seems quite straightforward, but care must be taken in site selection. In one instance, a combination of supply, technological, and economic problems resulting from poor advice led to unfavorable results. J.F. Chicken Lumber in Ossipee, New Hampshire, had an engineer on site dealing with emission problems. With his encouragement, they called in consultants to set up a cogeneration system in each of their plants. But the systems which they installed failed to generate enough steam to drive the turbines.

Since they had the turbines, they called in new consultants. They discovered that the company did not generate enough waste. In fact, both plants together had just enough residue for one cogenerator. But the profitability was too low anyway. The value of the electricity which could be generated was only marginally higher than the operation and maintenance costs. Thus the project was abandoned. This illustrates the need for qualified consultants at every stage in the process.

One final technological consideration also pertains to siting. If the secondary energy to be sold to other users is heat rather than electricity, the facility should be located close to these users to avoid uneconomic heat transmission losses.

Economic considerations. In spite of the need for new equipment, manpower, and interconnected electrical distribution and relay systems, all of which require additional capital outlays, cogeneration can be a very attractive means for reducing the cost of process steam for any facility which uses large amounts of steam in manufacturing. The paper industry relies very heavily on steam to reduce the moisture content of its raw material by 96 percent. Thus some means of reducing this cost is very profitable. This explains why so many cogeneration facilities are located in Maine. All of the large paper companies --Boise Cascade, Georgia-Pacific, International, and Scott-- are generating from 16 to 26 MW. But it can also be profitable for a company like Moosehead Manufacturing in Monson, Maine, which generates as little as 125 kW.

Financial considerations are still important, however, especially with regard to funding. The facility at S.D. Warren was planned under a 1978 grant from the Department of Energy to Wheelabrator Frye to study the development of energy alternatives. The original grant included some funds for building but those were eventually withdrawn. Subsequently, Scott Paper Co., the parent company of Warren, decided to proceed on their own and authorized $73 million for the project. Additional funds have advanced the start-up date by six months.

At this plant, current prices for chips will probably be less than $20 per ton. Warren could afford to pay up to $25 per ton (minus handling costs) and still be gaining financially over the use of oil. Even greater savings can be obtained if fuel is produced on site. Warren may also be able to use about half of the biomass to produce pulp if they can get the harvesters to fill the van with hardwood chips.

The PURPA legislation (mentioned in the first section) also provides substantial economic incentives. While only a few facilities actually generate excess electricity for sale to a utility, Warren will ultimately meet more than its own needs. Currently, Warren purchases about 6 MWh of electricity from Central Maine Power (CMP). When the new facility comes on line at the end of February 1982, CMP will be purchasing about 13 MWh from Warren. In addition to the income provided for Warren by the sale, the difference of almost 20 MWh provides a considerable additional source of power for the utility.

Legislation. As with all other wood-burning technologies, pollution abatement legislation is the primary concern. 50 percent of boiler costs are due to pollution controls. But the emission standards can be met with current technology. In fact, reduced sulfur dioxide emissions are generally a large incentive to adoption, as it is easier to meet pollution standards with wood than coal. At the Warren plant for example, sulfur emissions will be cut to 25 percent of their previous level.

The practicality of some regulations is more questionable. Maine frequently tries to outdo the federal government. Some regulations which companies objected to included the number of monitoring devices or the need to sweep streets. However, the economic advantages of wood use tend to more than outweigh the regulatory disadvantages.

The remaining applications are relatively recent innovations. As such, there is much less experience with them and less can be said in reference to how the many factors under consideration enhance or deter adoption. However, a few brief comments will be made regarding potential advantages and disadvantages of each of them.

Gasification

Wood gasification is a relatively new technology. Currently there are only two facilities in New England, only one of which is in the north. This unit is located at the Allen Rogers plant in Wentworth, New Hampshire. Its potential for adoption seems quite high but some difficulties need to be overcome.

Technology. Gasification is a process whereby wood chips are burned directly on electric grates, producing gas and a fine ash residue. The gas is then funneled and burned to create steam. There are some difficulties. The grates have had a tendency to break in the past. Grates made of a different alloy have just been installed at the Rogers plant. Hopefully the problem has been solved.

Another technical problem is that the process is extremely sensitive to feedstock quality. Green chips cannot be burned efficiently. The feeding mechanism cannot handle bark. Thus high-quality chips have to be gasified and this leads to resource competition with the paper industry.

Economic considerations. The costs per BTU for gasifiers are supposed to be substantially below other alternatives. The need to burn paper-quality chips currently detracts froms the exploitation of this possibility. Eventually with refinements in the burning process and the feeding mechanism, the problem should decrease. Further discussion of the economic aspects is difficult since this project is still on trial and is financed by a federal grant.

Fluidized Bed Burners

When the state of Vermont decided to switch to wood
as a means of heating the State Hospital and the State
Office complex, they decided to adopt a new technology as
a demonstration project. It is currently the only such
boiler operating in the region. The results have not been
entirely successful due to a number of technological
problems.

Technology. Fluidized bed burners are ideally a
means to burn solid fuels more efficiently. Air is
blown through a bed of sand and the sand and wood chips
become suspended over the bed. There are a number of
problems in actual practice.

The first problem encountered at this plant is that
the chips kept falling onto the bed. While this makes the
burn less efficient, it does not make the boiler inoper-
able. In fact, the operators have decided to burn dirctly
on the bed for the moment. This practice, while feasible,
negates any of the advantages of installing this technology.

The burner is also very sensitive to the moisture
content of the chips. One cannot burn chips of over 55
percent moisture content. This means that at many times
of the year they cannot burn green chips (since in the
winter the moisture content of chips is too high).

The operator of the facility also tried at one time
to burn whole tree chips. These would have been a little
bit cheaper than paper-quality chips. However, this
source has too many small limbs and twigs. The sticks
would get caught in the feeding mechanism causing it to
malfunction.

Economic considerations. In general, the costs of
fluidized bed burners are higher than for conventional
grate boilers. The controls are much more complicated.
Since there are more problems with particulate emissions,
there is a need for more sophisticated pollution abatement equipment. The economic advantages lie in the more
efficient use of the fuel, but, given the technological
problems, these have not yet been attained.

On the more positive side, the state government is
currently burning about 100 tons of wood chips per week
with a 40 percent moisture content or less. Each ton displaces about forty-five gallons of oil. Thus the plant is
saving a significant amount of oil each year. This does
not consitute a recommendation for adoption, however, unless the technological difficulties are solved. Other,
less expensive alternatives also displace large quanti-

ties of oil.

Wood Pellets

Pellets are probably the newest innovation in the wood energy market. While they are an extremely attractive fuel source, a number of marketing difficulties have hindered development. In fact, some companies have folded without even completing their start-up. More recently, inroads have been made and the market is beginning to turn around.

Technology. Wood pellets are an enhanced fuel with a uniform and predictable BTU output. They are easily packaged, transported, and can be stored for long periods without losing their efficiency. They are dry and have very good firing characteristics.

Economic considerations. Wood pellets are an economical, easy to use, efficient energy alternative for home, industry and commerce alike. Currently, the costs for installing household units to burn pellets may be a slight deterrent at $1,400 and up for the average household. But costs should decline as more experience is gained. The pellets sell for about $125 per ton in bags. Soon, it should be possible to sell them in bulk for about $105 per ton. Homeowners' usage will vary tremendously, of course, but for any user pellets are cost-competitive with wood. Given the advantages of less handling, cleanliness, and lessened·storage space, pellets become even more attractive.

The difficulties in starting up the market have been the traditional chicken-and-egg problems. Pelletizing is an energy-intensive process and as such it requires a large initial capital investment. Bankers are hesitant to loan money to an unproven industry without an established market. Potential producers have found it difficult to line up consumers who are hesitant to invest in the burning units. They need assurance of supplies. They want to know that if one company fails, they will be able to obtain pellets somewhere else. They also do not wish to be subject to monopolistic pricing practices.

There have recently been a couple of attempts to break this cycle. The first successful attempt was actually made by Shell Oil in Canada. To assure availability of buyers, Shell simply installed burning units on the consumers' premises. Shell has since expanded its market using this captive market as the starting base for production.

In New England, there have been unsuccessful attempts

although a market turn-around has recently begun. A company in Bangor, Maine, BioMass Energy Corporation, owns the rights to and manufactures Woodex pellets. The company's two divisions handle industrial and residential consumers seperately. Although Woodex pellets are currently manufactured at many sites in the U.S., the basic problem still remains of how to start up a franchise when the banks will not back the enterprise.

The franchise in Bangor was purchased by a group of individuals who were unable to install burning units for potential customers. They also knew that they could not hope to start selling a product which they did not yet have. They invested about $75,000 of their own money, borrowing the remaining $300'000 needed for building the plant from the Farmers Loan Guarantee and the banks. This was before money became tight and expensive, however.

Given the supply base, they then turned to the development of a customer base. Using aggressive marketing techniques, they began finding both industrial and residential users. They underwrote the costs of demonstration burners. They opened the doors of the plant to anyone interested in it. They integrated into the government network and they developed local distributors in surrounding states.

Today, the pellet production capacity of the first plant is all sold out. A second plant is being built with private funding and no problems are anticipated in marketing its output. Plans are also being developed for a third plant. It is assumed now that its output will be contracted for before the plant is even built.

It would appear that this technology will now grow rapidly. It should be able to make inroads in homes and industries which have traditionally used wood for fuel as well as in those that have hesitated to switch because of the difficulties involved. It should have a significant impact on the reduction of oil consumption in New England in the coming decade.

CONCLUSIONS

Wood energy has the potential to make a significant contribution to New England's energy needs. Even at current rates of consumption it displaces about six million barrels of oil each year. But it has been estimated that the equivalent of three billion barrels of oil, enough to meet all of the area's energy needs for nine years, currently stand in the region's forests. While we certainly do not wish to cut all of these trees at once, there is still an unused energy potential. With proper forest management techniques, economic incentives, and pollution

controls, forest resources can probably provide about 10
to 20 percent of the area's energy needs indefinitely with
a negligible environmental impact. Here we make a few
summary remarks concerning the efforts which should continue to be made in support of further wood use for energy purposes.

Environmental Considerations

State forest services and energy offices have been
conducting periodic assessments of forest reources. This
information is critical to the continued development of
the region's forests. However, to assure the availability
of supplies, more efforts such as S.D. Warren's programs
in support of individual landowners would take some of
the burden off the state. If large companies offered forest management assistance to individual landowners, it
would advance their interests as well as those of all New
England residents.

Technology

Technological considerations are not a significant
deterrent. While some newer innovations are still having
technical difficulties, these should eventually be
solved. For the serious potential adopter of wood burning
a variety of practical technologies are available.

Economic Considerations

The largest disincentives to adoption are the availability of accurate information and the capital needed in
most cases for starting up new operations. J.F. Chick is
an example of how inaccurate information can have harmful
results. Too many such unsuccessful attempts will discourage future users.

Many programs are available which provide information
to industrial users. These should be continued. The New
England Regional Commission and the various state energy
offices have a cooperative program which can include a
cost assessment, site visits to determine whether sufficient space is available, technical planning assistance,
and an assessment of cogeneration possibilities. Such
programs not only make enterprises aware of the possibility of using wood as a fuel. They also reduce the costs
involved in planning and designing a wood burning facility.

The biggest problem, though, is obtaining funds. A
large company like Scott Paper has excess capital, but
for a small enterprise the need for external funds can be

a significant deterrent. Two problems are interconnected. The first is the high costs involved in borrowing money today. The second is the skepticism of bankers towards investments in wood-burning equipment. A couple of practical steps could be taken to alleviate these problems. The first step would be for local renewable energy coalitions to employ economists who can assist in the development of accurate cost figures, equivalent to those for oil-based processes. This would not only reduce the distrust of bankers, but would also provide invaluable assistance to potential adopters.

Secondly, some intervention on behalf of renewable energy by the federal government would be valuable. Low interest loans would be ideal, but can scarcely be expected under today's political realities. However, the increased use of federal loan guarantees might reduce the risk involved and encourage bankers to loan money at favorable rates. This would involve minimal intervention by federal government and would probably be of little expense to taxpayers. It would, though, provide quite a boost to adoption of the wood alternative.

Legislation

Pollution standards are absolutely essential. We cannot be so shortsighted as to reduce these standards simply in order to increase economic incentives for wood. But the extent and nature of the requirements for meeting these standards should be constantly re-evaluated. Regulations should not be pecuniary in nature. Allowing industry the freedom to meet standards rather than enforce adherence to specific regulations seems to be a more practical method of achieving the same goal.

In sum, the economic advantages of wood use have already led to an increase in its consumption in industry and will most likely to continue to do so in the future. But some actions --dissemination of information and technical assistance, and financial assistance-- would facilitate this process. However, we must take care that in our rush to replace foreign oil we do not unintentionally overexploit our valuable forest resources.

NOTES

1. High (1980:14).
2. High (1980:14).
3. Bailey and Wheeling (1979).
4. Hewett (1978).
5. Hewett (1979).

6. High (1980:24). This is equivalent to $36 to $ 48
per cord or $10 to $13 per cubic meter.
7. Berger and Lohnes (1979).
8. Public Law 95-617 (1978:3149).
9. Hewett (1979).
10. Hewett (1979:12-13).
11. Berger and Lohnes (1979:2-15).
12. Chapman (1979).
13. Information on the use of wood for steam generation is given by Nadherny (1979).
14. Berger (1979:4-5).
15. Berger (1979:4-5).
16. Berger (1979:17).
17. Nadherny (1979:A1-A12).

BIBLIOGRAPHY

Bailey, M. and P. Wheeling 1979 New England Fuel Wood
    Survey. Broomall (Pa.): U.S. Department of Agricul-
    ture.
Berger, G.J. 1979 "Why Wood? An Introduction for Potential
    Industrial Wood Boiler Users." Resource Policy Center
    Publication Nr. 137. Hanover (NH): Thayer School of
    Engineering.
Berger, G.J. and J. Lohnes 1979 "A Users' Guide to Legal
    and Institutional Factors Affecting the Use of In-
    dustrial Wood Boilers in New England." Resource Poli-
    cy Center Publication Nr. 132. Hanover (NH): Thayer
    School of Engineering.
Chapman, E. 1979 Report to the Council of State Govern-
    ments. New York: Council of State Governments.
Hewett, Ch.E. 1978 "The Availability of Wood for a 50 MW
    Wood-Fired Power Plant in Northern Vermont." Resource
    Policy Center Publication Nr. 114. Hanover (NH):
    Thayer School of Engineering.
Hewett, Ch.E. 1979 "Institutional Constraints on the Ex-
    panded Use of Wood Energy Systems." Resource Policy
    Center Publication Nr. 155. Hanover (NH): Thayer
    School of Engineering.
High, C. 1980 "New England Returns to Wood." Natural His-
    tory, 89(2).
Nadherny, J. 1979 "Survey of Industrial Wood-Fired
    Boilers in New England: Analysis of Responses." Re-
    source Policy Center Publication Nr. 129. Hanover
    (NH): Thayer School of Engineering.
Public Law 95-617 1978 United States Statutes at Large.
    95th Congress, 2nd Session, Vol. 92, Part 3, pp.
    3117-3173.

9
Peat for Energy in Finland: History of a Development Process

Jan-Inge Lind

The development of the peat industry in Finland illustrates one of the ways a new energy industry can emerge and grow. In the following description and analysis of this development, I shall try to answer the following questions:

o How did a peat industry develop in Finland?
o Why did it happen?
o What were some of the critical events and the driving forces in the process?
o How were the developments affected by state policy and action?

THE FINNISH ENERGY SITUATION

In 1960, total energy consumption in Finland amounted to about 10.5 million tons of oil equivalent (mtoe). In 1976, the corresponding figure was about 23 mtoe. A 1977 forecast indicates a total energy consumption of about 38 mtoe by the year 2000.

The level of energy self-sufficiency during the last twenty years has been falling from around 60 percent to roughly 30 percent today. Energy produced from national resources has remained constant in absolute terms at about 7 mtoe. But dependency on oil has increased. It represents today about 50 percent of the energy supplied.

Finnish energy policy during the last years of the 1970s concentrated mainly on trying to raise the level

Jan-Inge Lind is a Doctor of Business Administration from the Lund School of Business Administration. He is now working as a project leader with the Scandinavian Institutes for Administrative Research in Lund (Sweden). His research focus has been on regional development and government promotion of new industry.

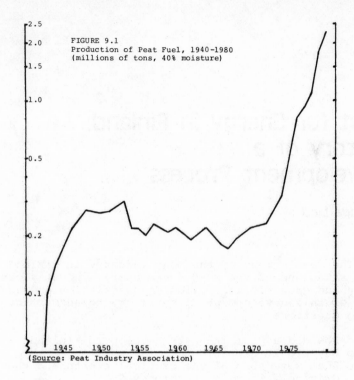

FIGURE 9.1
Production of Peat Fuel, 1940-1980
(millions of tons, 40% moisture)

(Source: Peat Industry Association)

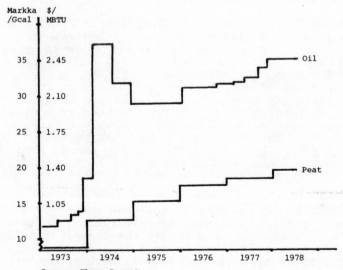

FIGURE 9.2
Price Developments for Heavy Fuel Oil and Peat, 1973-1978

Source: Ekono Report
Note: Prices include delivery costs.

of self-sufficiency and supporting various measures for
saving energy. Government action has consisted mainly of
financing aid in various forms, of planning and of research.

In 1977 about Fmk 7.1 billion[1] were spent on the
import of energy, corresponding to about 23 percent of
imports and 6 percent of GNP. The last two of these relative figures trebled during the preceding twenty years.

Long-term contracts for the import of electricity
and natural gas from the Soviet Union were drafted towards the end of the 1960. They were based on the expec-
tation that the rate of growth in the national economy
would continue throughout the 1970s. Since the rate of
growth in the economy has in fact declined, and since nuclear energy has emerged as a factor in Finnish energy
supplies, there is nominaly an energy surplus today.

Finland has about 10 million ha of peat bogs, the
fifth largest area in the world. It produced 3.1 million
tons of peat for fuel use in 1980, up from half a million
tons in 1975. The goal is to increase production by at
least 2 million tons per year to reach a sustainable production of 20 million tons sometimes in the late 1980s.
Peat is presently contributing approximately 3 percent of
total energy consumption. It would contribute between 6
and 10 percent in the year 2000, the latter if the state
intervenes sufficiently strongly. Finland is the third
largest user of peat for fuel in the world. But it is
still underutilizing its resource despite the rapid production increases over the last few years.[2]

It is not production prospects that set an upper
limit on the use of peat (and wood fuel) today; instead
it is the consumption prospects and the competition from
alternative uses for peat (and wood fuel). State planning
activities in the energy sector have greatly increased
over the last few years, and a major ambition today is to
diversify the base for the country's energy supply. The
State Fuel Center (VAPO) was responsible for about 85
percent of total peat extraction. The growth in peat production in Finland between 1925 and 1980 can be seen in
Figure 9.1. The price level of peat compared with other
fuels can be seen in Table 9.1. The figures refer to the
last quarter of 1977. A comparison of the prices for milled peat compared with the price of heavy fuel oil for
the period 1973-1978 appears in Figure 9.2.

Calculations of the profitability of different types
of power plants, carried out by Ekono (a Finnish engineering and consulting company) in 1978, indicate repayment periods for additional investment in the peat-fuel
alternative of between 4 and 11.6 years. The figures can
be seen in Table 9.2.

A recent report by the Ministry for Trade and Industry has described alternative developments for energy
supplies in Finland until the year 2000. A comparison

TABLE 9.1
Energy Prices (including delivery costs) in 1977 (Fourth Quarter)

Fuel	Price	Effective Calorific Value	Heat Price (mk/Gcal)
Power Plant Fuel			
Heavy Fuel Oil	388 mk/t	9.7 Gcal/t	40.00
Coal	190 mk/t	6.1 Gcal/t	31.15
Milled Peat	23 mk/m^3	1.0 Gcal/m^3	23.00
District Heating Fuel			
Heavy Fuel Oil	388 mk/t	9.7 Gcal/t	40.00
Coal	305 mk/t	6.5 Gcal/t	46.92
Wood Chips	58 mk/m^3	1.0 Gcal/m^3	22.00
Machine-made Peat	40 mk/m^3	1.2 Gcal/m^3	33.33
Milled Peat	22 mk/m^3	1.0 Gcal/m^3	22.00
Softwood Fuel	572 mk/m^3	8.6 Gcal/m^3	66.50
Anthracite	390 mk/t	7.4 Gcal/t	52.70
Birch Firewood	91 mk/m^3	1.4 Gcal/m^3	65.00
Peat Briquettes	200 mk/t	4.5 Gcal/t	44.45

Source: Ministry for Trade and Industry.

TABLE 9.2
Profitability Estimates for Different Power Plants[1]

Power Plant Type	Energy Production Costs (markka/MWh)		Payback Period[2]
	Peat	Oil	
Central Heating Plant (15 MW; Peak Load for 5500 h/a)	56	57	11.6
Industrial Steam Generation /45t/h; Peak Load for 6000 h/a)	47	52	7.2
Industrial Back-Pressure Power Plant (40/148 MW; Peak Load 7000 h/a)	44	52	
District Heating Cogeneration (60/125 MW; Peak Load 5500 h/a)[3]	52	58	

Source: Ekono Consulting Report.
Notes: 1. Assuming 8% interest and depreciation over 15 years.
2. For the additional investment in the peat alternative.
3. Estimate based on price for high-pressure steam.

between the scenario entitled "free adaptation to demand" and the one entitled "radical state intervention", which represent two extreme forms of energy development, are illustrated in Figure 9.3

FIGURE 9.3
Finland's Sources of Energy, 1960-2000

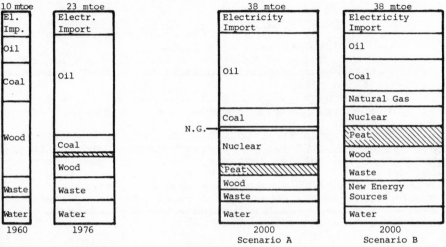

Scenario A = Free Adaptation to Demand
Scenario B = Radical State Intervention

At present there are about 15,000 ha of peat bog under production and 40,000 ha being planned in Finland. The planned increase in peat output of about 2 million m^3 of peat yearly requires opening up for production of 4,000 ha of peat bog annually. The aimed for goal of 20 million m^3 by the end of the 1980s will call for the preparation of a further 40,000-50,000 ha of peat bog. With a total area of 100,000 ha of peat bog, it would be possible to produce 20 million m^3 a year for twenty to twenty-five years.

THE DEVELOPMENT OF THE FINNISH PEAT INDUSTRY

The industrial use of peat in Finland started in the 1870s. But it was the energy shortage due to the loss of coal imports at the beginning of World War II which forced the government to become involved in energy planning and to manage a switch back to domestic energy resources. This was the beginning of the development which led to today's large-scale use of peat in Finland. We investigate here the dynamics of the development since 1939.

The development of the peat industry in the post-war period falls into five phases, each of which contains one or more key events crucial to the phase:

1. The shortage society during World War II when the authorities started to organize fuel energy supplies, among them peat.
2. The period of the hegemony of oil during which only one company continued to produce significant amounts of peat for burning in its boilers.
3. The new role for the state fuel company, VAPO, which included the task of developing peat bogs and marketing peat as a fuel.
4. The decision of the town of Kuopio, which led to the construction of the first peat-fired cogeneration plant.
5. The breakthrough of peat with production targets and peat output increasing with each oil price shock.

In each phase it is possible to identify a particular system structure and some of the factors and events which have led to the changes generating the next phase. Key driving factors have been entrepreneurial drive of important actors in the existing system structure and system imbalances such as unemployment, declining energy self-sufficiency, readily available unexploited peat, etc. (see Figure 9.4).

The Shortage Society

Peat has been dug for fuel in Finland since the middle of the 19th century. Its first industrial use occurred in the 1870s at the Wärtsilä Ironworks in Carelia, in eastern Finland. Until 1929, however, peat was of marginal importance; the energy supply was traditionally based on wood fuel and water power. The big increase in energy consumption resulting from industrialisation during the 1920s and 1930s was mainly satisfied by the import of coal.

During the shortages prevailing in the 1940s, the fundamental structure emerged which was to become the launching pad for the development of the peat industry in Finland.

During the war years 1939-1945 the responsible authorities in Finland became aware for the first time of the key role that energy supplies play in the functioning of our society. Evidence of this appeared already in 1940, with the establishment of the State Fuel Center, VAPO. VAPO's task consisted originally of providing the national railways with fuel. Peat was included in VAPO's product range from the beginning, being used among other things as engine fuel.

Several companies in the forest industry began to use peat as fuel during the war years. Boilers running

FIGURE 9.4
The Dynamics of the Peat System

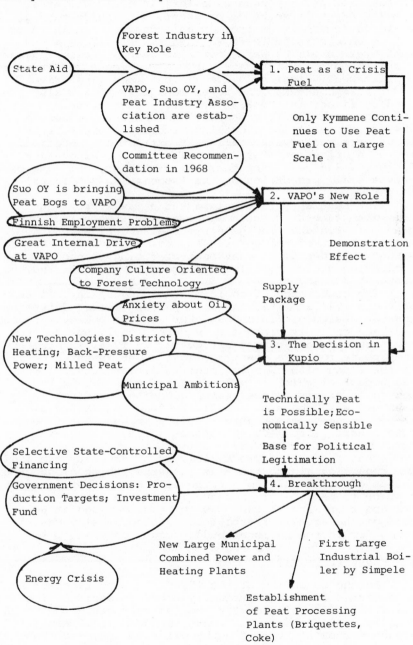

on waste wood and bark could be adapted to run on peat
with only slight adjustments; the peat was mainly purchased from private peat suppliers in the local area.
Kymmene AB, a large paper producer, also began to dig
peat and to use it as fuel on an industrial scale, and
they even continued to do so when all other companies
went over to oil as being more profitable and convenient.
Despite poor profitability, however, Kymmene continued to
exploit peat, digging in its own peat bog. The prime
mover in Kymmene was the power manager, who was also the
leading figure in the Peat Industry Association.

The Peat Industry Association was established in
1942, with initially about 100 members. These were in
large part relatively small peat-extracting companies.
Representatives of other groups, such as equipment manufacturers and peat consumers, joined later, but made up
only a small proportion of the Association's original
members.

The Finnish parliament passed a law supporting
the production of domestic fuels - i.e., wood fuel and
peat - in Finland. The government also decided on the
establishment of the enterprise Suo OY, although this remained only one among many peat-producing companies. The
production of sod peat in 1944 amounted to about 100,000
tonnes for the year.

The experience of an 18-month-long gap in coal supplies in 1944 and 1945 was an important factor determining the design of Finland's future energy policy. Finland
had been entirely dependent on German coal, but deliveries from Germany ceased altogether in 1944. In order to
compensate for this loss, the government invested heavily
in the production of solid fuel in Finland itself. But it
was wood fuel which largely replaced coal during the
period of crisis, since peat production could not be
launched with the same immediate effect. Nevertheless,
as can be seen from Figure 9.1, the production of peat
rose steadily from 100,000 tonnes in 1944 to a maximum of
300,000 tonnes in the early 1950s.

Peat production was decisively affected by the 1947
law regarding aid to the peat industry, which among other
things enjoined VAPO to acquire all the peat produced at
a price to be determined annually. At the same time the
transport of Finnish fuel was to be subsidised at 60 percent of the actual transport costs. The subsidy was allowed for in the national budget each year.

The Hegemony of Oil

At the beginning of the 1950s the importance of peat
as a source of energy gradually began to decline. The
rapid expansion of industry and infrastructure led to an
equally rapid increase in energy consumption. This increase was mainly satisfied by oil supplies, and the

technologies of oil refining and the distribution and use of oil quickly developed. Oil became the predominant source of energy for industry, domestic heating and transport. Except for the period of the Korean war and the Suez crisis, the price of oil nevertheless stayed at a competitive level until the end of the 1960s.

The only big energy consumer to remain loyal to peat during the period of oil's hegemony was the paper company Kymmene AB. To begin with the company had invested in peat because it had a surplus of labour, because there was a need for energy at the papermill, and because the company had a peat bog available close by on its own land. From wood, the natural alternative to peat, it was found most profitable to produce pulp and paper.

After oil had become the predominant fuel in other companies in the forest industry on grounds of profitability, Kymmene AB's steam plant manager, Mr. Zimmerman, still insisted on retaining peat as fuel. Under his supervision the digging technique was further developed and made more efficient. In 1958 the first boiler for solid fuel in powder form was installed at Kymmene. The boiler was of German manufacture, and the fuel technology was based mainly on the German experience with lignite. At that time peat was one of seven fuels used in the boiler. The peat was first dug and then ground to a powder before being fed into the boiler. In 1964 a second, similar boiler was installed at Kymmene.

During the 1950s considerable progress had been made in the technology of milled peat in the Soviet Union. The technique, which had been known in principle and used already before the war in Sweden and elsewhere, was introduced into Finland in 1958, when the first attempts to use Soviet-manufactured machines were made. Since fuel technology had already been oriented towards fuel in powder form, this provided the spur for various peat-related measures in Finland.

The national hydro-electric company, Imatran Voima OY, now launched a major study of a 30 MW peat-burning condensing power plant. At the same time the company bought the equity in the peat-producing state company Suo OY, which subsequently signed a series of long-term leases for a total of 15,000 hectares of peat bog. Digging and drainage was started over a large part of the bogs, which were to provide fuel for the condensing power plant. Planning and profitability analysis for the proposed power station continued until 1964, when it was finally stated that the project was not profitable since the price of oil was still so low. Nevertheless Suo OY continued to produce small quantities of peat for VAPO, but it was becoming an increasingly heavy burden on Imatran Voima OY.

Nor was the government entirely inactive as regards supporting the peat industry during this period. Among

other things it decreed in 1958 that all state-owned
buildings should be heated with Finnish fuel, and that
dispensation from this rule could only be obtained after
making special application to the Council of State.
Ironically enough, one of the first buildings which
sought and obtained dispensation from this rule was the
new main office of the Forest Board in the centre of
Helsinki.

Another important factor in the development of the
peat industry during this period was the rapidly increasing production of horticultural peat, which was partly
a result of the substantial demand for it on the export
markets.

The generous transport subsidy for Finnish fuel, introduced already in 1947, continued to apply until well
into the 1960s. However, due to new sulphate cooking
techniques, the sulphate industry was now able to use
birch chips as raw material, and this use increased rapidly. It was suddenly realized that the state was heavily subsidising the burning of this industry's major raw
material. As a result, the transport subsidy was quickly
abolished. It was an unfortunate consequence that this
also meant abandoning the subsidy on the transport of
peat, which immediately put the peat producers into a
difficult situation. The state company Suo OY suffered
with the others. Only after a long drawn-out and complicated process of legislation was the subsidy on the transport of peat reintroduced, and it remains in operation
today.

VAPO's New Role

After 1965 the finite nature of oil resources and
the need to be free of a one-sided dependence on oil
were mentioned increasingly often in the public debate.
Nuclear energy technology was advancing rapidly, but
there was still good reason to try to exploit more efficiently the national energy reserve that peat represented.

In 1967 a government commission was appointed to
suggest ways in which the Finnish peat industry should
and could be supported. The committee's main recommendation was that the state should assume a leading role in
developing the peat industry, that VAPO was the organisation through which this should be achieved, and that
Suo OY should be transferred from the state hydro-power
company Imatran Voima OY to VAPO. This last decision
appears to have been mainly dictated by employment considerations. That is, the government wanted to guarantee
work for about 100 peat workers employed by Suo OY,
which was then under threat of closure.

VAPO's output of wood fuel and railway sleepers had
been falling persistently since the end of the 1950s.

VAPO's Managing Director Kosti Ranta explains:

> The consumption of wood fuel had been falling steep-
> ly during the 1960s. The same applied to our other
> major product, railway sleepers for the National
> Railways. Thus there was a surplus of resources
> within VAPO's organisation.
>
> The age structure in VAPO was also pretty homoge-
> neous, most of our 300 employees had joined the
> organisation immediately after the war, so at the
> end of the 1960s they were in their fifties.
>
> This constellation of factors coincided with a na-
> tural desire in the organisation to get hold of
> something new and interesting to do, and a new
> operation such as that offered by peat digging ge-
> nerated great energy in our structure. Of course
> there had been others before us, but we felt we
> would be able to create a good deal of new know-how
> and a new way of operating.
>
> Also, of course, VAPO had its own field organisa-
> tion, consisting mainly of forestry people, and they
> had exceptionally good personal contacts with all
> the national agencies using Finnish fuel for heating.

Of course, Suo Oy was not immediately transformed
into a profitable business simply because the company was
transferred to VAPO. Nevertheless, access to a large area
of already drained peat bog offered opportunities for
rapid development in peat production, and VAPO immediately started acquiring the necessary equipment for the
production of milled peat. The organisation of the work
and the transport system was based on experience already
gained in forestry. The winter months were used for heavy transport on the bogs; and the supervision and training models used in forestry were applied.

The greatest worry was that there was no existing
demand for milled peat. This had to be created, and VAPO
launched a marketing campaign directed towards the
government, the local government sector and industry. It
was a case of winning decision-markers in key posts to
the acceptance of peat as an alternative. At this time
the small increases in the price of oil had not yet affected oil's superior competitiveness as an energy
source. VAPO's investments were financed from the national budget.

At the same time the engineering and consulting company, Ekono, conducted a major information campaign,
arranging confrontations between peat fuel specialists
on the one hand and government and municipal decision-
makers in key positions on the other. These contacts

resulted in an extensive investigation of the future
technical and economic possibilities of peat as a source
of energy. VAPO's central role in this development was
based on its role as an extended arm of the government,
and government policies gave VAPO a task to fulfill. What
was peculiar about the situation was that nobody knew
what all the peat would be used for that VAPO had been
told to start producing. And soon it proved that the
main problem was not on the production side; it lay fair
and square on the consumption side. Very little had been
done to investigate the conditions for making sensible
use of all the peat being produced. On the other hand,
without the government's decision and the budget allocations, neither VAPO nor anyone else would have been
able to get the peat industry growing to anything like
the extent it did.

Two factors seem to explain best this process which
generated the basis for a sustained expansion of the peat
industry: The choice of an appropriate industry organisation, and the right combination of entrepreneurial drive
and system imbalances.

Industry Organisation. The state acted as an 'orga-
niser' in order to bring about stability and order in
the peat industry. Actors such as the Peat Industry Association and Ekono, the consultants, and factors such as
the employment problem in Suo OY, problems of regional
development etc., all lay behind the appointment of the
commission in 1967 to investigate the future of peat.
The main result was a reorganisation from which VAPO
emerged as the key actor for trying to overcome the
technological and economic constraints. Thus an organisation structure started to evolve, and a certain way of
solving problems began to be institutionalised. In other
words, a social structure was being created in the industry. And since VAPO had been chosen as the instrument
for future developments, a culture rooted in forest
technology(relating to cutting, transport, supervision
of work, for example) came to dominate.

Imbalances and Entrepreneurial Drive. Chance partly
decided the choice of VAPO. And no one was particularly
aware that a social structure was thus acquired in the
bargain. But this combination brought together a number
of imbalances --unemployment and unexploited peat bogs--
and entrepreneurial drive in the form of a VAPO management eagerly looking for new opportunities. The existing
culture in VAPO formed by VAPO's involvement in the
forest industry came to influence the direction of the
peat industry's growth and the social structure emerging
there. The development however did not end here. First
efforts and successes on the part of VAPO quickly produced new imbalances even while ending other ones. VAPO's

success in expanding peat production rapidly made it
necessary to develop quickly new markets.

Up to this point the development process can also
be envisaged as an overlapping sequence of driving forces: first the entrepreneurial drive in the form of
Kymmene's peat enthusiast, then the production-oriented
force of VAPO's organisation, and subsequently the market
driving-forces which led Kuopio to build a peat-fired
cogeneration plant.

The Decision in Kuopio

During the 1960s several big municipal projects
for combined power and heating plants came into the
picture. The larger towns in the interior in Finland were
faced with major decisions on energy policy. Back-
pressure power, which had been developed on the industrial side, provided a combination of district-heating
technology and good profitability. Experiences in Helsinki particularly were here of decisive importance.
For the coastal towns investment in coal or oil was the
natural solution, but the towns in the interior became
seriously interested in investigating the peat alternative as well.

To anyone interested in investigating the peat
alternative, VAPO's new role as a reliable supplier of
milled peat meant the removal of a major source of uncertainty. The concrete example of Kymmene AB's long experience with peat fuel also made an impression on municipal decision-makers. As a result of municipal ambitions
combined with the first signs of rising oil prices, one
city council - in Kuopio - decided in favour of the peat
alternative.

The course of events, which resulted in the Kuopio
city council investing in a 30/60 MW combined power and
heating plant in 1969, started with discussions around
this question as early as 1965. Behind it lay a general
interest in the opportunities for using peat, and an ambition to launch an experimental plant. The decision to
build the plant sprang mainly from a desire on the part
of the city fathers to provide energy supplies with a
broader base and to assure Kuopio of access to fuel.
There was also a wish to promote employment in the local
region.

The economics of the boiler also seemed to be within
acceptable limits. At the time oil prices were in the
region of 7 markka per Gcal, and negotiations with VAPO
resulted in an agreement to supply peat at a competitive
price.

The initial capital cost of the boiler was also relatively low. A good deal of new technology had to be developed for the plant although the boiler manufacturer
adopted a lot of Russian and Irish technologies.

VAPO's willingness to accept responsibility for annual deliveries of about 400,000 m^3 of milled peat over a fairly long period of time, at a price that was guaranteed in relation to the level of oil prices, was of course necessary before the municipal politicians could make such a daring decision. VAPO came to an agreement the same year regarding substantial peat deliveries to G.A.Serlachius OY in Mänttä, who converted to peat one of the boilers in its mill. VAPO's earlier problem, which had been to find outlets for their increased peat production, was suddenly transformed: the problem now was how to fulfill the demand for over half a million cubic meters of milled peat within only two years.

At the same time as negotiations were going on in Kuopio, other negotiations were also in progress for the towns of Joensuu and Björneborg. However, in both cases, a decision was made in favor of Imatran Voima OY, which had offered very favorable deliveries of electricity on long-term contracts. This meant that the planned municipal combined electrical power and heating plants could be postponed for three to five years, and the corresponding peat consumption therefore failed to arise.

Another town, Jyväskylä was also considering investment in a peat-fired power and heating plant at this time. Although a decision was postponed until 1973, when some rise in the price of oil had already taken place, an oil-fired plant was eventually built. Economic estimates had shown that peat was still more expensive. The hoped for economic and political aid from the government for a peat plant could not be fully guaranteed, and that decided the case.

The Breakthrough

Up to 1971 progress in the peat industry was to a great extent due to the efforts of a few forceful individual actors. From the strictly economic point of view it was easy to attack the 'peat fanatics' and to accuse them of wasting capital and cherishing unrealistic ambitions. Tension between the supporters of oil and electricity on the one hand and the peat supporters on the other became increasingly marked. The problem, from the peat supporters' point of view was described by the managing director of VAPO as follows:

When you work in the public administration, the huge number of decision makers is often the greatest obstacle to pushing through anything new. You have to get a lot of key people at the highest political level and at the top levels of the civil service to support what you want. A few opponents won't really matter, so long as your supporters represent a broad enough range. Such breath is difficult to shape.

The government's decision in 1971 and 1973 to increase annual peat production to 10 million m^3 by 1980
was of decisive importance for the future development of
the peat industry. When oil prices had more than trebled
two years later, the target was increased to 20 million
m^3. No time limit was set for reaching this target. But
VAPO, which had been charged with implementing these decisions, received increased budget allocations and about
25,000 ha of peat bogs were transferred to it from the
Forest Board.

The Peat Industry Association played an active role
in preparing these government decisions. Investigations
to establish the profitability of energy investments
based on the peat alternative were undertaken only after
the decision to expand peat production had already been
taken. The engineering industry in collaboration with
VAPO and potential peat users invested in the development
of methods and equipment for peat digging and handling,
and for transportation systems, and for different uses
of peat as a fuel.

The financing of energy investments came to play an
increasingly prominent role. The government was able to
influence investments through the newly established State
Investment Fund (INRA), which quickly achieved a com-
manding role on the energy side. The government could
also conduct a selective financing policy when it came
to investment in energy by using the Bank of Finland
which is regulating international borrowing by Finnish
investors.

At this stage the public debate on energy policy and
national energy supplies really took off. Nuclear energy,
the import of natural gas, and the possible further expansion of the remaining hydroelectric potential aroused
widespread debate. The government began to pay more attention to energy issues, and an energy department was
established at the Ministry for Trade and Industry.

The traditionally energy-conscious forest industry
was still marking time, but experiments using peat in
existing boilers were started in various parts of the
country. A pulp and paper company, Yhtyneet Paperitehtaat
OY Simpele Bruk, in Carelia, had to replace an industrial
boiler. The new boiler would have to allow for paper and
cardboard production at twice the previous volume. The
options facing the company were either to build a combined gas and oil-fired boiler or to build a peat-fired
boiler. The nominal capacity of the boiler was 85 MW.
The decision process took the following form:

1. The natural gas alternative would have involved
building a 40 km long gas pipe from the recently
completed gas main at Imatra. However, the Neste

Company wanted Yhtyneet to finance half the initial capital cost for the pipe. To the north of the mill there are quite extensive peat bogs, which are also close to the main railway. The estimated investment for a peat boiler amounted to about 80 million markka; the corresponding cost of an oil/gas-fired furnace was about 45 million markka. The expected government investment subsidies amounted to about 5 million markka. Since Neste would not withdraw their demand that Yhtyneet should finance part of the gas pipe, and since negotiations with VAPO resulted in a satisfactory agreement, Yhtyneet decided in favor of peat.

2. The decisive factor in the negotiations with VAPO was that the price of peat was not linked to changes in oil prices. The contract was to run for seven years. The price for the calorific value of the peat was to be determined annually with one-third linked to wage costs, one-third to the transport cost index, one-sixth to the wholesale price index and one-sixth was fixed.

The situation after the boiler had been in operation for two years was that the technical problems were overcome. Profitability was satisfactory assuming a 10 percent rate of interest and depreciation over ten years. The main problems were on the transport and quality sides. There is a difference in handling ten truck-loads of peat per day, and turning on the tap on a gas pipe.

During 1974, too, a number of important investment decisions were made. The town of Uleåborg decided to invest in a large municipal heating and power plant. VAPO's negotiations with Outokumpu OY led to a decision to plan and build a plant for the manufacture of coke in Peräseinäjoki in Northern Ostrobothnia. The plant was to deliver coke to the new superrefined steelworks being built by Outokumpu Oy in Torneå. Several smaller peat-fired heating plants were also being built in different parts of the country. In 1976 the town of Tammersfors also decided to build a large peat-fired heating and power plant.

VAPO's peat production was now well under way, and the consumption of peat began to appear as a noticeable factor in the energy statistics. By 1977 peat already accounted for 1 percent of the country's energy supply and looked like continuing to increase by about 2 million m³ a year.

The production of coke in Peräseinäjoki was expanded to an annual capacity of 30,000 tonnes of coke and 30,000 tonnes of briquettes. The building of an additional 12 MW waste-heat power plant was also in full swing. It was to feed 3 MW into the national electricity grid. The heat was to be used for the heating of greenhouses to be built in the neighbourhood. A packing plant for horticultural peat was also planned.

Two briquette factories in eastern Finland have been planned for 1980 and 1981 using the experiences from Peräseinäjoki. The breakthrough for the peat industry as an established energy industry was confirmed by the decision in November 1978 according to which Kuopio was to build a new peat-fired heating and power plant for 60/120 MW alongside the earlier one. This decision was made despite a considerable supply of electric energy and competitive offers for long-term contracts from Imatran Voima OY. The size of the investment was to be about 170 million markka.

THE FUTURE OF THE FINNISH PEAT INDUSTRY

The dilemma of the peat industry is that non-peat forms of energy are apparently socially acceptable. Peat is not quite so acceptable. It is much better to be working in a factory than to work on a peat bog. Working with peat does not involve working with high technology near industrial centers. Peat people do not live in the cities. They work out in the wilds.

Yet all estimates predict a further increase in the production of peat. Achieving the goal of an annual peat production of 20 million m^3 during the 1980s appears to be realistic. The relative profitability of peat has already been demonstrated. Peat has other advantages than just those attaching to energy independence. It is environmentally clean because it contains no sulphur. It has positive implications for regional employment and development. Yet, several central problem areas can nevertheless be identified:

1. Certain physical characteristics of peat --its low energy value, difficulty in handling, the danger of explosion, etc.-- still call for considerable technological development.

2. Because of the seasonal nature of the work, the sensitivity to transport costs, and the labour intensity of peat production, much work still needs to be done to develop new organisational forms to achieve desired cost efficiency.

3. Negative socio-cultural reactions to certain characteristics of peat --non-industrial handling, dirt, unsophisticated technology, location in the wilds, etc.-- impede further growth.

4. There are still no systems for using sod peat for the heating of houses, small industry buildings, greenhouses, etc. Even some essential items, such as small, reliable boilers, still have to be developed.

5. The high capital intensity of the peat-burning plants makes their costs sensitive to the degree of utilisation. Normal operating time should be about 4,000-5,000 hours a year in order for the advantageous fuel cost to provide full economic competitiveness against oil.

6. The whole problem of pricing presupposes further development and rationalisation of the digging and the transport systems. Very important are guarantees of peat's future ability to compete with the price of oil. At this point the government's pricing policy for liquid fuels and transport services comes into the picture.

Actions under way in the public and private spheres are already providing some solutions to these problems. The relevant legislation is being reviewed with the goal of further facilitating the production of indigenous energy resources in full accordance with the aims of national energy policy. The new law regarding support for the production of solid fuels in Finland will provide more public investment capital than had hiterto been the case. The various government administrations are also further extending various forms of aid in support of urgently needed energy-related measures.

The forest industry places increasing emphasis on the ultimate achievement of a high degree of self-sufficiency as regards process energy. Thus several forest companies have conducted extensive investigations regarding the extraction and burning of peat. The rate of development as regards industrial peat consumption will depend mainly on the rate at which industrial power plants have to be renewed.

VAPO is said to be negotiating at present for contracts to supply peat corresponding to about 20 million m^3 per year. Thus demand is obviously not going to be a bottleneck in future developments. The fact that the whole of VAPO's managerial staff will reach retirement age within the next five years, and that the management of the organisation will soon be in completely new hands, will probably also affect the course of future events. At the same time the possible reorganisation of VAPO as a state-owned joint stock company is also being considered. This is chiefly justified in government circles by the fact that more that half of VAPO's output already goes to non-state buyers, and that substantial exports

of peat-based products are building up. Forecasts in the
public sector predict that the reorganisation of VAPO as
a limited company will be realised some time around the
beginning of the 1980s.
Most people in the peat industry are expecting
further diversification of the peat-based industry. New
technologies in combustion and processing such as wet
charcoal burning, briquetting, graphite and activated
carbon production, etc., will soon be complementing current processes.
The vitality of the emergent industry will of course
also be fundamentally affected by oil price trends and
the development of equipment costs at the user level.
At any rate the development of the peat industry is no
longer dismissed as a pointless enterprise. On the contrary, in both the public and the political debate, peat
seems to be sailing steadily with the wind.

CONCLUDING OBSERVATIONS

1. The peat industry in Finland has been dominated
by the state and its institutions. The most important instrument of the state has been without a doubt VAPO which
accounts for the largest part of peat production in Finland, determines pricing policy, and dominates development plans and investments. VAPO is financed annually
from the government budget.
Other important actors within the state's sphere of
influence have been financial institutions such as the
Bank of Finland and the State Investment Fund (INRA), and
the public energy companies (utilities) Neste and Imatran
Voima. The Defense Department has also played a role with
its concerns about military-industrial preparedness.
2. The reemergence of peat as a fuel in the 1970s
is in large part due to the municipalities. They played
a pioneering role in combining the back-pressure technology for cogeneration with the use of peat as a fuel. The
central feature of this development has been the ambition
of the municipalities to take over responsibility for
communal energy supply despite the availability and very
good offers of cheap electricity from the national electric utilities. The desire to use the energy question to
contribute to strengthening the local and regional economies has also contributed to this independent behavior.
Party political connections may also have accounted
for these municipal decisions in favor of peat. The municipal authorities who decided for peat and against
national electricity were linked through membership in
the same party to those members in the government who
stood behind the government's principal decision to support a growing exploitation of peat. This constellation

of forces facilitated the task of the municipal authorities to finance the building up of municipal, peat-based cogeneration facilities. The commitment to peat on the national level combined with the state's control over investment funds assured availability of scarce funds to those acting in agreement with national energy policy.

3. The forest industry too has increasingly seen in the last few years that peat can be useful to secure long-term access to energy. Profitability calculations in 1974 and 1975 for peat-burning industrial boilers had failed to show a sufficient return on investment compared to alternative possibilities.

The oil price jump after 1979 and the growing importance of energy self-reliance has started to change the evaluation of peat. The decision of Yhtyneet, one of the large paper manufacturers, to buy a large peat-burning furnace and boiler system and the initial operative experiences with it --which have been positive-- convinced the rest of the industry that the technical problems can be overcome and that profitability is acceptable. An important number of enterprises from the forest industry have negotiated new supply contracts with the peat industry or are in the process of doing so.

4. The Peat Industry Association has played a major role in the revival of peat as a fuel. Association members are all who in some way relate to peat: peat producers and distributors, consumers, equipment producers, etc. The peat producers formed initially the largest membership group. There were at one time over 100 of them, though most were small producers. Today this group counts only 28 members and VAPO is completely dominating the group. The consumers and equipment producers have come to play a more prominent role over the last few years as their number and importance to the well-being of the industry have been growing.

The efforts of the Association during the development period of the 1960s consisted above all in various actions designed to influence attitudes toward peat. After the breakthrough of peat, the Association has turned increasingly towards becoming more like other branch organisations. It organized a system of information exchange, it undertakes branch related studies and investigations, and it defends and lobbies for branch related interests.

5. Producers and distributors of equipment --such as peat cultivators and extraction equipment, transportation equipment furnaces and boilers-- are largely private enterprises. Equipment for the cultivation and digging of peat was initially imported in its entirety from the Soviet Union. Machines were often adapted to suit local conditions and two thirds of the equipment used in the peat industry today is locally produced.

The producers in Finland of large funace and boiler

systems had from the beginning no difficulty in designing and producing the specialized equipment needed for burning peat. The development of peat handling and transportation equipment has to a large extent only required the adaptation and organization of existing technology and enabled Finnish industry to build all the parts of a functioning system.

6. At the beginning of the 1970s the fact that various links in the peat-handling chain were actually functioning --thanks to the three actors Kymmene,the paper company, VAPO, the state-owned peat-producer, and Kuopio,the first municipality to adopt peat for cogeneration-- provided real evidence of the possibility of a breakthrough. This was reinforced by the political legitimacy which was conferred on peat by the concrete, time-related goals, the employment of VAPO as an instrument, and the government-regulated aid.

7. Further development involved a rapid increase in volume and peat appeared in the Finnish energy statistics. This too had the effect of a signal about the value of developing and considering the option of peat.

8. A profitable scale of peat production is now being achieved. Competition on the peat-digging side is beginning to appear as a result of municipal and even privately owned companies.

9. The reorganisation of VAPO as a state-owned joint stock company can be seen as the expression of a need to obtain a clearer economic picture of operations, to satisfy demands for a return on investment and to diversify and create new business opportunities based on peat. The opportunity to 'exploit' the accumulated competence of the peat industry, and to pay back the possible additional costs, will depend to a great extent on the response to the new problems and opportunities.

NOTES

1. There were about 4.7 Finnish markka per US$ during 1981.

2. Ireland, the second largest producer of peat for fuel in the world has only the twelfth largest peat reserves in the world. It was producing about 4.7 tonnnes of peat fuel per hectare of peat bog in 1980. The Soviet Union, the largest producer with the second largest reserves produced .5 tonnes per ha in 1980. Finland reached only .3 tonnes per hectare in 1980.

Part IV

Analysis, Theory, and Normative Conclusions

10
Selective Observations

Thomas Baumgartner and Tom R. Burns

The cases presented in the preceding chapters illustrate several general features of the introduction and development of new technologies: the roles played by different social agents, including the entrepreneurs who initiate production and distribution; the opportunities and barriers which entrepreneurs and other change agents recognize and deal with; and the complex processes of shaping and reshaping production, distribution and use (PDU) systems.

Generally, the introduction of a new technology entails a complex of innovations rather than a single technical innovation. Typically, some of these are of an organizational and socio-political character, for instance changing certain administrative rules and procedures or reformulating government policies. For instance, taxation rules and building codes had to be changed in connection with solar energy developments in both Israel and in California.

Even if technological innovation is based largely on old elements --as in the case of heat pumps and peat cogeneration-- new elements or combinations of elements are involved. In the case of heat pumps in Germany, it meant designing and producing small units and selling them to a new buyer group, owners of single or small multi-family houses. The use of peat for the generation of steam and of electricity in Finland involved a scaling up of the production and transportation of the resource. This implied a different method of harvesting peat, requiring new types of equipment as well as railroad rate changes to make the whole venture worthwhile. It also required the organization, for the first time, of large-scale peat production in one place.

Technological innovation always involves some risks, even if the proponents believe that these are minimal or even non-existent. The proponents of nuclear power have discovered this but so have the producers of heat pumps in Germany who find themselves with substantial unused

production capacity, contrary to all forecasts. Demand is
stagnating if not (temporarily?) falling partly due to
disappointments with early heat pump models, partly due
to the slump in housing construction, and possibly also because buyers wait for the appearance of the often announced new types of heat pumps.

Our studies suggest that one cannot know for certain
beforehand if the innovation(s) will succeed or not. The
uncertainty and risks are greater the more radical the
new technology or the more socio-technical systems organized around its production, distribution and use deviate
from established socio-technical systems. In these instances, change agents are likely to encounter more substantial and difficult to solve problems of a technical,
economic, and socio-political nature.

Of course, powerful actors or coalitions of actors
with ownership rights, a political mandate or technical
authority may push the new development because they can
effectively mobilize resources, economic as well as socio-
political. Ben Gurion, the Israeli prime minister during
the 1950s and 1960s   assured funding for
solar energy research which was far ahead of its time.
High-level political commitment to peat helped to push
aside barriers blocking the development of peat use in
Finland. The exploitation of geothermal energy made a
step forward only when the large electric utilities and
oil companies became interested and involved. In short,
radically different technologies, requiring substantial
changes in existing socio-technical systems, are very
difficult to introduce and develop without powerful
backing, at least if the technology is to succeed within
short spans of time.

The following paragraphs discuss a select number of
general and comparative observations based on the case
studies. Chapter 11 systematizes some of our observations
and research hypotheses into a theoretical framework relating to the introduction and development of new technologies. In Chapter 12 we go on to draw a few policy and
normative conclusions based on the empirical and theoretical research.

(1) Our case studies of the emergence and development of new energy technologies suggest that progress is
being made. However, there have been no major developments, certainly no indications that a transition to alternative energy systems is taking place. In the countries of our investigation, the developments described,
while promising, remain only marginal. This is, in part,
because nowhere are all the key actors fully committed
to the development of the technologies. They fail to
support such developments in a coherent manner.

(2) Nevertheless, one may draw some satisfaction

from the modest, although rather isolated, achievements
in the development of alternative energy systems described
in the case studies. Many of the technologies we have investigated were said to be too "expensive" or not commercially interesting. Nevertheless, entrepreneurs experi-
mented, solved problems, developed production and marketing strategies, increased efficiency and managed to establish infant industries. Knowledge has been accumulated.
Some diversification of energy production and energy saving systems has been achieved. This will be particularly
important when energy problems will become once again more prominent on the political agenda than at the present,
and efforts will have to be once more intensified to find
new energy sources and to improve energy economizing.

(3) A complex of different actors, policies, laws,
and rules as well as technical and economic conditions
influenced the shaping and development of the new industries and related socio-technical systems described in
our case studies. The social agents involved played different roles: inventors and scientists, entrepreneurs and
technicians, banks and financial intermediaries, government agencies, politicians, and socio-political movements,
as well as users and consumers.
In a complex social system, there are few genera-
lists. There must be communication and various forms of
cooperation across the boundaries of specialization and
the various phases of introducing and developing new socio-technical systems. Linkages among different types of
actors occurred through market networks, business and
ownership structures, through industry and public organizations, as well as through research and technical networks. Progress was especially marked --for example in
California and Denmark-- when movements interested in alternative energy technologies managed to cooperate with
business interests in the interest of common lobbying and
effective marketing of the products to sceptical consumers.
In some instances, the connections were initially
weak or non-existent, thereby slowing down or blocking
the technological developments. We found examples of weak
connections between those designing and producing the new
technologies and ultimate users (e.g. in the early phases
of solar energy developments in California); between policy-makers, on the one hand, and producers and users, on
the other (e.g. heat pumps in Germany); between entrepreneurs and technical experts capable of solving critical
problems (in the early phase of geothermal development in
California). In our view, weak linkages and, in general,
barriers to communication and mutual learning and cooperation among the various key actor groups are among the
critical factors slowing down or blocking technological
developments. As we shall discuss in Chapter 12, a major

challenge to entrepreneurs, policy-makers, administrators
and other change agents seeking to bring about new technological developments is to develop strategies to shape
forums and networks for communication and mutual learning,
with feedback across different spheres and on various levels. A related question concerns strategies to establish
institutions for improving coordination, reducing transaction costs, and minimizing unnecessary risks. We argue
later that the genuine risks in technology development
cannot be eliminated prematurely, but must be accepted as
part of the challenge. Nevertheless, communication and
cooperation are one way to help minimize risks.

(4) The motivation for introducing and developing
new energy technologies varies considerably among the
inventors, entrepreneurs and change agents involved. It
may derive largely from economic considerations, the hope
for economic gain through the exploitation of new sales
opportunities or the possibilities for cost reductions.
Other motives may be the challenge of technical problems
and the opportunity to solve interesting problems, the
desire for social recognition, political motives, ideal
interests (anti-nuclear feelings, environmental concerns,
worries about oil dependence and vulnerability).
In several instances, economic calculation has not
been the initial point of departure for actors (particularly engineers, policy-makers and environmentalists)
who were trying to facilitate the production and use of
alternative energy technologies. Instead they wished to
deal with a problem, for example reducing national oil
import dependence in the case of Finland, to solve interesting technical problems (in the case of early solar
research in Israel), or to shape developments competing
with nuclear energy development (in the case of the
ecological movements in Denmark and Germany).
Of course, the entrepreneurs and change agents have
had to obtain private or public economic backing to realize their visions. Sometimes they misjudge completely
the opportunities for and the feasibility of projects.
Resources they manage to obtain are lost: money, time
and human effort go into R&D, into prototype development,
or into trying to introduce new technology products onto
markets. But the developments are aborted, branches are
never established, markets dry up. Both heat pump (Chapter 6) and solar water heating developments (Chapter 4)
were once promising in California before the discovery
of cheap gas and oil interrupted further developments until the 1970s. Or companies with good ideas and promising
products go bankrupt, with long delays before others take up the development again. This happened in the case
of early geothermal developments in California (Chapter
7).

(5) Relative energy prices provide signals, but they are not always very reliable or valid signals:

o Many of the technologies we have investigated were said to be commercially doubtful. In each case, however, entrepreneurs innovated, solved problems, found new possibilities, increased efficiencies, and achieved some breakthroughs in reducing costs and marketing products with competitive prices.

o The "here and now" prices are particularly poor indicators or reflections of the potential of complex systems where new solutions and possible changes in production, distribution, and/or consumption processes may radically change the picture.

o Tax regulations, building codes, engineering norms, energy pricing policies, administrative regulations reducing or shifting risks make up complex rule regimes which typically bias cost calculations for or against alternative energy technologies.

o Price developments for conventional energy resources may be unstable, or diverge in the short and medium run from long-term trends. The ideas about prices and likely price developments used by buyers to make choices among different energy systems may also differ from the actually existing price relations and developments.

Such factor complexes make it very difficult to judge the long-term feasibility and profitability of alternative energy technologies, particularly in so much as there is, in general, a lack of data and analytical tools to investigate such complexes and the consequences of their restructuring.

This observation does not imply that cost and price questions can be ignored. Quite the contrary. But costs and prices cannot be calculated mechanically. They must be seen as rough indicators. In some instances, they are not only rough but highly unstable indicators of incompletely formed and rapidly changing socio-technical systems. The argument suggests that one should examine and analyze as thoroughly as possible --and repeat the process as conditions change-- the comparative socio-economic advantages and disadvantages of more or less different systems, for example conventional as compared to various alternative energy systems. This implies, in particular, looking at the subsidy structure (including hidden subsidies), tax structure, regulatory and infrastructure systems, as well as other special conditions which give unfair advantages --and a very distorted relative price picture-- to conventional energy sources, including nuclear, as compared to new, alternative sources. At the same time, it is apparent from our studies that a complex of technical, commercial, and socio-political problems must often be solved before one can obtain a relatively clear and stable picture of the cost and relative price structures of new energy technologies.

(6) Laws, norms, rules and policies shape and influence the ways new energy systems can be built up and used, how well they fit into established energy systems, and how effective they can be operated. In some instances, such constraints retard or prevent the adoption of the new energy technology: existing legal and policy requirements make them relatively uneconomic. Thus, construction policies and regulations can slow down the turnover of the building stock, and thereby retard the introduction of solar heating technology, although substantial gains might be possible from its introduction into new buildings. The absence of piping and radiators, or warm air ducts, in buildings, make the installation of solar heating systems prohibitively expensive except under the most ideal conditions (see Chapter 3).

The norms used by engineers and architects to calculate the size requirements for heating systems can lead to over-dimensioned, hence non-optimally operating heat pumps. This tends to make heat pumps less economic than they should be. The norms also led in the case of Germany to calculations of operating costs and returns which differed systematically from actual ones. On paper, the heat pump often looked unprofitable.

Confusion about policies and rules --or changes in these-- can often deter the rapid growth of new technology markets. We have seen this in the case of the substantial drop in the rate of expansion of heat pump sales in Germany (see Chapter 6): (a) There was considerable confusion about subsidy rules concerning who could receive subsidies, and under what conditions, for the installation of a heat pump; and (b) the definition of allowable costs for tax purposes was unclear.

Our case studies identified a number of other legal and rule changes which were important in facilitating the introduction of new energy technologies, among others:

ISRAEL (Solar): The building code was changed to require new (apartment) buildings to have pipes preinstalled which could be used to connect individual collectors on the roof with the respective apartments.

Also, the right of neighbors and municipal authorities to prevent, on aesthetic grounds, the installation of solar collectors was limited.

DENMARK (Wind): The electric utilities adhered to a policy to connect houses whose owners had installed a wind-

mill to the grid, to continue to sell electricity to them
and to purchase all excess electricity the owners
wished to sell. However, the utilities were beginning to
change these policies once windmills started to become
popular and it required public pressure to make the government induce the utilities to continue the original,
favorable policies.

NEW ENGLAND (Wood): A law was passed setting rates for
electricity sold to utilities by cogenerating plants
above the rates charged for electricity sold by utilities.
(In Vermont and Maine the difference was 2.8 cents, in
New Hampshire 1.7 cents per kWh.) This encouraged companies with access to wood (and wood wastes) to go into
the production of electricity.

CALIFORNIA (Solar): Municipalities obtained the right to
guarantee access to sunlight for solar collector owners.
    Local building ordinances were changed to require
builders to install solar collector systems for house
and swimming pool heating purposes.

Finland (Peat): Public buildings were required to burn
domestic energy resources, in practice wood or peat.

CALIFORNIA (Geothermal): Changes in the Federal leasing
law enabled the acquisition of claims to larger land
tracts, thus enabling developers to prevent others from
exploiting geothermal resources discovered and developed
by them. This change facilitated geothermal development
under the control of large companies in the late 1970s.

    Changes in building codes and ordinances are often
major determinants of the ease with which new energy systems spread, or are prevented from effectively spreading.
Building code adaptations may have to be made far ahead
of the actual market introduction of new energy equipment, for instance, solar energy systems. The future
fitting of solar warm water heaters to then existing
buildings would require changes in the building codes
such as: (a) Limiting if not prevention of the adoption
of electric resistance space heating; and (b) hot water
heating systems, including those using electricity,
should be designed and equipped with extra large pipes
and radiators, as required for the low water temperatures
typically produced by solar collectors.

    (7) The preceding points strongly suggest the impor-
tance of policy-makers and government agencies making
changes --or in preventing changes-- which can facilitate
new energy developments. In some instances, the changes
introduced, although small, even trivial, had substantial
impacts on the trends and rates of development.
    A general desire has been expressed in all of the
countries of our case studies to develop alternative ener-

gy sources, in particular renewable energy resources. Nevertheless, the studies suggest that the role of government may vary considerably, both in the nature of the
role it played and in the effectiveness with which it is
executed. In some instances, there has been a strong will;
laws and policies have been changed to facilitate successful alternative energy development (Israel, California, New England, Finland). In other cases, there has
been a will, but action has been somewhat ineffective,
even damaging (Germany). In some instances, there has
been a lack of interest or will to develop certain alternative energy systems, e.g., solar energy in Israel during the 1960s, small windmill electricity production in
Denmark, geothermal in the US until the late 1970s. Development continued in any case but at a slower rate and
burdened with unnecessary constraints.

Among other observations, the following are worth
stressing:

(a) Early support by the Israel government for solar research, even if only modest, laid the basic scientific
and technical foundation for solar energy development in
the 1970s.

(b) Government requirements that public buildings make
use of alternative energy sources for space or water
heating have been important policy tools in Finland, Israel, and California.

(c) Consistent legislation, tax and other policies oriented to particular alternative energy developments explain
in part the relatively successful development of solar
energy in Israel since the early 1970s, solar in California and peat in Finland. But confusion and inconsistency
in the subsidy and tax policies of German federal and
state governments increased uncertainty among potential
buyers of heat pumps. Government efforts to facilitate
heat pump development may have hurt as much as it helped.

(d) Legislation and policies directed at influencing the
behavior of utilities are particularly important instru-
ments, since, as we discuss later, utilities are strate-
gically important actors and power centers in most established conventional energy systems. In Denmark, utilities were forced to maintain their policy to connect windmills to the grid and purchase excess electricity at a
reasonable price. The US government's Public Utility Act
required utilities to purchase electricity from small
producers at rates which were reasonable, in the public
interest, and above the rates charged for electricity delivered. In addition, the utilities were forced to provide back-up service at a reasonable price. Cogenerators
and other small producers of electricity were exempted
from state and federal regulations concerning financing
and rates (which apply to utilities. Such changes were

important incentives to windmill development in Denmark and wood-burning cogeneration in New England respectively.

(e) Ownership legislation can be a particularly strategic factor encouraging alternative energy developments. Solar collector owners have been provided with "rights to sunlight" in Califorai. Changes in the mineral leasing law in the US allowed the leasing of larger single tracts of federal land, thus covering in most cases the whole of a geothermal resource area.

On the negative side, one may point out not only the failure of German authorities to establish and implement consistent policies for heat pump developments, but to instances of lack of interest or will to encourage certain alternative energy developments:

(i) During the 1960s, the Israel government stopped all research support. The state utility's policy to encourage the expansion of electric accumulator use for water heating purposes (in 1963) may have contributed to retarding growth of solar energy (although it had also an unintended pro-solar effect).

(ii) The Danish government, oriented to large-scale windmill design and testing, did little or nothing to help the small-scale windmill industry.

(iii) The US federal government dragged its feet about changing the minerals leasing law, in part out of a suspicion of oil company motivations, thereby blocking one of the important conditions for large-scale geothermal development in California and the US as a whole.

(iv) Failure to organize small forest owners --and to offer them substantial incentives to harvest their trees-- led to great uncertainty around the stability of wood supply in New England.

The role of government in technology development should be viewed in its larger context, the complex restructuring which the introduction of a new technology and the development of new socio-technical systems entails. Some of the change is under the direct influence of entrepreneurs and private change agents. But certain changes may require, or may be facilitated by, political and government action. The extent of this will vary from concrete case to case and from society to society, each with its particular legal, institutional, and political structures. Thus, the scope for government and political action in facilitating transitions to alternative energy systems should be specified as much as possible (as we shall try to do in the following two chapters).

Our cases reflect relatively successful technology developments where with a certain hindsight one might ask why didn't government authorities or policy-makers do more. "Winners" are difficult to pick. Neither government

authorities nor politicians are in particularly good positions to know which technology or particular design
will pay off and which will flop.

In the following chapters we shall examine more analytically the potential roles and strategies of government in technological developments. One of our main the-
sis is that there is no single role, but multiple roles
which must be distinguished in relation to concrete technical, economic, and socio-political problem solving
which goes on in technological developments.

(8) The shaping and development of alternative energy systems typically requires not only economic resources
but socio-political power. In many instances the actors
(small businessmen and entrepreneurs) who are prepared to
take initiatives and to try to shape new systems have
very limited access to either adequate economic resources
or political influence.

For successful or rapid development of new energy
systems, entrepreneurs and change agents must often
struggle to change laws, rules and policies which block
or hinder such development. Also, they may have to contend with hidden or even open opposition of powerful vested interests. A utility company, for instance, with its
special technical culture and its interests to protect
its investments and profit opportunities may act to ob-
struct the introduction of a new energy technology or
they may try to shape it so that it falls naturally under
its control. This is so unless utility decision-makers
have a strong professional interest in it or have few or
no alternative ways to expand and grow in the future.

In some instances, certain government agencies and
socio-political movements ally themselves with entrepreneurs to change policies and laws. This has been true for
the ecological and anti-nuclear movements in Denmark and
California. But most often the small entrepreneurs lack
access to or influence in the corridors of central power.
They are compelled to operate marginally and to do the
best they can under difficult circumstances. This can be
observed in the development of solar energy in Israel in
the 1950s and 1960s, and of wind energy in Denmark. Or
the small entrepreneur is forced to sell out to larger
companies with the economic and political clout to bring
about change. This has happened in the case of the geothermal development in California where oil companies
took over and managed to get the minerals leasing act
changed in ways favorable to geothermal development.

(9) Our research suggests that, in general, utilities are key actors in facilitating or hindering new
energy developments. This is because of:

o   their pricing policies;

o   their expertise and the information they command;

O   their business relationship with significant
    shares of energy consumers;

o   their power to set, or to influence the setting
    of, rules relating to energy production, pricing
    and distribution;

o   their ability to influence legislation and poli-
    cy concerning energy matters, in part because of
    established connections to politicians and go-
    vernment authorities, in part because of their
    positions of expertise and general authority on
    such matters.

Utility companies in Denmark and Israel resisted the
new energy developments. They feared negative consequences for their economic situation and market position due
to a spread of solar and wind energy technologies, respectively. PG&E in California became interested in concluding long-term delivery contracts with the geothermal
electricity producer once it became clear that he would
otherwise go ahead and constitute an independent utility
in the middle of PG&E's supply territory. Also, the
introduction of large-scale systems, e.g. large windmills
and windmill parks, which the utilities themselves could
manage and develop, is less likely to evoke their opposition, as developments in Denmark and New England suggest.
Utility support is hesitant or ambivalent in instances where the new technologies are not those they prefer to develop themselves. We have seen that PG&E in
California was not entirely negative toward efforts to
develop geothermal power. But it lacked technical competence in the area. It was slow to act and to exploit available opportunities, but changed its attitude once a
trusted engineer from a reputable electrical machinery
producer became involved with the geothermal company at
the Geysers.
At the same time, the case of PG&E suggests that utilities may be relatively positive toward new energy technologies when they lack possibilities of expanding conventional energy production at the same time that they
are faced with demand increases. Utilities are unlikely
to oppose a new energy development which is perceived by
them as being strictly marginal, such as the initial
windmill development in Denmark and the geothermal electricity production at the Geysers.

(10) Environmental, conservationist, or other socio-
political movements can play a major role in the introduction and spreading of new alternative energy systems.
They play such a role through engaging themselves in the
concrete processes of shaping a normative climate, and

through exercising or applying political pressure to create laws, rules and policies which facilitate the emergence of new energy systems. The case of wind energy in Denmark points up that a social movement can work together, directly and indirectly, with entrepreneurs and producers of alternative energy technologies and thus contribute to changing public opinion and to influencing government policies (and countering in part the policies of utilities). Similar cooperation helped in accelerate the spreading of solar energy in California.

On the other hand, the battle of the German ecological movement against the electric heat pump --seen as a tool used by the utilities to legitimize their nuclear power program-- at the same time that it supports the widespread use of the gas or diesel heat pump has not only reduced the sales of electric heat pumps, but has also affected the introduction of heat pumps generally. Potential buyers are obviously confused and prefer to wait until the claims and counterclaims become reconciled.

(11) Our case studies point up that it is extremely difficult, if not impossible, to know beforehand or to predict the specific designs the new technologies were to take and the form and character of the socio-technical systems in which they developed. Among other reasons, this is because:

o   A variety of possible or potential alternative energy systems may emerge, not a single, predetermined one.

o   The energy production, distribution and use systems emerging tend to develop special characteristics as a function of the societal contexts in which their development is taking place.

In general, technologies --and the socio-technical systems in which they become integral parts-- may take a variety of ways. Which ones will be successful --or which of several forms will be successful-- cannot be determined a priori (Callon, no date). This reflects the fact that technology developments, the introduction of new technologies into production, distribution and use, entail a variety of technical, economic, and socio-political problems which must be solved in concrete settings by a constellation of actors. The actors involved often give different priority to the various problems and support diverse solutions. Matters of contradictory assessment and judgement come into play. Alliances are formed; conflicts occur.

The resultant uncertainty must be managed by the social agents, in part simply through taking risks, in part by solving technical and economic problems and bringing about changes in government policies and regulations.

Such problem-solving entails processes of adaptation,
trial and error, and backtracking. Technological development is no clearly plannable activity, particularly in
its early phases.[1] As Nelson and Langlois (1983:815)
argue:

> In fact, it is an activity characterized as
> much by false starts, missed opportunities
> and lucky breaks as by brilliant insights
> and clever strategic decisions.

> Only in hindsight does the right approach
> seem obvious; before the fact, it is far from
> clear which of the bewildering array of op-
> tions will prove fruitful or even feasible.

(12) Policy and research concerning technological
development are often oriented toward "hardware", the
technical aspects, as well as toward the economic aspects,
the assessment of the likely markets and levels of demand.
Our studies point up the importance of "social technologies": organizational forms, rules and norms, policies
and attitudes which affect the introduction and development of new technology systems. This applies to the organization of research and development, to the planning and
organization of production and the use of technology, the
education of users, and the various institutional arrangements and policies which facilitate or hinder the transition to alternative energy systems. We have pointed out
earlier the significance of particular rule changes. We
also stressed the importance of communication and cooperative linkages among key actor groups who play different
roles in new technology developments (see Point 3).
Our studies suggest that new technology developments,
particularly those emerging in comsumer markets, are facilitated by programs and institutions which provide for:

o   Testing and quality certification of products
    and the provision of warranties. In Israel,
    equipment guarantees for five to seven years
    were provided in the 1960s. Certification and
    complaint procedures have been an important in-
    gredient in California's solar development. In
    both cases, these programs tended to reassure
    potential buyers who had become uncertain about
    the quality of products and of the installation
    work.

o   Equipment standardization consistent with the
    stage of technical development. The Standard
    Institute of Israel established and enforced
    from the mid-1970s quality standards for solar
    equipment and its production. (See Woodward
    (1984) concerning French government standardiza-
    tion of heat pumps and solar collectors through

certification.)

o   Education and training of installers and mainte-
    nance men in order to minimize equipment failure
    that could raise unnecessarily consumer doubts
    about and resistance to new energy products and
    systems. This has been a factor in the demand
    slump in the German heat pump market.

The preceding points suggest, on the one hand, the
complexity of technological development and, on the other
hand, the ability of entrepreneurs and other social
agents to solve complex problems in the course of such
development. In part they do this by muddling through!
Indeed, muddling through reflects the high uncertainty so
characteristic of new technological developments.

The following two chapters build on the empirical
work and the theoretical ideas presented thus far in the
book. Chapter 11 presents a theoretical framework with
which to analyze new technological developments (see also
Baumgartner et al, 1984 and Woodward, 1984). Particular
stress is put on diverse social agents engaged in such
developments, the spectrum of problems with which they
must contend, and the political, institutional and socio-
cultural factors which facilitate or impede technological
development. In Chapter 12 we outline several policy implications and strategies for alternative energy developments.

NOTES

1. Once the major technical, economic and socio-political problems associated with introducing a new technology and developing socio-technical systems based on it
have been solved, detailed prediction and planning become
feasible and useful policy tools. Indeed, production,
distribution, and use usually become more routinized and
rationalized under such conditions.

BIBLIOGRAPHY

Baumgartner, T., T.R. Burns and P. DeVillé 1984 The Sha-
    ping of Socio-Economic Systems. London: Gordon and
    Breach.
Callon, M. (no date) Introduction of the Electric Vehicle
    and Public Demand. Ms, Paris: Ecole des Mines.
Nelson, R.R. and R.N. Langlois 1983 "Industrial Innova-
    tion Policy: Lessons from American History."
    Science, 219:814-815.
Woodward, A. 1984 International Innovation in Energy.
    Communities' Conservation and Planning. Uppsala:
    Institute of Sociology.

11
Toward a Theory of New Technological Developments

Tom R. Burns and Thomas Baumgartner

THE CONCEPT OF TECHNOLOGICAL DEVELOPMENT

The introduction of a technology into social systems -- at least as more than a mere conception or idea -- entails producing, distributing, and using the technology. Technological development involves then not only the designing and redesigning of new technologies but the development of their production, distribution and use systems (PDU). This broader conception implies that the barriers or bottlenecks to technological development are not only scientific and technical, but commercial, socio-political and cultural.

Systems for producing, distributing and using a new or different technology must be either adapted from existing systems or established as new systems. Such systems are not mere ad hoc collections of elements. They are organized socio-technical systems. Entrepreneurs and other change agents engaged in the concrete process of adapting or building up and integrating the various relevant PDU systems: for instance, the production of generators, towers, blades and other components for electricity generating windmills, setting up and operating the windmills, and ultimately distributing the electricity and making use of it in appliances and other electrical equipment.

As pointed out in the preceding chapter, there are a variety of problems which must be dealt with, decisions made, and inventions and innovations shaped in the global social process of establishing and developing PDU systems for a new technology. In addition to inventions and innovations connected directly with the technology itself, there may be innovations in machinery, other equipment, forms of organizing production and distribution, rules and regulations about standardization, quality aspects, and patterns and concepts of utilization.

In the process of trying to establish and operate PDU systems, technical, production, marketing and utilization problems are discovered and solutions attempted.

Some attempts may succeed. Considerable uncertainty is typical about such matters as costs, quality, reliability, market demand, and so forth until actors have worked through the planning and practical activities. Many problem solving efforts end in failure. A few may result ultimately in 'marketable' ideas (in the broadest meaning) and the establishment and development of new industries and patterns of consumption around a new technology.

Our framework points up that technological development does not simply concern improvement in a furnace or a windmill but development of the systems to produce and distribute the furnace or windmill as well as those which utilize such 'products'. Competing systems, rather than competing products, is a central concept in our framework. Products as such compete only when they can be distributed and utilized more or less in the same systems.

CHANGE AGENTS, PROBLEM-SOLVING, AND SOCIAL LEARNING

A strategic factor in technological development is the availability or absence of entrepreneurs and other change agents to engage themselves in the process of introducing and developing new technologies. Actors in diverse roles are involved in this complex, collective problem-solving process: inventors, scientists, technicians, businessmen, bankers and other financial experts, marketing experts, consumers, politicians and administrators. Typically, these come into development processes in different ways and to some extent in different phases of the development process.

(1) A person or a group has an 'idea' or a concept of how to solve a problem or class of problems. The idea may be realized in the form of a technology design or model. In the world of technical ideas, we refer to such persons as inventors, for instance, engineers or scientists who invent a new technology. Even in the social and political worlds, it is appropriate to speak of social and political inventors, respectively, who come forth with social inventions, new organisational forms and institutional innovations as well as cultural elements.

(2) Entrepreneurs are social agents -- individuals, groups, and social organizations -- which implement an idea or put it into practice, for example, they produce and sell it on markets. In many instances, entrepreneurs attract capital for establishing and developing production and distribution systems; they do this through their connections, position of authority, or charisma. Administrative entrepreneurs in government agencies and networks play a similar role in developing technology production and distribution systems within the government sphere.

(3) Entrepreneurs and other actors with managerial and technical skills organize labor and production processes, often adapting the innovation into forms which can be more readily produced and marketed (identifying or dis-covering these forms is often a complex learning and trial-and-error process).

(4) Actors with marketing and organizational skills deal with problems of distribution and selling. Often this en-tails influencing and educating consumers and potential users.

(5) Political leaders and movements as well as government agents, play a role in many instances in shaping laws, policies or rules which facilitate the technological de-velopment.

A complex of technical, economic and socio-politi-cal problems must in many instances be solved -- and mul-tiple decisions made -- in the process of new technolo-gical developments. Some solutions are realized in tech-nical networks,[2] others in more business-oriented and financial organizations, networks and markets, still others in political and administrative institutions and arenas. Indeed, in the context of such organizational, network and market frames, the various special types of actors pointed out earlier are linked together, although many are formally independent: through market processes (flows of commodities and money), social networks inclu-ding networks of formal agreements and contracts, as well as through formal organizations such as enterprises, go-vernment agencies, political institutions. Thus, on the one hand, a technical-economic system such as electrici-ty supply based on hydropower links together waterfalls, power stations, electricity grids, and electric equipment and appliances in factories and households, respective-ly. On the other hand, market, network and organizatio-nal frames connect together diverse types of actors in both building up and operating such economic-technical systems. An energy PDU system is not usually based on a single social organization but a network of organizations (Lönnroth, 1978b).

In general, diverse actors with various capabili-ties and resources are involved in dealing with and sol-ving the complex of strategic problems in technological development. If some of these actors are not available -- or they are unwilling or unable to act in the circum-stances -- then the effective introduction of new tech-nologies will be blocked or seriously slowed down. Of course, blockage often occurs also because powerful ves-ted interests resist or impede solutions to strategic problems.

Efforts at innovation are carried out by actors who perceive that,through the changes,they can realize net gains, solve particular problems, or better satisfy their own needs or those of others (Davis and North,

1971). Typically, these various motives can only be distinguished analytically. In practice, they are found represented among the diverse actors involved in any technological development. Not infrequently, they are combined in complex mixes in single actors or groups, for instance an entrepreneur who is driven by an urge to solve a challenging technical problem, earn money and gain social recognition for his or her inventions.

Any given innovation or technological development is likely to activate multiple, in many instances incompatible norms and values. Often these are experienced as dilemmas by some of the actors involved. For example, energy substitution or conservation goals may be contradicted by aesthetic or environmental objectives, as pointed up in the case of developments making use of peat or coal as fuel. Such problems reflect the fact that innovation and technological development have multiple effects. These include effects directly related to actors' expressed goals or the problems with which they set out to deal. They also have unintended effects. Thus, the introduction and development of new energy technologies leads to non-energy consequences, such as environmental effects and socio-political reactions. Similarly, non-energy developments in society will typically have direct and indirect impacts on energy matters.

The effects of introducing and developing new technologies influence and alter the context of decision-making and strategic behavior of those involved in the development process. Information about the consequences, intended as well as unintended, of previous change efforts feed back to social agents leading them to support or oppose the development, to mobilize additional resources or alternatively to give up mobilization efforts, and to engage in intensified cooperation or to struggle in relation to the development process.

Social agents learn and reformulate their goals, strategies and engagements in the course of the development. New concepts, shifts in values, and changes in relevant 'rules of the game' and social institutions will be reflected sooner or later in the technological development. Often these changes occur at a slow pace and, occasionally, only after prolonged and costly struggles.

In general, feedback processes in connection with technological developments are characterized by delays, distortion and confusion, and blockage. Blocked or distorted feedback, or long delays in feedback, prevent learning and restructuring essential to effective technological development and the minimization of unnecessary uncertainty.

PHASES OF TECHNOLOGICAL DEVELOPMENT

One may conceptualize on a general, abstract level
the process of technological development as going from
an 'idea' or conception of how to solve a problem, possibly realized in the form of a technology design or model,
to the adaptation or establishment of systems to produce,
distribute and use the new technology. There may be processes of growth as the technology is improved and applied to new problems. Resource accumulation as well as
the attraction of additional resources to the development
process enables further improvements and growth. Ultimately, the growth process slows down and   stagnation
sets in. The industry becomes 'mature'.

The introduction of a new technology into production
and use is an historical process. The process goes
through several critical phases entailing a spectrum of
technical, economic as well as socio-political problems
which must be solved. The   problem complex differs from
case to case, and from society to society.

For analytical purposes, one may divide the introduction and development process into six phases or
problem sequences. Each phase is characterized by a critical or strategic problem complex.

(1) Recognition of a problem or class of problems to be
solved, a need to be satisfied, or economic, political,
or other social gains which can be realized through dealing with the problem.

(2) Discovery and technology invention processes. Here
attempts are made to invent or adapt a technology to
solve the problem to be addressed. In some instances, a
new idea or discovery, perhaps realized in a different
setting, leads to the identification of problems which
can be solved. In general, there are complex interplays
between the first two phases, and also to some extent,
between them and later phases. Phase 2 may be skipped
to the extent that a technological solution already
exists and the critical challenge is one of deciding to
apply the technology, adapting it to the specific context in which it is to be introduced.

(3) Fitting the technology and PDU systems. The technology may be redesigned and adapted to fit into established production, distribution and use systems. There is
a complex interplay between redesigning or restructuring
technologies and restructuring the socio-technical systems into which they will be introduced. The following
phases concern largely the structuring of production,
distribution and use systems.

(4) Development of production systems. This phase entails
the mobilization of capital and other resources necessary
to establish and develop capacity to produce the technology for sale in markets or for use in the public sector. Of course, the problems will be minimal in the case

TABLE 11.1
Phases of Technological Development, Key Problems, Strategic Actors, and Policy

PHASE	KEY PROBLEMS	STRATEGIC ACTORS	POLICY GOALS	POLICY STRATEGIES
1. PROBLEM OR OPPORTUNITY RECOGNITION	Specification of the nature of the problem or class of problems	Users, inventors	Facilitate efforts to specify and understand the problem	Organize forums, newsletters, and other forms of information exchange
2. TECHNOLOGY INVENTION OR CREATION	Knowledge and techniques to solve the problem not available	Inventors, scientists, engineers	Stimulation of creative processes of invention	Support basic research and R&D to generate knowledge, proposals and models
3. TECHNOLOGY APPLICATION AND ADAPTATION	Knowledge and useful ideas available, but technically feasible applications not yet available	Engineers, technicians, entrepreneurs	Support prototype development and applications	Provide incentives or resources for prototype construction and testing
4. PRODUCTION DEVELOPMENT	Knowledge and useful technologies exist and have been tried out and shown promise; design and finance production	Entrepreneurs, financial intermediaries, managers, technicians	Support attempts to produce the technology and the growth of production	Provide access to finance capital, tax benefits, subsidies; set production standards. Facilitate feedback for modifying and improving production and products. Encourage application to new problems
5. DISTRIBUTION DEVELOPMENT	Technology is in production. Problem of activating or creating distributional networks and shaping markets	Entrepreneurs, marketing experts	Assure effective distribution, stimulate and facilitate marketing	Establish programs to build up infrastructure and distributional networks; provide subsidies and loans to encourage market demand; also, stimulate through government purchases, rebates
6. UTILIZATION DEVELOPMENT	Users and potential users have limited knowledge about the new technology	Marketing experts, advertisers, educators, opinion leaders	Facilitate information spreading and advertising, consumer education	Education for consumers and potential consumers; quality guarantees provided; complaint procedures established

that unused production capacity can be exploited for this purpose. Otherwise strategic decisions have to be made, and support mobilized, to convert existing capacity;or to establish entirely new capacity suitable for producing the technology.

(5) Development of Distribution. In the case of market oriented production, existing systems of distribution, marketing and selling must be exploitable or new ones established. The former pose the fewest problems. Otherwise, considerable effort and resources may have to be channeled into establishing and developing suitable market systems. In the case of the public sector, suitable internal distribution systems may already be well-established, thus simplifying the development problem and minimizing 'transaction costs'.

(6) User-learning and adaptation processes. Customers and potential buyers must be informed and educated about the use or possible uses of the new technology. Such requirements may be minimal. On the other hand, in the case of radically different technologies, requiring potential users to substantially change practices, norms, and ways of thinking, the success or failure of a technological introduction will depend on effective communication and education. These processes may be carried out by producers, by established users, by government agencies or various combinations of these. Markets, networks and other infrastructures may or may not be available to exploit for such purposes.

The phase structure outline above is a highly simplified picture of technological development in a market or mixed economy system. One moves from ideas and conceptions which are translated into 'solutions' in the form of a particular technology, to producing marketable or usuable designs, selling them (or in the public sector budgeting them) and bringing them into use. It should be stressed that the different phases do not follow a linear sequence but overlap and feed forward and back between one another. A group of users, for instance, may take an initiative to invent and produce a technology to solve a problem they have encountered. Later, they may come to produce the technology for others. Or a technology used to solve a specific type of problem may become a 'solution looking for problems'. Its producers or users realize that it can be used for quite new problem sets, and this contributes to its further spread and development. Thus, the technology may come to be utilized and developed in ways which go far beyond the problem set with respect to which it was originally conceived and developed.

The general point we wish to stress is that the phases of technology branch development should not be viewed in a mechanical way. The concept of development phases is a means with which to organize and analyze data. In any given concrete investigation, one should be alert

to the overlaps, the interactions and feedback loops between and among the different phases of technological development. There are often long delays between one phase
and another, for instance between the time an invention
is made, on the one hand, and its introduction into production and use, on the other.

Each phase has certain strategic problem complexes
which must be dealt with and ultimately solved, if effective PDU systems for new technologies are to emerge and
develop. Our conception of technological development
stresses particularly the socio-political and cultural
factors involved in technological development. These are
usually equally as important as the purely techncial and
economic.

Diverse actors are involved in the overall process
of learning and unfolding associated with technological
development. Certain types of actors   tend to be more
prominent than others in any given phase. Thus, scientists and technicians are likely to be particularly important in the early phases. In many instances, the entire process is initiated by entrepreneurs or potential
users eager to solve particular types of problems. Knowledge about their needs and the nature of the problem to
be dealt with may be essential to the technical or scientific problem solving process. Thus, technical-scienti-
fical theory and knowledge is linked to practical applications through communication networks and information
exchange between different groups of social agents.

In Table 11.1 we make use of the phase development
concept, identifying strategic problems for the different phases. Ultimately, this provides a basis on which
to formulate policy goals and possible strategies of
change agents and policy-makers who wish to facilitate
the introduction of new technologies into production and
use.

Knowledge of the phases of technological development,
the strategic problems characteristic of each phase, and
the key actors who play a role in solving the strategic
problems in each phase is essential for those involved,
in terms of effectively exchanging essential information
and coordinating their activities. The complex of actors
is engaged in a collective effort of innovation, whose
final results, PDU systems for the new technology or for
a family of technologies, cannot be precisely delineated
beforehand. There is no blueprint of the future, only
the opportunity to exchange information and to engage in
collective learning and development. The social agents
involved can more effectively resolve misunderstandings
and conflicts and coordinate their activities, the better
they understand their roles and relationships to one
another during the development.

CONSTRAINTS ON AND FACILITATION OF NEW TECHNOLOGY DEVELOP-
MENT: CULTURAL AND INSTITUTIONAL FACTORS

Established institutional and cultural frames in a
society constrain or facilitate the introduction and development of new technologies. Each concrete setting --
with its particular historical, social, economic and technical conditions -- has its own particular configuration
of factors constraining and facilitating new technology
developments.

Cultural barriers to technological development are
likely under conditions such as the following:
(1) The new technology or the socio-technical system
based on it depart substantially from established or customary concepts of 'technological solutions' or socio-
technical system design. This is particularly problematic in social contexts which are intolerant of uncertainty or which place low value on innovative activity. But
it is also problematic in contexts where the new technology is ignored by those allocating R & D resources or
having technical authority in the society. As Wittrock
and Lindström (1982:41) point out in the case of Sweden,
interest in and support of research, development and prototype production of alternative fuels (peat, wood) and
energy conservation (heat pumps) among other alternative
energy technologies, have been meager and never sustained.
At best there has been periodic interest during crises
brought on by the threat to imported fuels (WW I and WW
II). As a result, research traditions have not been built
up in these areas. This has severely limited the knowledge base for further technological development. In general, alternative energy technologies continue to receive
substantially less R & D funds from public and private
sources than nuclear, coal and other large-scale energy
technologies. The sustained, massive commitments
to nuclear research and development have been essential
to the growth of nuclear power.
(2) The technology idea and its potential socio-technical systems are very abstract or complex, to the effect
that no actors are able or willing to translate the idea
into concrete terms whose value can be recognized or
whose implications for organizing production can be specified. Even if there are producers available, the complexity of the technology may appear forbidding to potential users at the same time that producers or other
change agents are not able or willing to engage in educating potential users.
(3) In general, there is a lack of 'cultural entrepreneurs' who feel the need and have the capability to translate the new into terms understandable or acceptable to
key groups in the society, whether producers, consumers
or policy-makers. Established concepts and ways of thinking block comprehension of the opportunities or the

unique value of the new technology. This problem is particularly acute when conventional technologies, and
'technical cultures' on which they are based, appear to
provide satisfactory results.
(4) Lack of knowledge or expertise is often a barrier
to actors with the motivation and even the power to initiate technological development. For instance, public
utilities are often reluctant to establish conservation
problems for consumers or to go into educating users in
small-scale alternative energy systems, since their conceptual frameworks, knowledge and skills usually do not
relate to such problems. At the same time, they may lack
a mandate or responsibility for such efforts.

Institutional barriers consist of the rule systems,
norms and established practices which block or make
highly costly the introduction and development of new
technologies. The type of production, distribution and
consumption systems built up in earlier periods of energy technology strongly influence the opportunity structures and relative advantages and disadvantages of future
energy developments. Lönnroth (1977:132) argues in such
terms:

> ..... the purely technical design of the
> energy system bears crucially upon the
> future freedom of action. The energy car-
> rier's task is to link up energy producers
> with users. Today we chiefly use electri-
> city and different fuels (heating oils,
> gasoline, town gase, etc.) as energy
> carriers, around which distribution systems
> are built up. Whether any one energy
> source can be used or not will very much
> depend on how it fits together with the
> energy carriers we have now. Solar col-
> lectors or thermal heat pumps for home
> heating will require a distribution sys-
> tem, e.g. circulating water. Direct elec-
> tric resistance heating thus impedes the
> introduction of solar collectors, while
> water as energy carrier admits of much
> greater flexibility...... So the free-
> dom of action toward the renewable alter-
> native will very much depend on whether
> we can adapt today's energy carriers (and
> the distribution system) to make them fit
> both the coal and/or breeder solution and
> the renewable solution. Examples of such
> energy carriers are water, methanol, per-
> haps hydrogen, and so forth. On the other
> hand, a continued rapid electrification
> presumably reduces the flexibility.

There are built-in barriers to the introduction of

of certain energy technologies and the establishment of socio-technical systems: the existing organization of production and distribution, established patterns of policies, rules and legislation. The latter may concern building codes and ownership laws, pricing rules for electricity, rates for back-up power, and so forth.

In general, contemporary socio-technical systems for producing and distributing energy are more favorable to the introduction and expansion of particular energy technologies than others. Kaijser(1982) points out that since nuclear power has a limited future in Sweden (after the referendum in 1980 which supported a phasing out of the Swedish nuclear program by 2010 at the latest), the power companies have oriented themselves to a major expansion of coal power (using imported coal) during the 1990s. This strategy suits them, precisely because such a development is compatible with their operations and their organizational and professional orientations, as opposed to smaller scale alternative technology systems or energy economizing.

A corollary to the above proposition is that certain combinations of energy supply systems may be more 'coherent' and fit together than others (see Chapter 2). Lönnroth argues (1978b:19):

> Large scale wind and large scale nuclear probably do not fit, among other reasons because of load management problems. In the same way large scale photovoltaics probably would lead to reduced load duration of a large nuclear program, and would thus also not be a good combination. Solar heating on a community basis is, on the same grounds, probably a bad fit with district heating, especially if the latter has a cogeneration plant on top of it. A more favorable combination seems to be nuclear and biomass. The former could be used for large scale district heating and electricity, while the latter could be used for small scale district heating, as fuel for processing industries and also as feedstock for synthetic liquid fuels (produced by a combination of biomass and nuclear process heat).

In general, many renewable energy sources do not fit well into conventional distribution and use systems -- in particular electric grids and the electrification of energy consumption. For instance, in order that wind energy systems would become more widely accepted, either (i) they must be coupled into electric grid systems or have other back-up systems so that voltage and amperage levels can be maintained; or (ii) appliances and other equipment

which use electricity must be redesigned to tolerate much
more variation in voltage and amperage than they are presently designed to do. In the absence of such radical redesign, entailing great costs, the constraints and incentives acting against the wide-spread use of small wind
generators are substantial. Similarly, the effective introduction and development of solar heating systems would
require changes in most existing building ordinances and
codes as well as changes in property ownership rights
(protection against 'shadowing').

ENTREPRENEURS AND THE MOBILIZATION OF SOCIAL POWER

The development of new technologies, particularly
radically new ones, requires the mobilization and exercise of economic and socio-political power, learning and
social restructuring; in shaping new enterprises, new
markets and industries, in establishing new public policies and laws, and so forth.

The changes which must be realized in order to introduce and develop a new technology in production, distribution and use are realized or carried out by social
agents. They must have sufficient authority, economic resources, and political power to do this, particularly in
instances where other social agents oppose them. A major
problem in new technological developments is that often
the actors who have the necessary knowledge, commitments
and will to shape something new, for instance to initiate
a transition to alternative energy systems, may lack the
resources and social power to realize this ambition. The
problem is particularly critical when changes must be carried out in several spheres of social activity in order
to establish effective production, distribution and use
systems (see Table 11.2). Entrepreneurs may be able to
attract finance capital and to establish production of a
new technology but lack the skills or political influence
to initiate changes in strategic government policies and
regulations. Conversely, socio-political actors may bring
about change in laws and government policies but fail to
influence business leaders and enterprises to start up
new businesses and branch developments based on a new
family of technologies; at the same time, the political
agents lack the knowledge or legitimacy to initiate business activity themselves.

Social power structures are critical factors in technological development for several reasons:
(1) Social power, whether based on technical authority,
command of economic resources, administrative power, or
political influence, is essential to bringing about many
of the changes -- technical, economic and socio-political
-- entailed in new technological development.
(2) Established power structures and vested interests in

TABLE 11.2   SOCIAL AGENTS AND TYPES OF TECHNOLOGICAL CHANGE

CHANGE AGENT CONDITIONS	TYPES OF CHANGES INVOLVED IN NEW TECHNOLOGICAL DEVELOPMENT		
	EVOLUTIONARY	RADICAL CHANGE IN SINGLE SPHERE	RADICAL CHANGE IN MULTIPLE SPHERES
NO COMMITTED ENTRE-PRENEUR OR CHANGE AGENT	No Change	No Change	No Change
COMMITTED CHANGE AGENT BUT WEAK IN AUTHORITY, RE-SOURCE CONTROL, SOCIO-POLITICAL POWER	Some Likelihood of Desired change	Change Unlikely	NO Change
COMMITTED CHANGE AGENT, POWERFUL IN ONE STRATEGIC SPHERE (has pro-perty rights, ac-cess to resources, or political mandate)	Change Likely	Change Likely if change agent's power is based in the relevant sphere. Otherwise, change uncertain	Change Very Uncertain (must be negotiated. Necessary changes readily blocked in spheres where change agent weak
COMMITTED CHANGE AGENT OR COALI-TION WITH NET-WORK OR ORGANIZED POWER ACROSS SPHERE	Change Likely	Change Likely	Change Likely

conventional technologies may block new developments, or, at least, they may distort or reorient them away from optimal forms. For instance, technical innovations are accepted or rejected on the basis of their degree of consistency with established concepts, norms and socio-political interests (in the latter case, for instance, in terms of the degree to which they are perceived to reinforce established positions of power and authority). Hence, public utilities tend to support large-scale energy innovation proposals, which fit into the existing systems under their control or which would be logical extensions of these systems. In Sweden for instance, electric space heating was up until the 1950s not acceptable. When nuclear power was introduced, a key proponent, the Swedish State Power Board, won the support of the building industry for this. Plumbing engineers and related groups in opposition lost out, in part because they were disorganized. In this way, the rapid expansion of nuclear power was combined with new electricity utilization systems which supported the rapid growth of nuclear electricity generation (Lönnroth,1978a).

Competing energy systems had their advocates. In particular, communal utilities in Sweden, as major producers and distributors of heat for district heating , have been interested in co-generation.[4] Lönnroth points out (1978b:8):

> The combined generation plants competed with nuclear in the generating market but also in the end-use market since CG (co-generation) required large district heating networks , and one of the primary markets for nuclear was electric space heating. Since the most rapidly growing market was the low-voltage market rather than industrial use, and since the distribution system to this market primarily was controlled by the cities, the State Power Board was understandable worrked by the plans of the cities. However, through long-term contracts, rate reduction, etc. (and through an earlier developed overcapacity of hydropower) the State Power Board managed to slow down the combined generation plants and thus secure a large market share for nuclear electricity.

The struggle between co-generation and nuclear power in the 1960s was a fight between two types of socio-technical systems: one, a cartel of electricity distributors (Swedish cities) and the other, the State Power Board and national utilities. The development of cogeneration required strong local authorities, able to plan heating markets through district heating but also in con-

trol of electricity distribution, while the nuclear energy system required a strong central institution able to
introduce nuclear reactors, adapt parts of the electricity supply system, develop new markets for electricty, and
so forth. The roles of the local authority and the central utility were quite different under the two technologies (Lönnroth, 1980).

Co-generation was blocked in Sweden largely because
electricity supply policies, rate setting, and regulatory
policies with respect to back-up power were under the
control of the State Power Board and national utilities.
The cities were faced with substantial uncertainty (determined
politically) about future electric supply policies, back-
up power and other conditions, which they lacked the power to overcome. This uncertainty and the risks it implied for large investments in co-generation (together
with the problems communes had in financing co-generation) effectively blocked co-generation development in
Sweden.

Today many powerful utilities and major energy
equipment companies try to exploit existing opportunities
to gain from developing new energy technologies such as
wind and solar, selecting paths of development which are
consistent with their ways of thinking, their modes of
organizing production and supply, and their positions of
authority and power. In cases when a new technology --
or new uses of a technology -- appear to threaten their
interests, they use their power and authority to block
it. Kaijser (1982:5) discusses the case of a public housing company in Gothernburg, Sweden, which installed heat
pumps based on outgoing ventillated air in some apartment
houses in a district-heated area. The heat pumps were
capable of supplying total end-use energy needs from
Spring to Autumn and of reducing annual energy needs by
about one-third. According to Kaijser, heat pumps of this
kind could easily be installed in about half of all
apartment houses in Sweden. On the other hand, since the
bulk of district heating (a very capital intensive system for producing and distributing energy) is directed
toward apartment houses, a widespread introduction of
these heat pumps would result in huge economic losses for
district heating systems, particularly in the absence of
expanding housing stocks and demand for heat. Not surprisingly, Gothenburg´s Energy Board (the authority in
charge of the district heating system) threatened to stop
the heat pumps through legal means. Kaijser points out
that such exercise of power based on vested interests and
different investment orientations have strategic implications for future energy developments in Sweden (1982:5):

      ...... If conservation proceeds at a slow
      pace, large-scale, capital intensive dis-
      trict heating systems with comparably low
      variable energy cost will be built during

the 1980s and render further energy conservation uneconomical. If, on the other
hand, (such) conservation proceeds rapidly, many of the investments in district
heating systems will become uneconomical
and will therefore be postponed.

In general, socio-political barriers to new technological development are of two types: (1) entrenched vested interests with considerable political and economic
power are able to block or undermine efforts to introduce
a new technology and to establish new, or reshape old,
socio-technical systems; (2) the introduction and development of alternative technology systems require restructuring in multiple spheres at the same time that the
entrepreneurs and change agents pushing for the new developments lack sufficient powers to bring about such extensive restructuring.

Some technological innovations require few changes
for their introduction. They can more or less be produced, distributed and used within existing arrangements.
They are more evolutionary in character. As long as
'entry-barriers' or entry costs are low, an entrepreneur
has clear opportunities to initiate the development process. Of course, barriers to entry or attempts to block
the innovation by powerful vested interests in the sphere
will raise development costs and risks considerably.

One may distinguish between frontier and well-organized areas. In the former there are weak or no major
vested interests to block or impede the introduction and
development of a new technology. On the other hand, in
well-organized or institutionalized areas, powerful vested interests may have to be won over or defeated in order to initiate new technological developments. To bring
about change in established socio-technical systems, an
entrepreneur or change agent must have the backing of,
for example, a large corporation, powerful labor unions,
key industries, or utilities, a configuration such as
that mobilized in the development of nuclear energy. Or,
they may require the backing of a political movement or
key government agency to bring about changes in laws,
policies, and ordinances suitable for new technological
developments.

In the case of alternative energy technologies, the
technical, economic and political influence of the entrepreneurs and change agents engaged in developing the
technologies is relatively weak: solar, bio-mass and
small-scale wind technologies are not generally backed
or pushed by powerful enterprises and industries. The
support of the environmental, anti-nuclear and related
social movements supporting 'soft and renewable energy
sources' tends to be in spirit, not in the actual technological development, including production and market

initiatives. At the same time, established energy industries and utility companies have powerful lobbies and
command considerable authority on energy matters in public forums.

Radically new technologies require shaping new and
different socio-technical systems. One is not simply
dealing with a slight variant or even a 'new product' but
a more 'global innovative complex'. The latter will often
require social and legal changes which cannot be carried
out by technicians or entrepreneurs, but only by policy-
makers and political agents. Wittrock and Lindström
(1982:12) have examined the Swedish govern-
ment´s role in the development of hydro-power and nuclear
power in Sweden (also, see Lönnroth (1977):

> The development of hydroelectric power and
> the R & D investment in the atomic energy
> endeavor both necessitated state involve-
> ment. The development of hydroelectric
> power was rendered more difficult by the
> prevailing legal provisions. It was nec-
> cessary to introduce, among other things,
> legislation in Government licensing in
> order to be able to develop the rivers and
> build up the distribution systems.......
> ... the development of a national nuclear
> technology was an undertaking requiring
> state financing and widespread political
> support.

In the case of hydro-power development there was an
available technology, capital, a market and interested
parties, and a growing industrial complex which could
overcome the obstacles of agricultural society. To introduce hydropower demanded intense legislation over a 20
year period in Sweden. Principles of right-of-way for
long-distance transmission had to be established along
with safety rules. Hydro-power installations required
changes in legislation in order to force landowners
into agreements. In effect, the expropriation of private
land for the public good was established. From the perspective of societal development, this was a struggle
between two social orders. The old water-law represented
an agrarian subsistance culture while the new was better
suited to an industrial order (Lönnroth, 1978b:7). The
changes in existing legislation and the enactment of new
laws made the new technology commercially viable
(Wittrock and Lindström, 1982).

The 'success' of nuclear power has depended heavily
on the socialization of R & D costs and ultimately other
costs, which in many instances have only slowly come to
be recognized: safety and security, waste disposal, de-
commissioning, and regulation generally. The initial socio-technical changes required for nuclear power develop-

ment were largely on the production side, substantially less (but not without significance as we have pointed out earlier) on the distribution and use side. Electric grids and electricity consumption patterns were already established. Ultimately, of course, socio-political factors, in particular public suspicion of nuclear power, fear of accidents, questions about security and disposal of nuclear waste and so forth has contributed to limiting the full development of nuclear power.

The development of hydro-power and nuclear systems appear to contrast sharply with that of domestic petroleum supply systems. Market, technology, and socio-economic conditions permitted the development of oil and gasoline supply systems. The latter could be handled largely through market mechanisms. That is, no major political or legal action -- and institutional restructuring -- were necessary domestically (see page 15 concerning international structuring).

In general, one may distinguish between radical and evolutionary technologies (Lönnroth,1978a:33):

> The latter can mostly be handled by the existing industries themselves, perhaps with some minor adaptation of legislation and regulation. The former frequently require much larger legislative changes, possibly the build-up of new institutions (or changed roles of existing institutions) and frequently require much more political action. In terms of the metaphor of the critical path, the evolutionary technologies have a critical path of expansion where conditions mainly are internal to or could be handled by the industry, while the more revolutionary technologies have a critical path where the conditions necessary for expansion cannot be met by the industry alone but requires rather extensive government involvement.

Of course, if the new technology is the 'brain-child' of large, powerful enterprises, they often have the economic and political power to assure political support. Large companies and labor unions (above all, in the construction industry), engineering groups and academic professions found supporters in the government (and in most instances the military) to develop nuclear power in many countries.

In other instances, private enterprises -- particularly smaller ones -- cannot mobilize the resources and put together the political coalition necessary to shape substantially new socio-technical systems (except in completely new areas of activity). They may lack the

the expertise or knowledge of steps to take.

The more such restructuring required, the greater the power resources necesssary to assure that problems can be dealth with, and unnecessary uncertainty reduced or eliminated. The question is not simply one of building individual plants but establishing new industries, training new cadres of specialists, settling issues concerning environmental standards, settling land use or other resources policy questions. The uncertainty which slows down or blocks technological develement may arise for diverse reasons: difficult technical problems, ignorance about potential users and about market demand, uncertainty about ownership and patent rights, instability or inconsistency in government policies, uncertainty about socio-political movements and political plans bearing on the introduction of the new technology and the shaping of socio-technical systems based on it.

Radically new technologies or socio-technical systems will typically have impacts on different areas of society, not simply production systems, markets, spheres of consumption, but government policy and regulation, education, and research. For this reason the restructuring is usually carried out by -- even requires for its success -- a 'coalition' of actors engaged across different social spheres and institutions in society. Such a coalition or movement carries through and integrates the technical, economic and socio-political problem-solving into more or less coherent PDU systems. These are not in the final analysis ad hoc collections of independent components, but systems which are largely shaped in relation to one another.

Inability to establish such a coalition or network across strategic spheres results in blockage of new technological development. Blockage is also likely if:
(1) a coalition of entrepreneurs and other change agents fails to formulate or develop an adequate model (theory) of effectively functioning socio-technical systems based on the new technology.
(2) the coalition is unwilling to pay the (opportunity) costs to restructure institutional arrangements, change policies and mobilize human and material resources in order to establish effective socio-technical systems based on the new technology.
(3) its social power is weak relative to actors or groups opposed to the introduction of the new technology and the development of new socio-technical systems.

In any concrete historical situation, these conditions are not fixed. Social learning, coalition formation, resource mobilization, commitments and strategies undergo change. Thus, an adequate theory of the technology-in-production and use may be formulated overtime. Change agents reassess the situation and commit themselves to bringing about the necessary economic and

socio-political changes. Resources, including expert resources, are mobilized to effectively overcome vested interests in the established socio-technical systems.

To sum up: the change agents who are necessary to
bring about a new technological development will vary
substantially from case to case, depending on the degree
and type of 'incompatibility' between the new technology and established production, distribution and use
systems, in particular (see Table 11.2):

(1) Minimum incompatibility. The technological innovation
is based on ideas, analytical tools and methods fitting
within conventional paradigms and ways of thinking. At
the same time, it can be produced, distributed and used
within established socio-technical systems, with at most
minor modifications. Technical, economic and socio-political problems and uncertainty will be minimal.

(2) Limited, radical incompatibility. In this case the
innovation fails to fit into at least one important
sphere. For instance, although there may be few technical or scientific problems, production, distribution or
ultimate use entails substantial problems,and restructuring would be necessary in one of these areas. Or there
may be laws or norms which make production of the technology problematic. If sufficient support or power can
be mobilized politically to bring about the necessary
legal or policy changes, the technological development
can take off.

(3) Extensive, radical incompatibility.The innovation requires complex restructuring in more than one sphere. New
forms of production, distribution and use may be required.
Often legal and policy changes are called for as well.
The technological development will not take place without substantial coordinated changes in several spheres.

(4) Revolutionary incompatibility. Such a technology requires complex, global restructuring. That is, substantial changes are required not only in immediate spheres
of production, distribution and use -- and in related
legal and policy areas -- but , for example, in military
and judicial systems.

The costs, economic and socio-political, tend to be
greater the more radical and extensive the changes entailed in trying to introduce and develop a new technology. The uncertainties and risks for entrepreneurs and
investors are correspondingly greater.

Radical technological changes call for powerful collective actors or coalitions which can initiate and carry
through the necessary changes in different spheres, in
part by mobilizing strategic resources. In obvious national emergencies there may be normative pressures and
social movements enabling the integration of different
interests and the mobilization of resources across insti-
utions and spheres of social activity. This is, in our
view a critical factor in the wartime and national emer-

gency successes of nation-states in radically re-orien-
ting production and establishing new, sometimes revolutionary socio-technical systems.

SUMMING UP: THE SOCIETAL CONTEXT OF NEW TECHNOLOGICAL DEVELOPMENT

A new technology is not developed and applied in the
abstract. It is proposed in relation to certain problems
or needs, as a means to solve problems or to meet needs.
The production, distribution and use systems based on a
technology or family of technologies develop in particular technical, economic and socio-political contexts.
These shape and regulate the innovation and problem-
solving processes, at the same time that the technological developments themselves lead to restructuring of
contexts.
Technologies are used in social activity such as
production and consumption. Their production, distribution and use should be viewed in their societal context.
These activities may to varying degrees fit into the
context of established PDU systems. Typically, when the
new technology is of the same general type as an established technology, its introduction entails no more than
a modification or adaptation of existing socio-technical
systems. The uncertainties and risks of introduction are
likely to be minimal.
On the other hand, the more a new technology radically departs from conventional types of technology, or
the more its introduction requires substantial restructuring of existing socio-technical systems for production,
distribution and use, the greater the level of uncertainty and the more opposition it is likely to generate from
vested interests in existing systems. Of course, there
may be attempts to redesign and adapt the technology to
enable it to fit more easily into existing arrangements.
Often, however, there are technical and economic limits
to such restructuring. Therefore, the stress is often
placed on reshaping the organizational arrangements,
practices and ways of thinking associated with established socio-technical systems. New socio-technical systems emerge, setting in motion processes of support as
well as opposition. The technological development may
'take off' or may be retarded or blocked as social groups
mobilize power resources and play out various roles and
strategies vis a vis the development process (Baumgartner
et al, 1984).
The introduction of new technologies entails complex problem-solving processes dealing with diverse technical, economic and socio-political problems. Inventors,
entrepreneurs, technicians, change agents of other types,
and even social movements play important roles in such

creative societal developments. The transformation of such
motive power into the introduction and development of new
socio-technical systems can only to a very limited extent
be planned and regulated in any strict sense. In the face
of high uncertainty associated with complex technical,
commercial and socio-political processes whose ultimate
outcomes are not predictable, a direct and dominant go--
vernment role is likely to be ineffective. A government
possess no 'transcendental truth' or blue-print for the
future (Callon, undated): it cannot 'pick winners' or
'weed out losers.'

Government policy-making, as we shall argue more
fully in the following chapter, should be directed toward
establishing the enabling conditions and incentives for
inventors, entrepreneurs, and other change agents, including consumer groups, to take initiatives and to in-
novate in introducing and developing alternative energy
systems. Governments may facilitate research and development as well as information exchange and learning generally. They may act to remove unnecessary barriers to
and costs of experimentation and efforts to develop alternative systems. They may encourage,through providing
incentives and risk-sharing measures, commercial, technical and scientific actors to take calculated risks.

A basic problem in market mediated technological
development is that often the payoffs, returns on investments, market demand, consumer reactions depend on government policies and socio-political conditions which entrepreneurs may be in no position to influence, for instance
through improvements in their production methods, improved quality control, rationalization and more effective
marketing strategies. Socio-political uncertainty and
turbulence increase the risks of investments and activities to develop new socio-technical systems and, thereby,
can slow down or block eventual technological development.

A climate of high socio-political or economic uncertainty makes enterprises and financial intermediaries
reluctant to make expensive commitments. The longer it
takes to develop, bring into production, and to market a
new technology, the less likely enterprises will invest
in them in times of great social instability and uncertainty. Exceptions would be most likely in rapidly expanding areas or areas with opportunities for extremely
large payoffs to make the risks appear worthwhile. The
general tendencies is for enterprises, particularly well-
established enterprises to devote their R & D budgets
and investments to new technologies which 'fit in' or
entail only modifications of existing types of technologies and socio-technical systems. In short, this means
to pursue an 'evolutionary path' of technological change.

Yet, times of great social instability and uncertainty are often those where there is a special need or chal-

lenge to develop new technologies as well as socio-technical systems, even revolutionary innovations. This paradox -- the gap between the challenge and the readiness
of key actors with resources to face the challenge in
creative, new ways -- is characteristic of the modern
energy crisis. The paradox is explained by the genuine
uncertainty in the situation, and the unwillingness of
powerful actors to take risks, at the same time that
risk-taking is absolutely essential to innovation and
new technological development. We wait suspended between
the old, which has lost the assuredness and wide-spread
support enjoyed earlier, and the new, which is still unknown and,therefore, cannot command widespread support,
in particular financial support. A certain immobiliza-
tion pervades our institutions. The question is: Can
human societies -- and their governments
and entrepreneurial groups eager to try to meet the challenge -- find effective ways and means to stimulate innovation and risk-taking.

NOTES

1. See Hughes(1983) concerning "the battle of the
electric supply systems", DC versus AC.

2. Wittrock (1980) points out the role such scientific and technical networks may play in formulating ideas
and making demands for new technological development
(and government support for it).

3. Coherent system combinations should be more economic, other things being equal.

4. Those communal utilities engaged in district
heating and electricity distribution had obvious opportunities and potential gains to make through co-generation.

BIBLIOGRAPHY

Baumgartner, T., T.R. Burns and P. DeVillé 1984 The Sha-
     ping of Socio-Economic Systems. London: Gordon and
     Breach.
Davis, L.E. and D.C. North 1971 Institutional Change and
     American Economic Growth. Cambridge: Cambridge
     University Press.
Hughes, T.P. 1983 Networks of Power. Baltimore: John
     Hopkins University Press.
Kaijser, A. 1982 "Energy Transition and the Building Sec-
     tor in Sweden." Paper presented at the 2nd Inter-
     national Conference on Societal Problems of the

278

Energy Transition, Dubrovnik, Yugoslavia, September,. 1982.

Lönnroth, M., P. Steen and T.B. Johansson 1977 Energy in Transition. Stockholm: Secretariat for Future Studies (Published in 1980 by University of California Press).

Lönnroth, M., T.B. Johansson and P. Steen 1980 Solar versus Nuclear . New York: Pergamon

Lönnroth, M. 1978a "The Oil Peak and Beyond." Stockholm: Beijer Institute and Secretariat for Future Studies.

---------- 1978b "Energy Futures for Sweden." Stockholm: Secretariat for Future Studies.

Wittrock, B. 1980 "Science Policy and Challenge to the Welfare State." West European Politics, 3:358-372.

Wittrock, B. and S. Lindström 1982 "Policy-Making and Policy-Breaking: Crisis, Technology and Energy Transition." Stockholm: University of Stockholm, Group for the Study of Higher Education and Research Policy. Report No. 23.

12
Policy and Normative Implications

Tom R. Burns and Thomas Baumgartner

In this chapter we outline several policy proposals and normative principles which are suggested by the research results presented in the preceding chapters. These should be viewed as tentative proposals. They are formulated in terms which go beyond our empirical and analytical results for purposes of stimulating debate and further research.

We begin by considering the problem of uncertainty associated with technological development. This leads into a discussion of the possible roles of the state. We conclude by considering a number of specific strategies and measures which government as well as other actors may utilize in order to facilitate the introduction and development of alternative energy technologies.

UNCERTAINTY AND OPENNESS

Uncertainty is substantial in connection with the introduction and development of new technologies. As Nelson and Langlois (1983:815) stress, policy must recognize uncertainty --and the different forms of uncertainty-- as a fact of life, and should not try to repress it or analyze it away. The uncertainty relates not only to the possibility of unforeseen technical problems but to complex production, marketing and socio-political problems which may arise. Uncertainty is real because in the case of new developments, the future can at best be known or anticipated only roughly. There is no sure blueprint of the socio-technical systems involving the new technology, the more so that the innovations are radical in character, require changes in different spheres (including legislative and policy shifts), or are opposed by powerful vested interests. In any case, blueprints must always be adjusted to a greater or lesser extent in the course of the technology introduction and development processes.

Reducing genuine uncertainty cannot be accomplished

through administration or edict. A learning and unfolding
process must be carried through by diverse actors who
possess essential technical, economic and socio-political
knowledge and capabilities and who collectively work out
the new technology and the socio-technical systems. This
process cannot be administered in the strict meaning and
should not be monopolized by a single actor or coalition
of actors. The process is best "organized" through relatively open information forums, networks, and markets
which may need to be reshaped in the course of the development.

Until genuine uncertainty can be significantly reduced, pluralism and openness toward alternative as well as
conventional energy systems should be the rule. If several energy technologies are available for development,
premature, administered choice among them is risky: flops
are more likely than winners. Similarly, during early
stages of the development of a given technology, heavy
commitment to any one design runs the risk of excluding
favorable or more optimal designs. These can only be identified in the course of the complex learning and unfolding process.

Open problem-solving --through information and knowledge forums, networks and markets-- is incompatible with
monopoly (Nelson and Langlois, 1983). Hence, conventional
energy utilities and related vested interests should not
be allowed to dominate or monopolize the development process. If they are to be involved in the new area, make
them compete with one another. If there is a single electricity monopoly, break up its R&D into regional and competing sections. Competitors, including the small and me-
dium-size competitors, should be encouraged by offering
for example substantial tax and other incentives.

Once major technical, production, commercial and socio-political uncertainties have been eliminated --or
greatly reduced-- then a more closed and administrative
approach may be entertained. In the meantime, a mixed
strategy is the strategy of choice: encourage and facilitate the learning and development processes through which
entrepreneurs and change agents, pursuing alternative
energy systems, are engaged. At the same time one should
exploit as well as critically examine conventional energy
systems.

As we have suggested earlier, some uncertainty connected with technological development may be unnecessary
and can and should be minimized. The uncertainty may arise from:

o   inconsistent or ambivalent government policies;
    legal confusion; rules and codes which are dif-
    ficult to interpret and not ready in time;

o   lack of adequate forums and institutions for in-
    formation exchange and cooperation in the dif-

ferent phases of technological development;

o   ambiguity, because of patent laws, lack of risk-
     spreading measures, etc., about the risks of in-
     vesting time, energy, and financial resources
     in technological development.

Such unnecessary uncertainty can be reduced through
suitable government action. This does not, however, war-
rant the suppression of the uncertainty associated in
technology development with the complex processes of
technical, economic, and socio-political assessment and
decision-making.

PUBLIC POWER: ITS USES AND ABUSES

New technological developments entail to a greater
or lesser extent the exercise of social power. In many
instances, such power is mobilized by political leaders,
government agencies as well as other political actors in
order to support, reorient, or block new technological
developments. Understanding technological development requires a conceptualization of the ambiguous role of governments, and political agents generally.
The policies, strategies, and programs of governments and political agents may be important for facilitating new technological developments by mobilizing resources, funding R&D, and supporting new branch developments
and employment opportunities. Support can also take less
direct forms and involve changes in laws, policies and
codes.
At the same time, the power of governments or political agents generally may interfere with and disorient
learning and innovation processes essential to new technological developments. With the best of intentions, they
may try to "choose winners", deciding on a direction of
development which leads prematurely to the reduction of
variety (and of uncertainty), locking the technological
development into non-optimal or even dead-end paths
(Nelson and Langlois, 1983). In some instances, opponents
to certain new technology developments manage to win the
support of the state to block important innovations, as
we have pointed out earlier about public utilities and
energy-intensive industries.
What general conclusion can be reached about the limitations on and possibilities of government actors to
advance or to hinder new technological developments?
First, government agencies and policy-makers can and
should become involved in processes of technological innovation and branch development. Secondly, the forms of
involvement, the possible effective roles and programs,
and the dilemmas and risks of involvement should be investigated and specified as much as possible.

In our view, a rough framework for specifying and
assessing government involvement in new technological developments can be formulated. Two critical dimensions
here are (i) the phase of technological development (determining the types and degree of uncertainty), and (ii)
the government's ultimate role in the eventual socio-
technical systems related to new technologies. Our argument is straight-forward and can be expressed in terms of
two principles.

Principle 1. The earlier the phase of development,
and the greater the technical, economic, and socio-political uncertainties, the less the government should be
involved in any direct or intimate way. In many instances,
there are entrepreneurs and change agents willing and capable of carrying through the development process,
if only they are left alone. At most, they require government assistance in breaking down some of the legal,
administrative and policy constraints and in overcoming
blockages set up by vested interests in conventional
technology systems.
In general, governments lack knowledge to make the
appropriate assessments and solve the scientific, technical, production, and commercial problems which are involved in technological developments before successful pro-
duction-distribution-use systems have been established.
As Callon (no date:23) has pointed out:

> To be effective, public demand must ... inter-
> vene (only) in sectors where any technological
> uncertainty has disappeared, when it is only
> a question of choosing between options and
> channels that are perfectely well known and
> foreseeable.

The state can reduce some of the risks and thereby facilitate exploration of new, interesting lines. It can encourage processes of research and invention, facilitate
contacts and communication among key groups of technicians and designers, managers, marketing experts, and
users and potential users. Such a "supportive" and more
indirect role is discussed more fully later.

Principle 2. The less the government is to be ultimately involved in the socio-technical systems which will
be established and developed in the process of technological change, the more strictly the government should
avoid being directly or intimately involved in the specific technical, production, marketing, and educational
processes associated with technological developments.
Conversely, it is legitimate and essential that the government is involved in the planning and the management
of systems in which it is already playing a major producer or consumer role or in which it will play such roles.

That is, it has concrete and specific interests in, or ultimate us of the technology for its own activities. In some instances, as in the case of the Finnish Fuel Board (VAPO) (see Chapter 9), the government is already involved for historical reasons in a system that is in the process of transformation. In other cases, it may become involved because the state is the only actor who can provide the financing and manage the research process. In many countries, nuclear energy development has been such a case, certainly in the development of the breeder option.[1]

Below we discuss three general role types and related strategies for government action. Finer distinctions can also be made as the specific technical, economic and socio-political contexts are specified.

1. Indirect Engagement: Meta-management Role.

Here the government's involvement is indirect and supportive, establishing laws, policies and infrastructure which will facilitate open and pluralist learning and development processes. Of course, policies and programs should be differentiated in terms of the phase of technological development at which they are directed.

The general principle here should be as follows: The greater the degree of technical, commercial, and socio-political uncertainty, the less the government administration should be directly or intimately involved in the development processes. It does not have the technical, economic or socio-political knowledge and judgement capability to engage in the complex assessment and sorting-out processes. In particular, it lacks in most instances the technical and economic knowledge to enable it to foresee or plan which technologies or technological developments will pay off and which will result in "flops." Its role in such development processes should be limited to providing resources to R&D, facilitating information exchange and learning, and removing unnecessary barriers to or cost burdens on alternative developments. Its policies, incentives, and subsidies should encourage scientific, technical, and commercial actors to experiment and to take calculated risks.

Such a meta-management role can be distinguished from direct and intimate involvement in complex technical, commercial and socio-political processes whose outcomes are not predictable. This role is found in cells (1), (2) and (3) in Table 12.1.

2. Direct Engagement in Pluralist Processes: Co-Determinatory Role. In cases government or government bodies are or will become active in producing, distributing and/or using the technology, government should be directly involved in the technological learning and unfolding processes, precisely as commercial interests are

TABLE 12.1
Matrix of Government Roles and Strategies

SPHERE	DEVELOPMENT PHASE		
	TECHNICAL DEVELOPMENT	PRODUCTION DEVELOPMENT	MARKETING AND UTILIZATION DEVELOPMENT
Largely private sphere	Facilitate R&D, prototype development, knowledge acquisition. Provide incentives to business to invest in R&D. Facilitate information exchange, e.g. between potential users and engineers/scientists. (1)	Facilitate development of means of production. Formulate policies and provide incentives to facilitate improvement in production and products, cost reductions, better quality, etc. (2)	Facilitate marketing and user education, learning processes. Regulate markets: quality control, standards, etc. (3)
Mixed private/ Public or Largely Public	Invest in R&D, either jointly with private enterprise or separately. Engage in dialogue with scientific and technical networks working on or interested in problems. Specify function of technology. (4)	Public utilities and enterprises determine production standards, organize and reorganize production, reduce costs, improve quality, etc. (5)	(Not relevant unless government wants to spread use of the technology in the public sector or sell on markets). (6)
		Government through its own production and/or consumption activities carries out its policies directly.	

involved in specifying technology function, standards, and other demands.

Government involvement should be participatory rather than administrative the more technical, economic or socio-political uncertainties are around the technological development. In the early stage of development, when technical uncertainty is high, government users or potential users, should be involved in defining their needs which the new technology is to satisfy. In general, the more government has special knowledge and competence in areas related to the technology development, for instance the knowledge of its own needs as an eventual distributor or user, the more it can be expected to be, and should be, involved actively in the development process. This role is found in cell (4) of Table 12.1.

3. <u>Direct Engagement: Management Role</u>. This role assumes that major technical, economic, and socio-political uncertainties have been resolved and that the government will be directly engaged in production and/or consumer roles. See cells (5) and (6) in Table 12.1

The engagement of government in the production, distribution, or utilization of the new technology may reflect a historical pattern, where the state has become heavily involved in such activity, accumulating considerable experience and expertise, as, for example, that of the Tennessee Valley Authority in the USA or of publically owned utilities in many European countries. Also government involvement may be motivated by the need to make large capital investments, for instance in the case of large windmills, wave power and district heating, which private interests are unable or unwilling to make. The risk here is that the government engages itself administratively in a development process where it lacks adequate knowledge and capability, or access to such resources, and mismanages the developments which it had intended to advance.

The government may have the knowledge and the resources (no small issue in these times of budget cutbacks and weakened public authority) to establish and operate new socio-technical systems. Nevertheless, it should not proceed --or should proceed with the greatest caution-- if it has not managed to gain <u>a public consensus or a mandate for its role</u>.

A major risk in the case of public (as well as of private) monopoly over the social learning and selection processes connected with technological development is that the latter will be prematurely closed. Awareness of this risk should be reflected in policy and institutional arrangements.

In general, failure to base the role of government and its strategies in technological development on considerations such as those outlined above (and in Chapter 11),

will lead not only to wastage of resources but to distorted developments, blockage or slow-down of transitions to
new energy systems.

SPECIFIC POLICY STRATEGIES AND MEASURES

A partial transition to alternative energy systems
is technically, economically and socially feasible and
probably desirable,   even   at   this stage of technological development. Questions remain about the degree to
which such a transition is possible in the short, medium
and long run. As we have argued in the first part of this
chapter, the technical, economic, and socio-political uncertainties are so substantial that precise answers cannot be given at this time. Answers will emerge in the
course of the concrete problem-solving processes in which
entrepreneurs and other change agents are enegaged. The
aim of policy-makers should be to encourage and facilitate such problem-solving efforts.

1. In countries with relatively low electricity and
fuel prices, one cannot expect substantial market-driven
initiatives and developments such as described in this
book. To the extent that governments wish to facilitate
the introduction and development of alternative energy
technologies, electricity and other fuel prices should be
increased to levels which would stimulate such a movement.
That is, there must be real incentives for entrepreneurs,
as well as users, to engage in developing alternative
energy technologies.
Regional, communal and employment policy considerations might countermand this argument. Policy-makers may
be reluctant or unwilling to risk the immediate threat to
employment and business interests which radical energy
policies designed to vigorously stimulate alternative
energy developments would entail. A second best strategy
would be to strongly support R&D and prototype development, as well as educational efforts, as part of prepara-
tions for the time and situation when market developments
or a new political climate make more radical policies and
restructuring feasible.

2. Efforts should be made to identify potential entrepreneurs --both producers and users-- who would be
most receptive to the idea of engaging in introducing alternative energy systems into production and use. Table
12.2 presents one such attempt.
One should be prepared, however, for unexpected
sources of entrepreneurship and change efforts in alternative energy developments, for instance from social
agents marginal to, and in some instances far from, the
field. We have observed the role of the environmental and

TABLE 12.2
Potential Producers and Users of Energy Technologies

Technology		Potential Producers	Potential Users
small		small metal-working workshops	farmers, isolated households
Windmills	large	ship building, large machinery manufacturers	communes, local and regional utilities
Wave Power		same as for large windmills	regional and natio- nal utilities
Solar		small metal-working workshops, plumbers	households, communal authorities (comm. buildings, pools), greenhouse operators, small manufactuerers
Biomass (Wood,Peat)		furnace manufac- turers, construc- tion firms	same as above plus cogeneration plants, local and regional utilities

anti-nuclear movements in wind energy development in Denmark, and of oil companies in the development of geothermal energy in California. Also, car and truck engine manufacturers plan to produce diesel heat pumps on a large
scale in Germany. In general, the key actors may often
not be found in the relevant branch. Indeed, utilities,
business enterprises, and government agencies in the
"energy branch" are often slow or reluctant to shift
their perspectives, business ideas and production and
marketing systems.

3. Potential blocking agents should be identified
and neutralized as much as possible. Laws, regulations
and policies can be reformulated so as to make, for instance, the utilities interested in the new developments.
In particular, policies should be directed toward providing incentives and "rules of the game" which would induce utilities to become interested in promoting the development of alternative energy technologies. In particular, the policies and rules governing them should reorient
them toward perceiving renewable energy sources as well
as energy-saving measures as opportunities, not threats.
Lönnroth (1977:133) writes:

> Today's technology for energy supply is em-
> bedded in an organizational structure which

--we think-- sees alternatives as threats,
especially the renewable energy sources.
Efforts should be made as to change the
tasks performed by today's energy suppliers,
that they perceive neither renewable energy
resources nor energy-saving measures as a
threat. On the contrary, the suppliers
should be made to have an interest in promoting them.

Today's energy system is better organized to
introduce coal and breeder reactors than renewable energy resources. That is why we
think that we must, first, find and stimulate
entrepreneurs who can undertake the different renewable energy resources, and second,
create sufficiently powerful integrating
bodies. The latter should be mandated to
weigh measures for saving energy, introducing renewable energy sources, etc., against
the use of those energy sources whose growth
one wants to limit (oil, nuclear, hydro-
power, etc.).

4. Governments should try to systematically establish --or encourage the establishment and development
of-- journals and forums (such as annual conferences and
fairs) drawing together inventors, entrepreneurs, potential users, policy-makers, and so forth, interested in
particular energy technologies such as solar, wind and
biomass. Also, "trade associations", similar to the
Finnish Peat Association, should be encouraged to form.
Their purpose would be to facilitate exchange of information , learning, joint ventures and other forms of cooperation as well as to act as a lobbying agent for interests engaged in the development of a particular alternative energy system. Of course, the government itself
should accept such associations as legitimate spokesmen
and take notice of their analyses and arguments to the
same extent that they listen to utilities and other conventional energy lobbyists.

5. In setting up concrete programs for facilitating
the introduction of alternative energy technologies, governments should make every effort to keep the procedures
for application (for grants, subsidies, loans, etc.) simple. Handling time should be short. Simplicity and quick
handling with a minimum of red tape will tend to encourage smaller enterprises and users. Economic regulation
and reporting should as much as possible be combined with
taxation reporting. Policies and rules may be established
nationally, but applications should be administered locally. The number of support programs should be kept

small. In federal systems, inconsistent or confusing policies and regulations must be avoided (see Chapter 6).

6. Rules and regulations should be established in
such a way as to allow maximum flexibility. This is particularly important concerning the sorts of development
under consideration here. As a result of experience from
earlier phases of the development of alternative energy
systems, it will be necessary to make changes in rules
and regulations. It should be possible to make them as
quickly as possible but as infrequently as feasible
(see again Chapter 6 for a negative example). A suitable
model here is providing a legal framework which permits
departments and other agencies to specify details. Such
rules and regulations could be changed on relatively
short notice.

7. In order to facilitate changes and adjustments in
rules and regulations, an information assessment system
should be established to provide continual feedback on
results and consequences of policies and programs. This
system should operate in such a way that it is not interpreted as an instrument of control of producers and users
of alternative energy technologies.[2]

8. In connection with the emergence of the production of alternative energy technologies, governments
should make sure that quality control and guarantee programs are established and that the agencies charged with
surveying product and service qualities are recognized
and trustworthy. These steps can contribute greatly to
reducing the uncertainty and hesitations among potential
users. Producers should not be allowed to misuse these
programs to limit competition.

9. Governments should develop strategies to educate
users and potential users of new energy technologies to
work toward changing attitudes and patterns of consumption so as to increase receptivity to the use of alternative energy technologies. Here local network organizations (idea organizations, including conservation groups),
interest organizations (such as houseowner and tenant
associations) as well as communes and local governments
can play an active role, particularly if the latter formulate policies and strategies to act concretely to bring
about changes in consumer attitudes and practices.

10. It is essential that economically weak groups be
enabled and encouraged to make use of economic incentives
for the purchase and use of alternative energy technologies in spite of the relatively higher investment costs.
Progressive tax rebates and/or subsidies are relevant
measures.

11. Government policy should be concerned with identifying areas where greater knowledge and additional research and development is required, for example:

o   knowledge of how new alternative energy systems
     would fit into existing electricity and fuel
     systems. The characteristics and capabilities of
     combined systems should be of particular inte-
     rest: biomass-using furnaces and electricity;
     biomass combined with gas; interactions of wind-
     mill systems and hydropower systems; back-up and
     system steering problems with different combina-
     tions;

o   knowledge of the user side and of the possibili-
     ties of structuring user demand so that it para-
     llells much better production patterns and the
     level of back-up available. Of particular inte-
     rest would be ways to reduce the "strictness of
     demand" for electricity and for hot water;

o   knowledge of societal consequences, economic,
     political, organizational and institutional of
     different alternative energy systems.

These three items point up the importance of energy systems research and evaluation.

In a number of instances it is not so much research
that is needed but practical testing and adaptation of
alternative energy technologies to regional and local
conditions. Biomass systems are commercially viable and
capable of playing some role in peripheral areas. Wind
and solar are also already commercially viable in some
regions. The gap between R&D and ultimate users should be
bridged. The latter need to be engaged earlier, possibly
by offering incentives and involving them in prototype
and early product assessment.

12. Governments should give consideration to more
effective ways of utilizing available but limited resources for developing new, renewable energy resources. A
variety of strategies are feasible.

(i) Offers of substantial prizes for inventions and
for applications of alternative energy technologies to
specific needs. Large awards could be offered at regular
intervals in one or more areas. Competitions could be made international if the awards were large enough and well-
advertised. Such prices would stimulate many times over
the creative activity and investments that the same sums
given out in typical R&D grants would do. They also would
act on public opinion and on the interests and ambitions
of students and young researchers.

(ii) Finance demonstration projects and organize the
dissemination of operating results to appropriate

target groups (such as engineers, architects, planners, and users).

(iii) Support for study trips of engineers, entrepreneurs and other practitioners to visit and learn about alternative energy developments in other countries.

(iv) Scholarship support for advanced graduate students and young researchers and engineers to study and engage in research and development both at home and abroad. Select x persons each year to work on biomass energy, y persons on wind energy, etc. But select also a number of people to work in the general are of energy science.

(v) Establish R&D as well as educational programs in univeristies and centers of higher education, with stress on the recruitment and training of younger researchers. These efforts should also include the building up and maintenance of competence in environmental and social sciences.

13. The transition to new energy systems will be difficult. The high energy consuming economies of the OECD countries evolved when oil cost $2 or less a barrel. They cannot be expected to function smoothly when the price of oil or its equivalent is 10 to 15 times as much (Brown, 1981). Also, the context for reaching strategic decisions about energy supply and distribution has become more complex and conflict-laden. The controversies and difficulties surrounding nuclear power, large-scale hydropower projects, and coal-fired facilities point this up.

Socio-political problems and conflicts relating to ecological, aesthetic, and land-use issues are likely to intensify as wind, solar, peat, biomass, or other energy systems become more widespread, as new designs and developments emerge, and as people learn about some of the consequences, both negative and positive, of the new energy developments.

One of the strategic problem facing modern societies today is to discover and develop technologies which are, on the one hand, economically and technically feasible and, on the other hand, socially and ecologically acceptable. A major challenge facing research and development is to shape new conceptual frameworks and tools of analysis --along with the educational and research settings-- to define and analyze technological development from a more global and integrated perspective.

THE NEW OUT OF THE OLD

This book has examined several instances of the development of alternative energy technologies and the shaping of new markets and industries. Such developments, in our view, will continue. Eventually conventional energy systems, energy-intensive industries, and other related industries will fade or be radically restructured. Resources, including engineering and management expertise, will be shifted from the stagnating or doomed industries to the new, for example, to those described in this book. New types of knowledge, skill and infrastructure will emerge and develop, such as professional knowledge and skills around wind, solar, biomass, energy conservation and energy systems analysis. Eventually the education and growth of new types of energy professions and occupations will become more systematic.

Today we are witnessing the emergence of the new out of the old. How long this process will take, and what ultimate forms the new will assume, cannot be foreseen. Knowledge of the social process, however, will enable us to tolerate uncertainty and to develop strategies to deal with it as well as the confusion and conflict that invariably arise in connection with technological transformations.

NOTES

1. It should be stressed that the government, through this involvement, tends to bias the technology development in the direction of large-scale systems (in relation to the resource base of the actors and the country).

2. But there is a dilemma: Information used for control may lead some to negative feelings of being controlled. Others may be positively influenced and stimulated to improve themselves.

BIBLIOGRAPHY

Brown, L.R. 1981 Building a Sustainable Society. New York: W.W. Norton.

Callon, M. (no date) Introduction of the Electric Vehicle and Public Demand. Ms, Paris: Ecole des Mines.

Lönnroth, M., P. Steen and T.B. Johansson 1977 Energy in Transition. Stockholm: Secretariat for Future Studies. (Published in 1980 by University of California Press.)

Nelson, R.R. and R.N. Langlois 1983 "Industrial Innovation Policy: Lessons from American History." Science, 219:814-815.